RESPONSES TO STAYING ALIVE:

'Truly startling and powerful poems' – MIA FARROW

'These poems distil the human heart as nothing else...*Staying Alive* celebrates the point of poetry. It's invigorating and makes me proud of being human' – JANE CAMPION

'*Staying Alive* is a blessing of a book. The title says it all. I have long waited for just this kind of setting down of poems. Has there ever been such a passionate anthology? These are poems that hunt you down with the solace of their recognition' – ANNE MICHAELS

'*Staying Alive* is a magnificent anthology. The last time I was so excited, engaged and enthralled by a collection of poems was when I first encountered *The Rattle Bag*. I can't think of any other anthology that casts its net so widely, or one that has introduced me to so many vivid and memorable poems' – PHILIP PULLMAN

'Usually if you say a book is "inspirational" that means it's New Agey and soft at the center. This astonishingly rich anthology, by contrast, shows that what is edgy, authentic and provocative can also awaken the spirit and make its readers quick with consciousness. In these pages I discovered many new writers, and I've decided I'm now in love with our trouble-some epoch if it can produce poems of such genius' – EDMUND WHITE

'A vibrant, brilliantly diverse anthology of poems to delight the mind, heart and soul. A book for people who know they love poetry, and for people who think they don't' – HELEN DUNMORE

'*Staying Alive* is a wonderful testament to Neil Astley's lifetime in poetry, and to the range and courage of his taste. It's also, of course, a testament to poetry itself: to its powers to engross and move us, to its ability to challenge and brace us, and to its exultation. Everyone who cares about poetry should own this book' – ANDREW MOTION

'This is a book to make you fall in love with poetry...Go out and buy it for everyone you love' – CHRISTINA PATTERSON, *Independent*

'I do

Reading Group
Collection

BEING ALIVE

the sequel to *Staying Alive*

edited by

NEIL ASTLEY

BLODAXE BOOKS

ISBN: 1 85224 675 8

First published 2004 by
Bloodaxe Books Ltd,
Highgreen,
Tarset,
Northumberland NE48 1RP.

www.bloodaxebooks.com
For further information about Bloodaxe titles
please visit our website or write to
the above address for a catalogue.

Bloodaxe Books Ltd acknowledges
the financial assistance of
Arts Council England, North East.

Cover printing by J. Thomson Colour Printers Ltd, Glasgow.

Printed in Great Britain by
Bell & Bain Limited, Glasgow, Scotland.

CONTENTS

3 Family

5 Men and Women

6 Being and Loss

7 Daily Round

9 Mad World

10 Ends and Beginnings

INTRODUCTION

If I read a book and it makes my whole body so cold no fire
can ever warm me, I know *that* is poetry. If I feel physically
as if the top of my head were taken off, I know *that* is poetry.

EMILY DICKINSON

Being Alive is the sequel to *Staying Alive,* which became Britain's
most popular poetry book within a fortnight of publication in 2002.
Staying Alive didn't just reach a broader readership, it introduced
thousands of new readers to contemporary poetry, giving them an
international gathering of poems with emotional power, intellectual
edge and playful wit. It also brought many readers back to poetry,
people who hadn't read poetry for years because it hadn't held their
interest.

Staying Alive was taken up by readers because it gave them
hundreds of thoughtful and passionate poems about living in the
modern world. This companion anthology is for all those people
who've wanted more poems that touch the heart, stir the mind
and fire the spirit. *Being Alive* is about being human: about love
and loss, fear and longing, hurt and wonder.

While this new anthology has been conceived as a sequel to
Staying Alive, the power and range of the selection are such that
it can be read just as fruitfully on its own. Like *Staying Alive,* it
is a "bridge" anthology, a book designed to make its readers want
to read more work by the poets it features, and I would hope that
new readers who come first to *Being Alive* would make *Staying
Alive* their next port of call. This would not be a backward step
but rather a broadening out from *Being Alive.*

Being Alive takes readers on a journey through the world of
contemporary poetry, stopping off for encounters and meetings.
Many of the poems seem almost alive to the living world, alert to
what they sense and summon up through language. Reading and
re-reading them, I feel the jolt of a live connection, a quickening
of consciousness. I hope this is something which readers will share,
and that *Being Alive* will pass Emily Dickinson's now famous test
for true poetry, that it makes you feel as if the top of your head
has been lifted off.

Housman described how poetry affected him in similarly physical
terms: 'Experience has taught me, when I am shaving of a morning,
to keep watch over my thoughts, because, if a line of poetry strays
into my memory, my skin bristles so that the razor ceases to act.'

Those two comments were very much in my mind when I was choosing poems for *Being Alive*. I wanted to give readers as many hair-raising, head-lifting poems as possible in the one book, but to vary the selection with different kinds of poems, balancing heart-rending, gut-wrenching poems of explosive power with gentler, playful, witty, thought-provoking poems of tenderness and sensuality. All these are poems which I feel *had* to be written. And because they were *necessary* poems for the writers, I hope readers will find them as compelling as I do. There are a lot of modern poems which don't engage me as a reader, either because they're too clever for their own good or too simplistic in their sentiments. The American poet William Stafford once said: 'I don't want to write good poems. I want to write *inevitable* poems – to write the things I will write, given who I am.' That's the kind I look for, poems which the poet *needed* to write, poems whose integrity derives from an honest and truthful engagement with living language and with living in the world.

These aren't poems which just confirm what we already know. Another American poet, James Tate, said: 'What we want from poetry is to be moved, to be moved from where we now stand. We don't just want to have our ideas or emotions confirmed. Or if we do, then we turn to lesser poems, poems which are happy to tell you killing children is bad, chopping down the rainforest is bad, dying is sad.' In other words, good poetry doesn't offer simple solace or poetic medication, it opens up the senses, it disturbs, questions and challenges. These poems make the reader less settled yet more whole, more alert to the world, more alive, more in touch with being human.

Paul Muldoon puts it rather well: 'The point of poetry is to be acutely *dis*comforting, to prod and provoke, to poke us in the eye, to punch us in the nose, to knock us off our feet, to take our breath away.' *Being Alive* and *Staying Alive* include many breathtaking poems by all kinds of writers from many different countries, classes, cultural backgrounds and literary traditions. These take the reader by surprise because the voice, style, stance or angle of approach are often quite different from what's expected.

When I first had the idea for *Staying Alive*, it was for a diverse and lively book to introduce new readers to contemporary poetry as well as to show existing poetry readers (whose access to international poetry is restricted by the narrowness of British publishing) a wider range of poems from around the world. I had no thoughts then of a sequel, but I also had no idea that the book would be championed so enthusiastically that readers would want a companion anthology.

Staying Alive was my response to the findings of a readership survey. This presented a damning picture of how poetry was viewed

18

by the general public: how people whose knowledge of modern poetry was very limited would dismiss it as obscure, difficult, dull, boring or pretentious. Modern poetry, according to their comments, was irrelevant and incomprehensible, so they didn't bother with it, not even readers of literary fiction and people interested in other arts which use language, such as theatre and film; and not even people who read Shakespeare and the classics: one of the most surprising findings of that research was that only 5% of the poetry books sold in British bookshops were by living poets.

Staying Alive was my attempt to show all those people who love literature and language and traditional poetry that contemporary poetry *is* relevant to their own lives; and that much of it is lively, imaginative and accessible to intelligent readers who might not have given it much of a chance before. And that didn't involve "dumbing down", but choosing lucid poems to entice new readers. There's no conflict here between "access" and excellence.

Staying Alive won thousands of new readers for poetry largely because of word of mouth: reader power. And those readers didn't just buy one copy for themselves, they bought more and more to give to friends and family as presents. *Staying Alive* is still being discovered by new readers. Two years after the book appeared, I'm still receiving letters, postcards and e-mails expressing people's appreciation, messages of support and thanks, all saying how much *Staying Alive* had helped or stimulated them and fired up their interest in poetry. These responses are not untypical:

ROB MARCHMENT: 'I just wanted to say that I am completely blown away by your anthology!... I feel as if I have reconnected with the flesh and blood of poetry once again.'

ANTHEA MATTISON: 'I am writing to thank you, as a reader, for showing me a way back to poetry after years of alienation.'

JONATHAN WOOD: 'I have read hardly any poetry in my 46 years. I found it disconcerting and difficult...I have been moved to tears and laughter by the poems I read in the last two days and carry the book everywhere...thank you for publishing and editing this wonderful anthology. I have found a new world.'

MAGGIE BUTT: 'It is a joy to read something celebratory in a world where it is fashionable to talk everything down. Our students arrive at University with a curiously ambivalent attitude to poetry. Many say they "hate it", but most write it. I think your book will go a long way to persuading them they don't "hate it" after all.'

JOHN McDONAGH: 'It will be a staple in my First year course for a while to come. Indeed, this course is crucial in the college as the students have a choice whether or not to do English in the first few

The Horses of Meaning

Let their hooves print the next bit of the story:
Release them roughmaned
From the dark stable where
They rolled their dark eyes, shifted and stamped –

Let them out, and follow the sound, a regular clattering
On the cobbles of the yard, a pouring round the corner
Into the big field, a booming canter.

Now see where they rampage,
And whether they are suddenly halted
At the check of the line westward
Where the train passes at dawn –

If they stare at land that looks white in patches
As if it were frayed to bone (the growing light
Will detail as a thickening of small white flowers),
Can this be the end of their flight?
The wind combs their long tails, their stalls are empty.

EILÉAN NÍ CHUILLEANÁIN

Symposium

You can lead a horse to water but you can't make it hold
its nose to the grindstone and hunt with the hounds.
Every dog has a stitch in time. Two heads? You've been sold
one good turn. One good turn deserves a bird in the hand.

A bird in the hand is better than no bread.
To have your cake is to pay Paul.
Make hay while you can still hit the nail on the head.
For want of a nail the sky might fall.

People in glass houses can't see the wood
for the new broom. Rome wasn't built between two stools.
Empty vessels wait for no man.

A hair of the dog is a friend indeed.
There's no fool like the fool
who's shot his bolt. There's no smoke after the horse is gone.

PAUL MULDOON

Not the Furniture Game

His hair was a crow fished out of a blocked chimney
and his eyes were boiled eggs with the tops hammered in
and his blink was a cat flap
and his teeth were bluestones or Easter Island statues
and his bite was a perfect horseshoe.
His nostrils were both barrels of a shotgun, loaded.
And his mouth was an oil exploration project gone bankrupt
and his last smile was a caesarean section
and his tongue was an iguanodon
and his whistle was a laser beam
and his laugh was a bad case of kennel cough.
He coughed, and it was malt whisky.
And his headaches were Arson in Her Majesty's Dockyards
and his arguments were outboard motors strangled with fishing-line
and his neck was a bandstand
and his Adam's apple was a ballcock
and his arms were milk running off from a broken bottle.
His elbows were boomerangs or pinking shears.
And his wrists were ankles
and his handshakes were puff adders in the bran tub
and his fingers were astronauts found dead in their spacesuits
and the palms of his hands were action paintings
and both thumbs were blue touchpaper.
And his shadow was an opencast mine.
And his dog was a sentry-box with no one in it
and his heart was a first world war grenade discovered by children
and his nipples were timers for incendiary devices
and his shoulder-blades were two butchers at the meat-cleaving
        competition
and his belly-button was the Falkland Islands
and his private parts were the Bermuda triangle
and his backside was a priest hole

25

and his stretchmarks were the tide going out.
The whole system of his blood was Dutch elm disease.
And his legs were depth charges
and his knees were fossils waiting to be tapped open
and his ligaments were rifles wrapped in oilcloth under the floorboards
and his calves were the undercarriages of Shackletons.
The balls of his feet were where meteorites had landed
and his toes were a nest of mice under the lawn-mower.
And his footprints were Vietnam
and his promises were hot-air balloons floating off over the trees
and his one-liners were footballs through other people's windows
and his grin was the Great Wall of China as seen from the moon
and the last time they talked, it was apartheid.

She was a chair, tipped over backwards
with his donkey jacket on her shoulders.

They told him,
and his face was a hole
where the ice had not been thick enough to hold her.

SIMON ARMITAGE

A Song of Lies
(for Maelíosa Stafford)

In a boat without oars we rowed for land
On the shore a weasel was singing
A white cat was washing clothes
A gravestone walked in circles

In a land without soil we planted trees
Each leaf was bigger than my head
Birds nested in the roots
The fruit fell and never landed

From a tree without wood we built a house
In the best room the dead were laughing
A spinning wheel spun by itself
Crickets churned by the fire

In a house without talk we told stories
Every tale was longer than eternity
The next was older than the world
God disappeared up the chimney

From a story without words we made a dog
She had a million pups in a grain of wheat
Every pup was older than its mother
So we made a boat to drown them

VINCENT WOODS

Mappa Mundi

I

In the land of mutual rivers,
it is all a conversation: one flows uphill, one flows down.
Each ends in a bottomless lake which feeds the other
and the boatmen who sail up, down, round and round
never age, growing half a day older, half a day younger
every time... as long as they never step on land.

II

In the land of always autumn
people build their houses out of fallen leaves
and smoke, stitched together with spiders' webs.
At night they glow like parchment lanterns and the voices
inside cluster to a sigh. Tell us a story, any story, except
hush, please, not the one about the wind.

III

In the land where nothing happens twice
there are always new people to meet;
you just look in the mirror. Echoes learn to improvise.
So it's said... We've sent some of the old
to investigate, but we haven't heard yet. When we
catch up with them, we might not know.

IV

In the land of sounds you can see
we watch the radio, read each other's lips, dread
those audible nightfalls. We pick through the gloom
with one-word candles *home... however... only... soon...*
while pairs of lovers hold each other, speechless,
under the O of a full black moon.

V

In the land of hot moonlight
the bathing beaches come alive at midnight.
You can tell the famous and rich by their silvery tans
which glow ever so slightly in the dark
so at all the best parties there's a moment when the lights go out
and you, only you, seem to vanish completely.

VI

In the land of migratory words
we glance up, come the season, at telegraph wires
of syllables in edgy silhouette against a moving sky
like code, unscrambling. Any day now they'll fall into place
and be uttered. Then the mute months. The streets
without names. The telephone that only burrs.

PHILIP GROSS

The Poem

It discovers by night
what the day hid from it.
Sometimes it turns itself
into an animal.
In summer it takes long walks
by itself where meadows
fold back from ditches.
Once it stood still
in a quiet row of machines.
Who knows
what it is thinking?

DONALD HALL

Saint Francis and the Sow

The bud
stands for all things,
even for those things that don't flower,
for everything flowers, from within, of self-blessing;
though sometimes it is necessary
to reteach a thing its loveliness,
to put a hand on its brow
of the flower
and retell it in words and in touch
it is lovely
until it flowers again from within, of self-blessing;
as Saint Francis
put his hand on the creased forehead
of the sow, and told her in words and in touch
blessings of earth on the sow, and the sow
began remembering all down her thick length,
from the earthen snout all the way
through the fodder and slops to the spiritual curl of the tail,
from the hard spininess spiked out from the spine
down through the great broken heart
to the sheer blue milken dreaminess spurting and shuddering
from the fourteen teats into the fourteen mouths sucking and
            blowing beneath them:
the long, perfect loveliness of sow.

GALWAY KINNELL

Celebration

Rise, small bird, to the top of the tree
and clasp the topmost branch with your feet,
sing out from your throat
your torrent of glorious notes
and then your melody re-enact:
remind me, earthbound, of some basic facts –
say if love leaves me I'll hardly lose my mind
and though grief is great so's the music of life.

29

Rise and tell to us poor creatures
by your bursting *joie de vivre* and sweetness
that the cows low sweetly in river fields
with grass and wild flag up to their ears
chewing the cud with contented sighs,
trust and patience in the solemn eyes
though the butcher awaits them and liver-fluke
hides in the cresses of every brook.

Tell how headscarved women pray the ritual
in Minard at John the Baptist's well.
Come from Dingle and Camp, they start to sweat
in their crimplene dresses in August heat.
The fat one starts the Rosary chanting,
decades rise and fall in a rustic mantra
like corncrake-call or hum of bees
while fruitflies dust with eggs the blackberries.

Tell how a dolphin-like English girl
in a yellow bikini rides the sea-swell,
strides to the door of her caravan,
dries herself, striped towel in hand.
Tell how her belly is sun-browned,
her breasts like grapefruit full and round,
a hairbrush in her hand, a tube of *Loxene* gel –
a Venus without her scallop-shell.

Rise and sing though unaware
that a middle-aged woman is on her way,
depressed in the sand dunes, pushing for miles
a pram which contains a retarded child.
Her face is a picture of defeat,
her elastic stockings killing in the heat
but even worse, she'd know greater pain
without them from her varicose veins.

Sing out loud from the shade of your oak,
mistle thrush with your speckled throat
dazzling my eyes, sing while you can
to the still child in the small pram.
He will clap his hands and start to laugh
conveying this delight to his Mam:
'From your brooding take some ease,
hear the small bird on the top of the trees!'

The woman breaks through the fog around her,
her courage and sense again have found her.
In the flash of an eye a sun ray will fall
and she will smile through her self-pitying pall.
I prefer that smile to her depressed face –
you, small bird, deserve all praise,
your song is a witness to the pain and joy
that goes in hand with just being alive.

NUALA NÍ DHOMHNAILL
translated from the Irish by Michael Hartnett

At the Fishhouses

Although it is a cold evening,
down by one of the fishhouses
an old man sits netting,
his net, in the gloaming almost invisible,
a dark purple-brown,
and his shuttle worn and polished.
The air smells so strong of codfish
it makes one's nose run and one's eyes water.
The five fishhouses have steeply peaked roofs
and narrow, cleated gangplanks slant up
to storerooms in the gables
for the wheelbarrows to be pushed up and down on.
All is silver: the heavy surface of the sea,
swelling slowly as if considering spilling over,
is opaque, but the silver of the benches,
the lobster pots, and masts, scattered
among the wild jagged rocks,
is of an apparent translucence
like the small old buildings with an emerald moss
growing on their shoreward walls.
The big fish tubs are completely lined
with layers of beautiful herring scales
and the wheelbarrows are similarly plastered
with creamy iridescent coats of mail,
with small iridescent flies crawling on them.

Up on the little slope behind the houses,
set in the sparse bright sprinkle of grass,
is an ancient wooden capstan,
cracked, with two long bleached handles
and some melancholy stains, like dried blood,
where the ironwork has rusted.
The old man accepts a Lucky Strike.
He was a friend of my grandfather.
We talk of the decline in the population
and of codfish and herring
while he waits for a herring boat to come in.
There are sequins on his vest and on his thumb.
He has scraped the scales, the principal beauty,
from unnumbered fish with that black old knife,
the blade of which is almost worn away.

Down at the water's edge, at the place
where they haul up the boats, up the long ramp
descending into the water, thin silver
tree trunks are laid horizontally
across the gray stones, down and down
at intervals of four or five feet.

Cold dark deep and absolutely clear,
element bearable to no mortal,
to fish and to seals... One seal particularly
I have seen here evening after evening.
He was curious about me. He was interested in music;
like me a believer in total immersion,
so I used to sing him Baptist hymns.
I also sang 'A Mighty Fortress Is Our God'.
He stood up in the water and regarded me
steadily, moving his head a little.
Then he would disappear, then suddenly emerge
almost in the same spot, with a sort of shrug
as if it were against his better judgment.
Cold dark deep and absolutely clear,
the clear gray icy water... Back, behind us,
the dignified tall firs begin.
Bluish, associating with their shadows,
a million Christmas trees stand
waiting for Christmas. The water seems suspended
above the rounded gray and blue-gray stones.

I have seen it over and over, the same sea, the same,
slightly, indifferently swinging above the stones,
icily free above the stones,
above the stones and then the world.
If you should dip your hand in,
your wrist would ache immediately,
your bones would begin to ache and your hand would burn
as if the water were a transmutation of fire
that feeds on stones and burns with a dark gray flame.
If you tasted it, it would first taste bitter,
then briny, then surely burn your tongue.
It is like what we imagine knowledge to be:
dark, salt, clear, moving, utterly free,
drawn from the cold hard mouth
of the world, derived from the rocky breasts
forever, flowing and drawn, and since
our knowledge is historical, flowing, and flown

ELIZABETH BISHOP

Tremors

We took turns at laying
An ear on the rail –
So that we could tell
By the vibrations

When a train was coming.
Then we'd flatten ourselves
To the banks, scorched
Vetch and hedge-parsley,

While the iron flanks
Rushed past, sending sparks
Flying. It is more and more
A question of living

With an ear to the ground:
The tremors, when they come,
Are that much greater –
For ourselves, and others.

Nor is it any longer
A game, but a matter
Of survival: each explosion
Part of a procession

There can be no stopping.
Though the end is known,
There is nothing for it
But to keep listening.

STEWART CONN

Night Journey

Now as the train bears west,
Its rhythm rocks the earth,
And from my Pullman berth
I stare into the night
While others take their rest.
Bridges of iron lace,
A suddenness of trees,
A lap of mountain mist
All cross my line of sight,
Then a bleak wasted place,
And a lake below my knees.
Full on my neck I feel
The straining at a curve;
My muscles move with steel,
I wake in every nerve.
I watch a beacon swing
From dark to blazing bright;
We thunder through ravines
And gullies washed with light.
Beyond the mountain pass
Mist deepens on the pane;

We rush into a rain
That rattles double glass.
Wheels shake the roadbed stone,
The pistons jerk and shove,
I stay up half the night
To see the land I love.

THEODORE ROETHKE

The Orient Express

One looks from the train
Almost as one looked as a child. In the sunlight
What I see still seems to me plain,
I am safe; but at evening
As the lands darken, a questioning
Precariousness comes over everything.

Once after a day of rain
I lay longing to be cold; and after a while
I was cold again, and hunched shivering
Under the quilt's many colors, gray
With the dull ending of the winter day.
Outside me there were a few shapes
Of chairs and tables, things from a primer;
Outside the window
There were the chairs and tables of the world...
I saw that the world
That had seemed to me the plain
Gray mask of all that was strange
Behind it – of all that *was* – was all.

But it is beyond belief.
One thinks, 'Behind everything
An unforced joy, an unwilling
Sadness (a willing sadness, a forced joy)
Moves changelessly'; one looks from the train
And there is something, the same thing
Behind everything: all these little villages,
A passing woman, a field of grain,

The man who says goodbye to his wife –
A path through a wood full of lives, and the train
Passing, after all unchangeable
And not now ever to stop, like a heart –

It is like any other work of art.
It is and never can be changed.
Behind everything there is always
The unknown unwanted life.

RANDALL JARRELL

Ithaka

As you set out for Ithaka
hope your road is a long one,
full of adventure, full of discovery,
Laistrygonians, Cyclops,
angry Poseidon – don't be afraid of them:
you'll never find things like that on your way
as long as you keep your thoughts raised high,
as long as a rare excitement
stirs your spirit and your body.
Laistrygonians, Cyclops,
wild Poseidon – you won't encounter them
unless you bring them along inside your soul,
unless your soul sets them up in front of you.

Hope your road is a long one.
May there be many summer mornings when,
with what pleasure, what joy,
you enter harbours you're seeing for the first time;
may you stop at Phoenician trading stations
to buy fine things,
mother of pearl and coral, amber and ebony,
sensual perfume of every kind –
as many sensual perfumes as you can;
and may you visit many Egyptian cities
to learn and go on learning from their scholars.

Keep Ithaka always in your mind.
Arriving there is what you're destined for.
But don't hurry the journey at all.
Better if it lasts for years,
so you're old by the time you reach the island,
wealthy with all you've gained on the way,
not expecting Ithaka to make you rich.

Ithaka gave you the marvellous journey.
Without her you wouldn't have set out.
She has nothing left to give you now.

And if you find her poor, Ithaka won't have fooled you.
Wise as you will have become, so full of experience,
you'll have understood by then what these Ithakas mean.

C.P. CAVAFY
translated from the Greek by Edmund Keeley & Philip Sherrard

What If This Road

What if this road, that has held no surprises
these many years, decided not to go
home after all; what if it could turn
left or right with no more ado
than a kite-tail? What if its tarry skin
were like a long, supple bolt of cloth,
that is shaken and rolled out, and takes
a new shape from the contours beneath?
And if it chose to lay itself down
in a new way; around a blind corner,
across hills you must climb without knowing
what's on the other side; who would not hanker
to be going, at all risks? Who wants to know
a story's end, or where a road will go?

SHEENAGH PUGH

Poetry of Departures

Sometimes you hear, fifth-hand,
As epitaph:
He chucked up everything
And just cleared off,
And always the voice will sound
Certain you approve
This audacious, purifying,
Elemental move.

And they are right, I think.
We all hate home
And having to be there:
I detest my room,
Its specially-chosen junk,
The good books, the good bed,
And my life, in perfect order:
So to hear it said

He walked out on the whole crowd
Leaves me flushed and stirred,
Like *Then she undid her dress*
Or *Take that you bastard*;
Surely I can, if he did?
And that helps me stay
Sober and industrious.
But I'd go today,

Yes, swagger the nut-strewn roads,
Crouch in the fo'c'sle
Stubbly with goodness, if
It weren't so artificial,
Such a deliberate step backwards
To create an object:
Books; china; a life
Reprehensibly perfect.

PHILIP LARKIN

The Last of the Fire Kings

I want to be
Like the man who descends
At two milk churns

With a bulging
String bag and vanishes
Where the lane turns,

Or the man
Who drops at night
From a moving train

And strikes out over the fields
Where fireflies glow,
Not knowing a word of the language.

Either way, I am
Through with history
Who lives by the sword

Dies by the sword.
Last of the fire kings, I shall
Break with tradition and

Die by my own hand
Rather than perpetuate
The barbarous cycle.

Five years I have reigned
During which time
I have lain awake each night

And prowled by day
In the sacred grove
For fear of the usurper,

Perfecting my cold dream
Of a place out of time,
A palace of porcelain

Where the frugivorous
Inheritors recline
In their rich fabrics
Far from the sea.

But the fire-loving
People, rightly perhaps,
Will not countenance this,

Demanding that I inhabit,
Like them, a world of
Sirens, bin-lids
And bricked-up windows –

Not to release them
From the ancient curse
But to die their creature and be thankful.

DEREK MAHON

The Appointment

After he'd crossed seven borders
on trains, in cars, on foot,
and each language he heard
meant less to him than the last,
he came to a wooded lake,
and he knew, looking at it,
that in winter it froze over,
that people walked across it
to the island in the middle
where bonfires were lit
and dozens danced and sang
to fresh-made music,
laughing amid the snow –
he knew, because he'd seen this
in a recurring dream,
and he'd been among them
dancing alone.

And now he'd come here
but not in winter,
so he jumped in and swam,
and a red-tailed hawk
led him to the island,
where among the silver birch
he found a lantern
and a two-stringed guitar
which he practised on
till he plucked out a jig
that set his feet tapping
and got him singing,
louder and louder,
out across the water
to the listening town –
when he lit the lantern
he knew the boats would come.

MATTHEW SWEENEY

The Mayo Tao

I have abandoned the dream kitchens for a low fire
and a prescriptive literature of the spirit;
a storm snores on the desolate sea.
The nearest shop is four miles away –
when I walk there through the shambles
of the morning for tea and firelighters
the mountain paces me in a snow-lit silence.
My days are spent in conversation
with deer and blackbirds;
at night fox and badger gather at my door.
I have stood for hours
watching a salmon doze in the tea-gold dark,
for months listening to the sob story
of a stone in the road, the best,
most monotonous sob story I have ever heard.

I am an expert on frost crystals
and the silence of crickets, a confidant
of the stinking shore, the stars in the mud –
there is an immanence in these things
which drives me, despite my scepticism,
almost to the point of speech,
like sunlight cleaving the lake mist at morning
or when tepid water
runs cold at last from the tap.

I have been working for years
on a four-line poem
about the life of a leaf;
I think it might come out right this winter.

DEREK MAHON

Echoes

I

I am describing to you on the phone
Stonechats backlit by an October sunset
A pair that seems to be flirting in the cold.
I am looking out of the bedroom window.
They fluster along the fuchsia hedge and perch
On bare twigs the wind has stripped for them.

II

As beautiful bog asphodel in flower
Is bog asphodel in seed. Or nearly.
An echo. Rusty-orange October tones.
This late there are gentians and centaury
And a bumble bee on a thistle head
Suspended, neither feeding nor dying.

III

Forty-two whoopers call, then the echoes
As though there are more swans over the ridge.

MICHAEL LONGLEY

No Matter What, After All, and That Beautiful Word So

This was the time of their heaviest migration,
And the wild geese for hours sounded their song
In the night over Syracuse, near and far,
As they circled toward Beaver Lake up beyond
Baldwinsville. We heard them while we lay in bed
Making love and talking, and often we lay still
Just to listen. 'What is it about that sound?'
You said, and because I was in my customary
Umbrage with reality I answered, 'Everything
Uncivilised,' but knew right away I was wrong.
I examined my mind. In spite of our loving
I felt the pressure of the house enclosing me,
And the pressure of the neighboring houses
That seemed to move against me in the darkness,
And the pressure of the whole city, and then
The whole continent, which I saw
As the wild geese must see it, a system
Of colored lights creeping everywhere in the night.
Oh the McDonald's on the strip outside Casper,
Wyoming (which I could indistinctly remember),
Was pressing against me. 'Why permit it?'
I asked myself. 'It's a dreadful civilisation,
Of course, but the pressure is yours.' It was true.
I listened to the sound in the sky, and I had no
Argument against myself. The sound was unlike
Any other, indefinable, unnameable – certainly
Not a song, as I had called it. A kind of discourse,
The ornithologists say, in a language unknown
To us; a complex discourse about something
Altogether mysterious. Yet so is the cricketing
Of the crickets in the grass, and it is not the same.
In the caves of Lascaux, I've heard, the Aurignacian
Men and women took leave of the other animals, a trauma
They tried to lessen by painting the animal spirits
Upon the stone. And the geese are above our window.
Christ, what is it about that sound? Talking in the sky,
Bell-like words, but only remotely bell-like,
A language of many and strange tones above us

In the night at the change of seasons, talking unseen,
An expressiveness – is that it? Expressiveness
Intact and with no meaning? Yet we respond,
Our minds make an answering, though we cannot
Articulate it. How great the unintelligible
Meaning! Our lost souls flying over. The talk
Of the wild geese in the sky. It is there. It is so.

HAYDEN CARRUTH

Migratory

Near evening, in Fairhaven, Massachusetts,
seventeen wild geese arrowed the ashen blue
over the Wal-Mart and the Blockbuster Video,

and I was up there, somewhere between the asphalt
and their clear dominion – not in the parking lot,
its tallowy circles just appearing,

the shopping carts shining, from above,
like little scraps of foil. Their eyes
held me there, the unfailing gaze

of those who know how to fly in formation,
wing-tip to wing-tip, safe, fearless.
And the convex glamour of their eyes carried

the parking lot, the wet field
troubled with muffler shops
and stoplights, the arc of highway

and its exits, one shattered farmhouse
with its failing barn... The wind
a few hundred feet above the grass

erases the mechanical noises, everything;
nothing but their breathing
and the perfect rowing of the pinions,

and then, out of that long, percussive pour
toward what they are most certain of,
comes their – question, is it?

Assertion, prayer, aria – as delivered
by something too compelled in its passage
to sing? A hoarse and unwieldy music

which plays nonetheless down the length
of me until I am involved in their flight,
the unyielding necessity of it, as they literally

rise above, ineluctable, heedless,
needing nothing... Only animals
make me believe in God now

– so little between spirit and skin,
any gesture so entirely themselves.
But I wasn't with them,

as they headed toward Acushnet
and New Bedford, of course I wasn't,
though I was not exactly in the parking lot

either, where the cars nudged in and out
of their slots, each taking the place another
had abandoned, so that no space, no desire

would remain unfilled. I wasn't there.
I was so filled with longing
– is that what that sound is for? –

I seemed to be nowhere at all.

MARK DOTY

Close-up on a Sharp-shinned Hawk

Concentrate upon her attributes:
the accipiter's short
roundish wings, streaked breast, talons fine

45

and slender as the x-ray of a baby's hand.
The eyes (yellow in this hatchling
later deepening to orange then
blood red) can spot
a sparrow at four hundred metres and impose
silence like an overwhelming noise
to which you must not listen.

Suddenly, if you're not careful, everything
goes celluloid and slow
and threatens to burn through and you
must focus quickly on the simple metal band around her leg
by which she's married to our need to know.

DON MCKAY

Inventing the Hawk

She didn't believe the words
when she first heard them, that blue
bodiless sound entering her ear.
But now something was in the air,
a sense of waiting as if
the hawk itself were there
just beyond the light, blinded
by a fine-stitched leather hood
she must take apart with her fingers.
Already she had its voice,
the scream that rose from her belly
echoed in the dark inverted
canyon of her skull.

She built its wings, feather by feather,
the russet smoothness of its head,
the bead-bright eyes,
in that moment between sleep and waking.

Was she the only one
who could remember them,

who knew their shape and colours, the way
they could tilt the world with a list of wings?
Perhaps it was her reason for living
so long in this hard place
of wind and sky, the stunted trees
reciting their litany of loss
outside her window.

Elsewhere surely someone was drawing
gophers and mice out of the air.
Maybe that was also her job,
so clearly she could see them.
She'd have to lie here forever,
dreaming hair after hair,
summoning the paws (her own heart
turning timid, her nostrils twitching).

Then she would cause the seeds
in their endless variety – the ones
floating light as breath,
the ones with burrs and spears
that caught in her socks
when she was a child,
the radiant, uninvented blades of grass.

LORNA CROZIER

The Hawk

On Sunday the hawk fell on Bigging
  And a chicken screamed
  Lost in its own little snowstorm.
And on Monday he fell on the moor
  And the Field Club
  Raised a hundred silent prisms.
And on Tuesday he fell on the hill
  And the happy lamb
  Never knew why the loud collie straddled him.
And on Wednesday he fell on a bush

And the blackbird
Laid by his little flute for the last time.
And on Thursday he fell on Cleat
And peerie Tom's rabbit
Swung in a single arc from shore to hill.
And on Friday he fell on a ditch
But the questing cat,
That rival, rampant, fluttered his flame.
And on Saturday he fell on Bigging
And Jock lowered his gun
And nailed a small wing over the corn.

GEORGE MACKAY BROWN

The southern skua

The skua flew into our heads in 1968 –
a new kind of poetry, a scavenging predator
frequently attacking humans,
flying through the streets of seaside towns,
foraging with seagulls. This bird
has few predators. One was found
in Tasmania, its beak embedded in the skull
of a spotted quoll, dragged
into a clearing by devils. They form clubs
and proclaim their territory
by various displays and loud aggressive calls;
they are agile metaphysicians,
sweeping along lines of projective verse,
echoing each other's songs.
Although the skua breeds on Black Mountain
it is migratory and dispersive, its call
a series of low quacks and thin whinnying squeals.
They are omnivorous and critical creatures;
animal liberationists never mention
the habits of skua. If you read skua poetry, beware:
one could fly out from the page
and change the expression on your face.

ROBERT ADAMSON

48

2

Taste and See

Poems show us that we are both more and less than human,
that we're part of the cosmos and part of the chaos,
and that everything is a part of everything else.

JULIA CASTERTON

Poetry speaks to something in us that so wants to be filled.
It speaks to the great hunger of the soul.

LUCILLE CLIFTON

DENISE LEVERTOV'S POEM (51) 'O Taste and See' tells how the world 'is not with us enough', urging us to connect with 'all that lives' through all our senses. Elizabeth Bishop's primary sense in her poems is sight: she transforms the world through close observation as though seeing is believing. In this section there are many poems about the world and its fruits drawing fully on all the senses, offering 'a mouthful of language to swallow' in Peter Davison's 'Peaches'.

Tony Harrison has said that his poem 'A Kumquat for John Keats' (54) 'asks what an undeniable capacity for joy tastes like in a world which is full of pain, misery, despair, hunger and possible extinction'. His sweet and sour kumquat is emblematic of a whole world. 'In the very temple of Delight,' writes Keats, 'Veiled Melancholy has her sovran shrine,' but the kumquat shows how Melancholy dwells *in* Delight, how joy exists in a world of pain. As a gloss on his poem, Harrison quotes Keats's mouthwatering descriptions of eating fruit from two of his letters, including: 'Talking of Pleasure, this moment I was writing with one hand, and with the other holding to my mouth a Nectarine – good god how fine...' He wants to share his celebration of the sensual with Keats, offering him the kumquat at the same time as he's writing his own epistle.

This section's encounters (see earlier commentary, 21) are with animals, following those earlier poems about birds; again, these are more than nature poems, they are poems in which a meeting brings a quickening of consciousness, a live connection. This is what Lawrence believed we lose in our modern world, cut off from life's natural cycle, our senses and consciousness deadened.

A series of poems embracing the whole world leads to a final group giving all kinds of different views of God, with God both in the world and missing from the world. These themes are picked up again in section 9, 'Mad World'. In 'The Ikons' (93) James K. Baxter refers to 'the darkness' as both 'God' and 'Te Whaea', a Maori word meaning both the Source and the Mother of God.

The Simple Truth

I bought a dollar and a half's worth of small red potatoes,
took them home, boiled them in their jackets
and ate them for dinner with a little butter and salt.
Then I walked through the dried fields
on the edge of town. In middle June the light
hung on in the dark furrows at my feet,
and in the mountain oaks overhead the birds
were gathering for the night, the jays and mockers
squawking back and forth, the finches still darting
into the dusty light. The woman who sold me
the potatoes was from Poland; she was someone
out of my childhood in a pink spangled sweater and sunglasses
praising the perfection of all her fruits and vegetables
at the roadside stand and urging me to taste
even the pale, raw sweetcorn trucked all the way,
she swore, from New Jersey. 'Eat, eat,' she said,
'Even if you don't I'll say you did.'
                                        Some things
you know all your life. They are so simple and true
they must be said without elegance, meter and rhyme,
they must be laid on the table beside the salt shaker,
the glass of water, the absence of light gathering
in the shadows of picture frames, they must be
naked and alone, they must stand for themselves.
My friend Henri and I arrived at this together in 1965
before I went away, before he began to kill himself,
and the two of us to betray our love. Can you taste
what I'm saying? It is onions or potatoes, a pinch
of simple salt, the wealth of melting butter, it is obvious,
it stays in the back of your throat like a truth
you never uttered because the time was always wrong,
it stays there for the rest of your life, unspoken,
made of that dirt we call earth, the metal we call salt,
in a form we have no words for, and you live on it.

PHILIP LEVINE

The First Green of Spring

Out walking in the swamp picking cowslip, marsh mangold,
this sweet first green of spring. Now sautéed in a pan melting
to a deeper green than ever they were alive, this green, this life,

harbinger of things to come. Now we sit at the table munching
on this message from the dawn which says we and the world
are alive again today, and this is the worlds birthday. And

even though we know we are growing old, we are dying, we
will never be young again, we also know we're still right here
now, today, and, my oh my! don't these greens taste good.

DAVID BUDBILL

O Taste and See

The world is
not with us enough.
O taste and see

the subway Bible poster said,
meaning **The Lord**, meaning
if anything all that lives
to the imagination's tongue,

grief, mercy, language.
tangerine, weather, to
breathe them, bite,
savor, chew, swallow, transform

into our flesh our
deaths, crossing the street, plum, quince,
living in the orchard and being

hungry, and plucking
the fruit.

DENISE LEVERTOV

From Blossoms

From blossoms comes
this brown paper bag of peaches
we bought from the boy
at the bend in the road where we turned toward
signs painted *Peaches*.

From laden boughs, from hands,
from sweet fellowship in the bins,
comes nectar at the roadside, succulent
peaches we devour, dusty skin and all,
comes the familiar dust of summer, dust we eat.

O, to take what we love inside,
to carry within us an orchard, to eat
not only the skin, but the shade,
not only the sugar, but the days, to hold
the fruit in our hands, adore it, then bite into
the round jubilance of peach.

There are days we live
as if death were nowhere
in the background; from joy
to joy to joy, from wing to wing,
from blossom to blossom to
impossible blossom, to sweet impossible blossom.

LI-YOUNG LEE

Peaches

A mouthful of language to swallow:
stretches of beach, sweet clinches,
breaches in walls, pleached branches;
britches hauled over haunches;
hunched leeches, wrenched teachers.
What English can do: ransack

the warmth that chuckles beneath
fuzzed surfaces, smooth velvet
richness, plashy juices.
I beseech you, peach,
clench me into the sweetness
of your reaches.

PETER DAVISON

Blackberry Eating

I love to go out in late September
among the fat, overripe, icy, black blackberries
to eat blackberries for breakfast,
the stalks very prickly, a penalty
they earn for knowing the black art
of blackberry making; and as I stand among them
lifting the stalks to my mouth, the ripest berries
fall almost unbidden to my tongue,
as words sometimes do, certain peculiar words
like *strengths* or *squinched* or *broughamed*,
many-lettered, one-syllabled lumps,
which I squeeze, squinch open, and splurge well
in the silent, startled, icy, black language
of blackberry eating in late September.

GALWAY KINNELL

Blackberrying

Nobody in the lane, and nothing, nothing but blackberries,
Blackberries on either side, though on the right mainly,
A blackberry alley, going down in hooks, and a sea
Somewhere at the end of it, heaving. Blackberries
Big as the ball of my thumb, and dumb as eyes
Ebon in the hedges, fat

With blue-red juices. These they squander on my fingers.
I had not asked for such a blood sisterhood; they must love me.
They accommodate themselves to my milkbottle, flattening their sides.

Overhead go the choughs in black, cacophonous flocks –
Bits of burnt paper wheeling in a blown sky.
Theirs is the only voice, protesting, protesting.
I do not think the sea will appear at all.
The high, green meadows are glowing, as if lit from within.
I come to one bush of berries so ripe it is a bush of flies,
Hanging their bluegreen bellies and their wing panes in a Chinese
    screen.
The honey-feast of the berries has stunned them; they believe in
    heaven.
One more hook, and the berries and bushes end.

The only thing to come now is the sea.
From between two hills a sudden wind funnels at me,
Slapping its phantom laundry in my face.
These hills are too green and sweet to have tasted salt.
I follow the sheep path between them. A last hook brings me
To the hills' northern face, and the face is orange rock
That looks out on nothing, nothing but a great space
Of white and pewter lights, and a din like silversmiths
Beating and beating at an intractable metal.

SYLVIA PLATH

A Kumquat for John Keats

Today I found the right fruit for my prime,
not orange, not tangelo, and not lime,
nor moon-like globes of grapefruit that now hang
outside our bedroom, nor tart lemon's tang
(though last year full of bile and self-defeat
I wanted to believe no life was sweet)
not the tangible sunshine of the tangerine,
and no incongruous citrus ever seen
at greengrocers' in Newcastle or Leeds
mis-spelt by the spuds and mud-caked swedes

a fruit an older poet might substitute
for the grape John Keats thought fit to be Joy's fruit,
when, two years before he died, he tried to write
how Melancholy dwelled inside Delight,
and if he'd known the citrus that I mean
that's not orange, lemon, lime or tangerine,
I'm pretty sure that Keats, though he had heard
'of candied apple, quince and plum and gourd'
instead of 'grape against the palate fine'
would have, if he'd known it, plumped for mine,
this Eastern citrus scarcely cherry size
he'd bite just once and then apostrophise
and pen one stanza how the fruit had all
the qualities of fruit before the Fall,
but in the next few lines be forced to write
how Eve's apple tasted at the second bite,
and if John Keats had only lived to be,
because of extra years, in need like me,
at 42 he'd help me celebrate
that Micanopy kumquat that I ate
whole, straight off the tree, sweet pulp and sour skin –
or was it sweet outside, and sour within?
For however many kumquats that I eat
I'm not sure if it's flesh or rind that's sweet,
and being a man of doubt at life's mid-way
I'd offer Keats some kumquats and I'd say:
You'll find that one part's sweet and one part's tart:
say where the sweetness or the sourness start.
I find I can't, as if one couldn't say
exactly where the night became the day,
which makes for me the kumquat taken whole
best fruit, and metaphor, to fit the soul
of one in Florida at 42 with Keats
crunching kumquats, thinking, as he eats
the flesh, the juice, the pith, the pips, the peel,
that this is how a full life ought to feel,
its perishable relish prick the tongue,
when the man who savours life's no longer young,
the fruits that were his futures far behind.
Then it's the kumquat fruit expresses best
how days have darkness round them like a rind,
life has a skin of death that keeps its zest.

History, a life, the heart, the brain
flow to the taste buds and flow back again.
That decade or more past Keats's span
makes me an older, not a wiser man,
who knows that it's too late for dying young,
but since youth leaves some sweetnesses unsung,
he's granted days and kumquats to express
Man's Being ripened by his Nothingness.
And it isn't just the gap of sixteen years,
a bigger crop of terrors, hopes and fears,
but a century of history on this earth
between John Keats's death and my own birth –
years like an open crater, gory, grim,
with bloody bubbles leering at the rim;
a thing no bigger than an urn explodes
and ravishes all silence, and all odes,
Flora asphyxiated by foul air
unknown to either Keats or Lemprière,
dehydrated Naiads, Dryad amputees
dragging themselves through slagscapes with no trees,
a shirt of Nessus fire that gnaws and eats
children half the age of dying Keats...

Now were you twenty five or six years old
when that fevered brow at last grew cold?
I've got no books to hand to check the dates.
My grudging but glad spirit celebrates
that all I've got to hand 's the kumquats, John,
the fruit I'd love to have your verdict on,
but dead men don't eat kumquats, or drink wine,
they shiver in the arms of Proserpine,
not warm in bed beside their Fanny Brawne,
nor watch her pick ripe grapefruit in the dawn
as I did, waking, when I saw her twist,
with one deft movement of a sunburnt wrist,
the moon, that feebly lit our last night's walk
past alligator swampland, off its stalk.
I thought of moon-juice juleps when I saw,
as if I'd never seen the moon before,
the planet glow among the fruit, and its pale light
make each citrus on the tree its satellite.

Each evening when I reach to draw the blind
stars seem the light zest squeezed through night's black rind;

the night's peeled fruit the sun, juiced of its rays,
first stains, then streaks, then floods the world with days,
days, when the very sunlight made me weep,
days, spent like the nights in deep, drugged sleep,
days in Newcastle by my daughter's bed,
wondering if she, or I, weren't better dead,
days in Leeds, grey days, my first dark suit,
my mother's wreaths stacked next to Christmas fruit,
and days, like this in Micanopy. Days!

As strong sun burns away the dawn's grey haze
I pick a kumquat and the branches spray
cold dew in my face to start the day.
The dawn's molasses make the citrus gleam
still in the orchards of the groves of dream
The limes, like Galway after weeks of rain,
glow with a greenness that is close to pain,
the dew-cooled surfaces of fruit that spent
all last night flaming in the firmament.
The new day dawns. O days! My spirit greets
the kumquat with the spirit of John Keats.
O kumquat, comfort for not dying young,
both sweet and bitter, bless the poet's tongue!
I burst the whole fruit chilled by morning dew
against my palate. Fine, for 42!

I search for buzzards as the air grows clear
and see them ride fresh thermals overhead.
Their bleak cries were the first sound I could hear
when I stepped at the start of sunrise out of doors,
and a noise like last night's bedsprings on our bed
from Mr Fowler sharpening farmers' saws.

TONY HARRISON

Crab Apple Jelly

Every year you said it wasn't worth the trouble –
you'd better things to do with your time –
and it made you furious when the jars

were sold at the church fête
for less than the cost of the sugar.

And every year you drove into the lanes
around Calverton to search
for the wild trees whose apples
looked as red and as sweet as cherries,
and tasted sourer than gooseberries.

You cooked them in the wide copper pan
Grandma brought with her from Wigan,
smashing them against the sides
with a long wooden spoon to split
the skins, straining the pulp

through an old muslin nappy.
It hung for days, tied with string
to the kitchen steps, dripping
into a bowl on the floor –
brown-stained, horrible,

a head in a bag, a pouch
of sourness, of all that went wrong
in that house of women. The last drops
you wrung out with your hands;
then, closing; doors and windows

to shut out the clamouring wasps,
you boiled up the juice with sugar,
dribbling the syrup onto a cold plate
until it set to a glaze,
filling the heated jars.

When the jars were cool
you held one up to the light
to see if the jelly had cleared.
Oh Mummy, it was clear and shining
as stained glass and the colour of fire.

VICKI FEAVER

A Jar of Honey

You hold it like a lit bulb,
a pound of light,
and swivel the stunned glow
around the fat glass sides:

it's the sun, all flesh and no bones
but for the floating knuckle
of honeycomb
attesting to the nature of the struggle.

JACOB POLLEY

Sweetness, Always

Why such harsh machinery?
Why, to write down the stuff
and people of every day,
must poems be dressed up in gold,
in old and fearful stone?

I want verses of felt or feather
which scarcely weigh, mild verses
with the intimacy of beds
where people have loved and dreamed.
I want poems stained
by hands and everydayness.

Verses of pastry which melt
into milk and sugar in the mouth,
air and water to drink,
the bites and kisses of love.
I long for eatable sonnets,
poems of honey and flour.

Vanity keeps prodding us
to lift ourselves skyward
or to make deep and useless
tunnels underground.

So we forget the joyous
love-needs of our bodies.
We forget about pastries.
We are not feeding the world.

In Madras a long time since,
I saw a sugary pyramid,
a tower of confectionery –
one level after another,
and in the construction, rubies,
and other blushing delights,
medieval and yellow.

Someone dirtied his hands
to cook up so much sweetness.

Brother poets from here
and there, from earth and sky,
from Medellín, from Veracruz,
Abyssinia, Antofagasta,
do you know the recipe for honeycombs?

Let's forget all about that stone.

Let your poetry fill up
the equinoctial pastry shop
our mouths long to devour –
all the children's mouths
and the poor adults' also.
Don't go on without seeing,
relishing, understanding
all these hearts of sugar.

Don't be afraid of sweetness.

With us or without us,
sweetness will go on living
and is infinitely alive,
forever being revived,
for it's in a man's mouth,
whether he's eating or singing,
that sweetness has its place.

PABLO NERUDA
translated from the Spanish by Alastair Reid

For Desire

Give me the strongest cheese, the one that stinks best;
and I want the good wine, the swirl in crystal
surrendering the bruised scent of blackberries,
or cherries, the rich spurt in the back
of the throat, the holding it there before swallowing.
Give me the lover who yanks open the door
of his house and presses me to the wall
in the dim hallway, and keeps me there until I'm drenched
and shaking, whose kisses arrive by the boatload
and begin their delicious diaspora
through the cities and small towns of my body.
To hell with the saints, with the martyrs
of my childhood meant to instruct me
in the power of endurance and faith,
to hell with the next world and its pallid angels
swooning and sighing like Victorian girls.
I want this world. I want to walk into
the ocean and feel it trying to drag me along
like I'm nothing but a broken bit of scratched glass,
and I want to resist it. I want to go
staggering and flailing my way
through the bars and back rooms,
through the gleaming hotels and the weedy
lots of abandoned sunflowers and the parks
where dogs are let off their leashes
in spite of the signs, where they sniff each
other and roll together in the grass, I want to
lie down somewhere and suffer for love until
it nearly kills me, and then I want to get up again
and put on that little black dress and wait
for you, yes you, to come over here
and get down on your knees and tell me
just how fucking good I look.

KIM ADDONIZIO

61

Wild strawberries

What I get I bring home to you:
a dark handful, sweet-edged,
dissolving in one mouthful.

I bother to bring them for you
though they're so quickly over,
pulpless, sliding to juice,

a grainy rub on the tongue
and the taste's gone. If you remember
we were in the woods at wild strawberry time

and I was making a basket of dockleaves
to hold what you'd picked,
but the cold leaves unplaited themselves

and slid apart, and again unplaited themselves
until I gave up and ate wild strawberries
out of your hands for sweetness.

I lipped at your palm –
the little salt edge there,
the tang of money you'd handled.

As we stayed in the wood, hidden,
we heard the sound system below us
calling the winners at Chepstow,
faint as the breeze turned.

The sun came out on us, the shade blotches
went hazel: we heard names
bubble like stock-doves over the woods

as jockeys in stained silks gentled
those sweat-dark, shuddering horses
down to the walk.

HELEN DUNMORE

Horses

From the window I saw the horses.

I was in Berlin, in winter. The light
was without light, the sky without sky.

The air white like wet bread.

And from my window a vacant arena,
bitten by the teeth of winter.

Suddenly, led by a man,
ten horses stepped out into the mist.

Hardly had they surged forth, like flame,
than to my eyes they filled the whole world,
empty till then. Perfect, ablaze,
they were like ten gods with wide pure hoofs,
with manes like a dream of salt.

Their rumps were worlds and oranges.

Their color was honey, amber, fire.

Their necks were towers
cut from the stone of pride,
and behind their transparent eyes
energy raged, like a prisoner.

And there, in the silence, in the middle
of the day, of the dark, slovenly winter,
the intense horses were blood
and rhythm, the animating treasure of life.

I looked, I looked and was reborn: without knowing it,
there, was the fountain, the dance of gold, the sky,
the fire that revived in beauty.

I have forgotten that dark Berlin winter.

I will not forget the light of the horses.

PABLO NERUDA
translated from the Spanish by Stephen Mitchell

The Horses

I climbed through woods in the hour-before-dawn dark.
Evil air, a frost-making stillness,

Not a leaf, not a bird –
A world cast in frost. I came out above the wood

Where my breath left tortuous statues in the iron light.
But the valleys were draining the darkness

Till the moorline – blackening dregs of the brightening grey –
Halved the sky ahead. And I saw the horses:

Huge in the dense grey – ten together –
Megalith-still. They breathed, making no move,

With draped manes and tilted hind-hooves,
Making no sound.

I passed: not one snorted or jerked its head.
Grey silent fragments

Of a grey silent world.

I listened in emptiness on the moor-ridge.
The curlew's tear turned its edge on the silence.

Slowly detail leafed from the darkness. Then the sun
Orange, red, red erupted

Silently, and splitting to its core tore and flung cloud,
Shook the gulf open, showed blue,

And the big planets hanging – .
I turned

Stumbling in the fever of a dream, down towards
The dark woods, from the kindling tops,

And came to the horses.
                    There, still they stood,
But now steaming and glistening under the flow of light,

Their draped stone manes, their tilted hind-hooves
Stirring under a thaw while all around them

The frost showed its fires. But still they made no sound.
Not one snorted or stamped,

Their hung heads patient as the horizons
High over valleys, in the red levelling rays –

In din of the crowded streets, going among the years, the faces,
May I still meet my memory in so lonely a place

Between the streams and the red clouds, hearing curlews,
Hearing the horizons endure.

TED HUGHES

Horses at Christmas

In our little house Creedence were singing
about the old cotton fields, the baby
was flat on his back in front of the fire,
eyes swimming with flame.
Christmas morning, and you were at church.
I thought of going to join you late,
but instead took the baby up to the horses.
Out in the field he started crying.
Maybe I should have taken him to the bath
of stone, the discipline of a saviour, the sanctuary
of hymns –
                    But the horses saved us.
To be close to them, so tough and nothing
to do with us, and their breathing all over him,
and the flaking mud on their necks
where they had rolled, and the sucking of hooves
as they walked the sodden field.
The horses with their long heads,
underwater eyes, watched us watch them.

Then they turned, drumming the field,
leaving us alone – the damp morning
all about, the soaked grass under foot,
the baby's diaphanous ears going pink in the cold
as silence bowed back to earth.

HENRY SHUKMAN

Calf

Outside my window a cow is giving birth.
Wrapped up in plastic, the calf dives feet-first
Onto the rain-sodden, trampled turf.

And at once it is desperate to be upright;
Heaves, flops, kicks as if sky was its birthright,
And not even the sudden slide from dark into daylight

Tugs like the gravity that drags it back to earth.

KATRINA PORTEOUS

How Everything Adores Being Alive

What
    if you were
        a beetle,
            and a soft wind

and a certain allowance of time
    had summoned you
        out of your wrappings,
            and there you were,

so many legs
   hardening,
      maybe even
         more than one pair of eyes

and the whole world
   in front of you?
      And what if you had wings
         and flew

into the garden,
   then fell
      into the up-tipped
         face

of a white flower,
   and what if you had
      a sort of mouth,
         a lip

to place close
   to the skim
      of honey
         that kept offering itself –

what would you think then
   of the world
      as, night and day,
         you were kept there

oh happy prisoner –
   sighing, humming,
      roaming
         that deep cup?

MARY OLIVER

In Praise of the Great Bull Walrus

I wouldn't like to be one
of the walrus people
for the rest of my life
but I wish I could spend
one sunny afternoon
lying on the rocks with them.
I suspect it would be similar
to drinking beer in a tavern
that caters to longshoremen
and won't admit women.
We'd exchange no
cosmic secrets. I'd merely say,
'How yuh doin' you big old walrus?'
and the nearest of
the walrus people
would answer,
'Me? I'm doin' great.
How yuh doin' yourself,
you big old human being, you?'
How good it is to share
the earth with such creatures
and how unthinkable it would have been
to have missed all this
by not being born:
a happy thought, that,
for not being born is
the only tragedy
that we can imagine
but never fear.

ALDEN NOWLAN

Cleaning the Elephant

Thirsty and pale, her face lowered in concentration,
she doesn't seem to mind my sweeping
insects and dung from her corrugated flesh,
permitting me even to brush her soft hairy nape,
where I dream of squatting barefoot one day,
like a figure in a scroll, to feel the immutable
place of thought, if an elephant has thought.
'What is the smell of being human?' I want to ask,
like Plato, desiring to witness the truth
as both elephant and embodiment,
pushing out everything else – as when a soul,
finding its peculiar other, pushes out
the staple of life, which is suffering,
and a red sun wraps everything in gold.

HENRI COLE

The Bull Moose

Down from the purple mist of trees on the mountain,
lurching through forests of white spruce and cedar,
stumbling through tamarack swamps,
came the bull moose
to be stopped at last by a pole-fenced pasture.

Too tired to turn or, perhaps, aware
there was no place left to go, he stood with the cattle.
They, scenting the musk of death, seeing his great head
like the ritual mask of a blood god, moved to the other end
of the field, and waited.

The neighbours heard of it, and by afternoon
cars lined the road. The children teased him
with alder switches and he gazed at them
like an old, tolerant collie. The women asked
if he could have escaped from a Fair.

The oldest man in the parish remembered seeing
a gelded moose yoked with an ox for plowing.
The young men snickered and tried to pour beer
down his throat, while their girl friends took their pictures.

And the bull moose let them stroke his tick-ravaged flanks,
let them pry open his jaws with bottles, let a giggling girl
plant a little purple cap
of thistles on his head.

When the wardens came, everyone agreed it was a shame
to shoot anything so shaggy and cuddlesome.
He looked like the kind of pet
women put to bed with their sons.

So they held their fire. But just as the sun dropped in the river
the bull moose gathered his strength
like a scaffolded king, straightened and lifted his horns
so that even the wardens backed away as they raised their rifles.
When he roared, people ran to their cars. All the young men
leaned on their automobile horns as he toppled.

ALDEN NOWLAN

The Fish

I caught a tremendous fish
and held him beside the boat
half out of water, with my hook
fast in a corner of his mouth.
He didn't fight.
He hadn't fought at all.
He hung a grunting weight,
battered and venerable
and homely. Here and there
his brown skin hung in strips
like ancient wallpaper,
and its pattern of darker brown
was like wallpaper:

shapes like full-blown roses
stained and lost through age.
He was speckled with barnacles,
fine rosettes of lime,
and infested
with tiny white sea-lice,
and underneath two or three
rags of green weed hung down.
While his gills were breathing in
the terrible oxygen
– the frightening gills,
fresh and crisp with blood,
that can cut so badly –
I thought of the coarse white flesh
packed in like feathers,
the big bones and the little bones,
the dramatic reds and blacks
of his shiny entrails,
and the pink swim-bladder
like a big peony.
I looked into his eyes
which were far larger than mine
but shallower, and yellowed,
the irises backed and packed
with tarnished tinfoil
seen through the lenses
of old scratched isinglass.
They shifted a little, but not
to return my stare.
– It was more like the tipping
of an object toward the light.
I admired his sullen face,
the mechanism of his jaw,
and then I saw
that from his lower lip
– if you could call it a lip –
grim, wet, and weaponlike,
hung five old pieces of fish-line,
or four and a wire leader
with the swivel still attached,
with all their five big hooks
grown firmly in his mouth.

A green line, frayed at the end
where he broke it, two heavier lines,
and a fine black thread
still crimped from the strain and snap
when it broke and he got away.
Like medals with their ribbons
frayed and wavering,
a five-haired beard of wisdom
trailing from his aching jaw.
I stared and stared
and victory filled up
the little rented boat,
from the pool of bilge
where oil had spread a rainbow
around the rusted engine
to the bailer rusted orange,
the sun-cracked thwarts,
the oarlocks on their strings,
the gunnels – until everything
was rainbow, rainbow, rainbow!
And I let the fish go.

ELIZABETH BISHOP

The Peace of Wild Things

When despair for the world grows in me
and I wake in the night at the least sound
in fear of what my life and my children's lives may be,
I go and lie down where the wood drake
rests in his beauty on the water, and the great heron feeds.
I come into the peace of wild things
who do not tax their lives with forethought
of grief. I come into the presence of still water.
And I feel above me the day-blind stars
waiting with their light. For a time
I rest in the grace of the world, and am free.

WENDELL BERRY

Gift

A day so happy.
Fog lifted early, I worked in the garden.
Hummingbirds were stopping over honeysuckle flowers.
There was no thing on earth I wanted to possess.
I knew no one worth my envying him.
Whatever evil I had suffered, I forgot.
To think that once I was the same man did not embarrass me.
In my body I felt no pain.
When straightening up, I saw the blue sea and sails.

CZESLAW MILOSZ
translated from the Polish by the author

Not-Yet

Morning of buttered toast;
of coffee, sweetened, with milk.

Out the window,
snow-spruces step from their cobwebs.
Flurry of chickadees, feeding then gone.
A single cardinal stipples an empty branch –
one maple leaf lifted back.

I turn my blessings like photographs into the light;
over my shoulder the god of Not-Yet looks on:

Not-yet-dead, not-yet-lost, not-yet-taken.
Not-yet-shattered, not-yet-sectioned,
not-yet-strewn.

Ample litany, sparing nothing I hate or love,
not-yet-silenced, not-yet-fractured, not-yet-   .

Not-yet-not.

I move my ear a little closer to that humming figure,
I ask him only to stay.

JANE HIRSHFIELD

A Pre-Breakfast Rant

Dull, dull hungry cloth-head dullard! Each day
I'm dull, even this ache is dull (though fatal). Each night
I climb on my lover and we ride
nowhere we haven't been before.
Dull the knife, dull the mirror,
dull each pane of glass around us.
Nothing here is sharp, clear or dangerous,
and even you, my blood's sugar,
have plummeted, disgusted, out of focus.
Let me stand at the window once more and stare
till the world's no longer *out there*.

True world, where are you hiding? Whose crime
makes you hide so? Is it the light yet murderous
force of habit, settling like grime on the mirror,
that lets you slip away? Yes,
the world is hid behind itself, smirking slightly,
as though we're in a murder mystery
where the killer and the clue are right in this room
and we're looking (for God's sake, they can be nowhere else!)
and we can see nothing, so well is everything hidden
as itself. The way I looked at you last night on the floor
and could not see what I saw before...

Open up, true world! I'm banging on
your pane that you might part
or shower down daggers to cut me to ribbons.
I can bear anything but this dull that I am,
unburnished, non-reflective, stupified, numb!
This cloth I've somehow spread over the world –
when I turn back from the kettle,
may it be whipped away: reveal again
the morning laid out like a shining breakfast table
with as many places as there are appetites
for this day about to – truly – begin.

ANDREW GREIG

Hunger for Something

Sometimes I long to be the woodpile,
cut-apart trees soon to be smoke,
or even the smoke itself,

sinewy ghost of ash and air, going
wherever I want to, at least for a while.

Neither inside nor out,
neither lost nor home, no longer
a shape or a name, I'd pass through

all the broken windows of the world.
It's not a wish for consciousness to end.

It's not the appetite an army has
for its own emptying heart,
but a hunger to stand now and then

alone on the death-grounds,
where the dogs of the self are feeding.

CHASE TWICHELL

Talking to God on the Seventh Day

You're not so sure about this world?
Listen. Take another look:

            the joyful reckless
barking dogs, convinced of doom, hysterical,
or only proud to own the yard,
the block, the wind –
            the raised welt of their voices
roughening your dreams.

The new leaves slightly bent, like
                fingers on guitar,
rippling their chord of twigs –
and the still-bare
slingshot branches,
        naked as the tails of rats,
liminal as roots.

The squirrel crushed in the road,
        its tail still
waving, in the wind of
passing cars, a flag,

and the blackest of black crows,
        breaching the body
with its surgeon beak –

black needles of its feet so pleased
with death,
        which is also meat, and life.
Another squirrel, its rapid jaws

                muttering around a nut:
                My number not up yet not yet bub not yet –

Now tell me why you ever thought
you could improve on this

                music, this hunger.

RUTH L. SCHWARTZ

Hunger

Digging into the apple
with my thumbs.
Scraping out the clogged nails
and digging deeper.

Refusing the moon color.
Refusing the smell and memories.
Digging in with the sweet juice
running along my hands unpleasantly.
Refusing the sweetness.
Turning my hands to gouge out chunks.
Feeling the juice sticky
on my wrists. The skin itching.
Getting to the wooden part.
Getting to the seeds.
Going on.
Not taking anyone's word for it.
Getting beyond the seeds.

JACK GILBERT

Dark Pines Under Water

This land like a mirror turns you inward
And you become a forest in a furtive lake;
The dark pines of your mind reach downward,
You dream in the green of your time,
Your memory is a row of sinking pines.

Explorer, you tell yourself this is not what you came for
Although it is good here, and green;
You had meant to move with a kind of largeness,
You had planned a heavy grace, an anguished dream.

But the dark pines of your mind dip deeper
And you are sinking, sinking, sleeper
In an elementary world;
There is something down there and you want it told.

GWENDOLYN MacEWEN

Toxicity

Can acupuncture cure the sadness of organs
Can the liver forget sadness when the needles enter,
its field of memory,
words of politic, the mining this week of the ports
of Nicaragua, Corinto & Puerto Sandino
Nicaragua of the liver & the pancreas,
Nicaragua of the heart,
the small cells of the kidneys teeming
The cords of energy severed in the body,
the body poisoned by underwater mines
In a country never seen, fish boats
pulling drag-nets under water,
risking explosion,
can acupuncture cure the sadness of the liver, now?

What is fucked-up in the body, what is blocked
& carried rolled in the intestine,
what suffocates so badly in the lungs,
adhering, we talk about it, *toxicity*, your body standing
at the sink & turned to me,
near but not near enough, not near enough, Gail
What if the blocked space in the liver is just sadness,
can it be cured then?
Can the brain stop being the brain?
Can the brain be, for a few minutes, some other organ,
any organ, or a gland, a simple gland with its fluids,
its dark edges light never enters, can it let us alone?
When I think of the brain I think
how can something this dark help us
together
to stay here, as close as possible, avoiding underwater minefields,
the ships of trade churning perilously toward us,
the throb of their motors calling the mines up,
as close as our two skins

ERIN MOURÉ

78

Planet Earth

It has to be spread out, the skin of this planet,
has to be ironed, the sea in its whiteness;
and the hands keep on moving,
smoothing the holy surfaces.

PABLO NERUDA
'In Praise of Ironing'

It has to be loved the way a laundress loves her linens,
the way she moves her hands caressing the fine muslins
knowing their warp and woof,
like a lover coaxing, or a mother praising.
It has to be loved as it it were embroidered
with flowers and birds and two joined hearts upon it.
It has to be stretched and stroked.
It has to be celebrated.
O this great beloved world and all the creatures in it
It has to be spread out, the skin of this planet.

The trees must be washed, and the grasses and mosses.
They have to be polished as if made of green brass.
The rivers and little streams with their hidden cresses
and pale-coloured pebbles
and their fool's gold
must be washed and starched or shined into brightness,
the sheets of lake water
smoothed with the hand
and the foam of the oceans pressed into neatness.
It has to be ironed, the sea in its whiteness

and pleated and goffered, the flower-blue sea
the protean, wine-dark, grey, green, sea
with its metres of satin and bolts of brocade.
And sky – such an O! overhead – night and day
must be burnished and rubbed
by hands that are loving
so the blue blazons forth
and the stars keep on shining
within and above
and the hands keep on moving.

It has to be made bright, the skin of this planet
till it shines in the sun like gold leaf.
Archangels then will attend to its metals
and polish the rods of its rain.
Seraphim will stop singing hosannas
to shower it with blessings and blisses and praises
and, newly in love,
we must draw it and paint it
our pencils and brushes and loving caresses
smoothing the holy surfaces.

P.K. PAGE

The Ball

As long as nothing can be known for sure
(no signals have been picked up yet),

as long as Earth is still unlike
the nearer and more distant planets,

as long as there's neither hide nor hair
of other grasses graced by other winds,
of other treetops bearing other crowns,
other animals as well-grounded as our own,

as long as only the local echo
has been known to speak in syllables,

as long as we still haven't heard word
of better or worse mozarts,
platos, edisons somewhere,

as long as our inhuman crimes
are still committed only between humans,

as long as our kindness
is still incomparable,
peerless even in its imperfection,

as long as our heads packed with illusions
still pass for the only heads so packed,

as long as the roofs of our mouths alone
still raise voices to high heavens –

let's act like very special guests of honor
at the district-firemen's ball,
dance to the beat of the local oompah band
and pretend that it's the ball
to end all balls.

I can't speak for others –
for me this is
misery and happiness enough:

just this sleepy backwater
where even the stars have time to burn
while winking at us
unintentionally.

WISLAWA SZYMBORSKA
translated from the Polish by Stanislaw Baranczak and Clare Cavanagh

The Passionate World

is round. For days we sail, for months,
and still the way is new; strange stars.
Drawn to you, taut over time,
ropes connect this floating floor
to the wind, fraying into sound.

To arrive is to sleep
where we stop moving.
Past the shoal of clothes
to that shore, heaped with debris
of words. A hem of salt,
white lace, on sea-heavy legs.

Love longs for land. All night
we dream the jungle's sleepy electricity;
gnashing chords of insects swim in our ears
and we go under, into green. All night
love draws its heavy drape of scent against the sea
and we wake with the allure of earth in our lungs,
hungry for bread and oranges.
Salamanders dart from your step's shadow, disappear
among wild coffee, fleshy cacti, thorny succulents and
flowers like bowls to save the rain.
We are sailors who wake when the moon intrudes
the smoky tavern of dreams, wake to find a name on an arm
or our bodies bruised by sun or the pressure of a hand,
wake with the map of night on our skin,
traced like moss-stained stone.

Lost, past the last familiar outpost,
flat on deck, milky light cool on our damp hair,
we look up past the ship's angles to stars austere
as a woodcut, and pray we never reach
the lights of that invisible city, where,

landlocked, they have given up on our return.
But some nights, woken by wind,
looking up at different stars,
they are reminded of us, the faint taste of
salt on their lips.

ANNE MICHAELS

World Truffle

This time the mycorrhizal infection
at the crooked roots of a hazelnut tree
meets a set of conditions so knotted and invisible
it feels like good will, or magic,
when the truffle begins its warty branches
that grow away from the sun.

This time it doesn't stop with one fairy ring
and dissolute spores, but fingers its way
beneath the turf and under the fence
and past the signs for Truffle Reserve:
Harvest Regulated by the State Forestry Department,
out through Umbria, up the shank of Italy;
it enmeshes the skin of the Alps.
In time its pale filaments have threaded Europe and,
almost as stubborn as death, are probing
sand on one side and burrowing on the other
through the heated muttering bed of the sea.
Its pregnant mounds rise modestly
in deserts, rain forests, city parks;
yellow truffle-flies hover and buzz
at tiny aromatic cracks in Panama and the Aleutians.
It smells like wood smoke, humus and ore,
it smells of sex. It smells like ten thousand years.
It smells of a promise that a little tastes better than all,
that a mix and disguise is best.
Young dogs whiff it, twist in the air
and bury their faces in loam;
tapirs and cormorants sway in its fragrance,
camels open their nostrils for it,
coatimundi and honey badgers start digging,
lemurs bark and octopi embrace.
Humans sense nothing unusual. Yet some of them –
teachers raking leaves in Sioux City,
truck drivers stretching their legs in Ulan Bator –
take a few deep breaths and, unaware,
begin to love the world.

SARAH LINDSAY

You, Andrew Marvell

And here face down beneath the sun
And here upon earth's noonward height
To feel the always coming on
The always rising of the night:

To feel creep up the curving east
The earthly chill of dusk and slow
Upon those under lands the vast
And ever-climbing shadow grow

And strange at Ecbatan the trees
Take leaf by leaf the evening strange
The flooding dark about their knees
The mountains over Persia change

And now at Kermanshah the gate
Dark empty and the withered grass
And through the twilight now the late
Few travelers in the westward pass

And Baghdad darken and the bridge
Across the silent river gone
And through Arabia the edge
Of evening widen and steal on

And deepen on Palmyra's street
The wheel rut in the ruined stone
And Lebanon fade out and Crete
High through the clouds and overblown

And over Sicily the air
Still flashing with the landward gulls
And loom and slowly disappear
The sails above the shadowy hulls

And Spain go under and the shore
Of Africa the gilded sand
And evening vanish and no more
The low pale light across that land

Nor now the long light on the sea:

And here face downward in the sun
To feel how swift how secretly
The shadow of the night comes on...

ARCHIBALD MacLEISH

Look and See

This morning, at waterside, a sparrow flew
to a water rock and landed, by error, on the back
of an eider duck; lightly it fluttered off, amused.
The duck, too, was not provoked, but, you might say, was
laughing.

This afternoon a gull sailing over
our house was casually scratching
its stomach of white feathers with one
pink foot as it flew.

Oh Lord, how shining and festive is your gift to us, if we
only look, and see.

MARY OLIVER

Stationery

The moon did not become the sun.
It just fell on the desert
in great sheets, reams
of silver handmade by you.
The night is your cottage industry now,
the day is your brisk emporium.
The world is full of paper.

Write to me.

AGHA SHAHID ALI

The Present

For the present there is just one moon,
though every level pond gives back another.

But the bright disc shining in the black lagoon,
perceived by astrophysicist and lover,

is milliseconds old. And even that light's
seven minutes older than its source.

And the stars we think we see on moonless nights
are long extinguished. And, of course,

this very moment, as you read this line,
is literally gone before you know it.

Forget the here-and-now. We have no time
but this device of wantoness and wit.

Make me this present then: your hand in mine,
and we'll live out our lives in it.

MICHAEL DONAGHY

Blessing

The skin cracks like a pod.
There never is enough water.

Imagine the drip of it,
the small splash, echo
in a tin mug,
the voice of a kindly god.

Sometimes, the sudden rush
of fortune. The municipal pipe bursts,
silver crashes to the ground

and the flow has found
a roar of tongues. From the huts,
a congregation: every man woman
child for streets around
butts in, with pots,
brass, copper, aluminium,
plastic buckets,
frantic hands,

and naked children
screaming in the liquid sun,
their highlights polished to perfection,
flashing light,
as the blessing sings
over their small bones.

IMTIAZ DHARKER

The Rain

All night the sound had
come back again,
and again falls
this quiet, persistent rain.

What am I to myself
that must be remembered,
insisted upon
so often? Is it

that never the ease,
even the hardness,
of rain falling
will have for me

something other than this,
something not so insistent –
am I to be locked in this
final uneasiness.

Love, if you love me,
lie next to me.
Be for me, like rain,
the getting out

of the tiredness, the fatuousness, the semi-
lust of intentional indifference.
Be wet
with a decent happiness.

ROBERT CREELEY

So Much Happiness

It is difficult to know what to do with so much happiness.
With sadness there is something to rub against,
a wound to tend with lotion and cloth.
When the world falls in around you, you have pieces to pick up,
something to hold in your hands, like ticket stubs or change.

But happiness floats.
It doesn't need you to hold it down.
It doesn't need anything.
Happiness lands on the roof of the next house, singing,
and disappears when it wants to.
You are happy either way.
Even the fact that you once lived in a peaceful tree house
and now live over a quarry of noise and dust
cannot make you unhappy.
Everything has a life of its own,
it too could wake up filled with possibilities
of coffee cake and ripe peaches,
and love even the floor which needs to be swept,
the soiled linens and scratched records...

Since there is no place large enough
to contain so much happiness,
you shrug, you raise your hands, and it flows out of you
into everything you touch. You are not responsible.

You take no credit, as the night sky takes no credit
for the moon, but continues to hold it, and share it,
and in that way, be known.

NAOMI SHIHAB NYE

Happiness

There's just no accounting for happiness,
or the way it turns up like a prodigal
who comes back to the dust at your feet
having squandered a fortune far away.

And how can you not forgive?
You make a feast in honor of what
was lost, and take from its place the finest
garment, which you saved for an occasion
you could not imagine, and you weep night and day
to know that you were not abandoned,
that happiness saved its most extreme form
for you alone.

No, happiness is the uncle you never
knew about, who flies a single-engine plane
onto the grassy landing strip, hitchhikes
into town, and inquires at every door
until he finds you asleep midafternoon
as you so often are during the unmerciful
hours of your despair.

It comes to the monk in his cell.
It comes to the woman sweeping the street
with a birch broom, to the child
whose mother has passed out from drink.
It comes to the lover, to the dog chewing
a sock, to the pusher, to the basket maker,
and to the clerk stacking cans of carrots
in the night.

It even comes to the boulder
in the perpetual shade of pine barrens,
to rain falling on the open sea,
to the wineglass, weary of holding wine.

JANE KENYON

The Third Body

A man and a woman sit near each other, and they do not long
At this moment to be older, or younger, or born
In any other nation, or any other time, or any other place.
They are content to be where they are, talking or not talking.
Their breaths together feed someone whom we do not know.
The man sees the way his fingers move;
He sees her hands close around a book she hands to him.
They obey a third body that they share in common.
They have promised to love that body.
Age may come; parting may come; death will come!
A man and a woman sit near each other;
As they breathe they feed someone we do not know,
Someone we know of, whom we have never seen.

ROBERT BLY

On Pilgrimage

May the smell of thyme and lavender accompany us on our journey
To a province that does not know how lucky it is
For it was, among all the hidden corners of the earth,
The only one chosen and visited.

We tended toward the Place but no signs led there.
Till it revealed itself in a pastoral valley
Between mountains that look older than memory,
By a narrow river humming at the grotto.

90

May the taste of wine and roast meat stay with us
As it did when we used to feast in the clearings,
Searching, not finding, gathering rumors,
Always comforted by the brightness of the day.

May the gentle mountains and the bells of the flocks
Remind us of everything we have lost,
For we have seen on our way and fallen in love
With the world that will pass in a twinkling.

CZESLAW MILOSZ
translated from the Polish by Czeslaw Milosz & Robert Hass

The Summer Day

Who made the world?
Who made the swan, and the black bear?
Who made the grasshopper?
This grasshopper, I mean —
the one who has flung herself out of the grass,
the one who is eating sugar out of my hand,
who is moving her jaws back and forth instead of up and down —
who is gazing around with her enormous and complicated eyes.
Now she lifts her pale forearms and thoroughly washes her face.
Now she snaps her wings open, and floats away.
I don't know exactly what a prayer is.
I do know how to pay attention, how to fall down
into the grass, how to kneel down in the grass,
how to be idle and blessed, how to stroll through the fields,
which is what I have been doing all day.
Tell me, what else should I have done?
Doesn't everything die at last, and too soon?
Tell me, what is it you plan to do
with your one wild and precious life?

MARY OLIVER

The God Who Loves You

It must be troubling for the god who loves you
To ponder how much happier you'd be today
Had you been able to glimpse your many futures.
It must be painful for him to watch you on Friday evenings
Driving home from the office, content with your week –
Three fine houses sold to deserving families –
Knowing as he does exactly what would have happened
Had you gone to your second choice for college,
Knowing the roommate you'd have been allotted
Whose ardent opinions on painting and music
Would have kindled in you a lifelong passion.
A life thirty points above the life you're living
On any scale of satisfaction. And every point
A thorn in the side of the god who loves you.
You don't want that, a large-souled man like you
Who tries to withhold from your wife the day's disappointments
So she can save her empathy for the children.
And would you want this god to compare your wife
With the woman you were destined to meet on the other campus?
It hurts you to think of him ranking the conversation
You'd have enjoyed over there higher in insight
Than the conversation you're used to.
And think how this loving god would feel
Knowing that the man next in line for your wife
Would have pleased her more than you ever will
Even on your best days, when you really try.
Can you sleep at night believing a god like that
Is pacing his cloudy bedroom, harassed by alternatives
You're spared by ignorance? The difference between what is
And what could have been will remain alive for him
Even after you cease existing, after you catch a chill
Running out in the snow for the morning paper,
Losing eleven years that the god who loves you
Will feel compelled to imagine scene by scene
Unless you come to the rescue by imagining him
No wiser than you are, no god at all, only a friend
No closer than the actual friend you made at college,
The one you haven't written in months. Sit down tonight

And write him about the life you can talk about
With a claim to authority, the life you've witnessed,
Which for all you know is the life you've chosen.

CARL DENNIS

The Ikons

Hard, heavy, slow, dark,
Or so I find them, the hands of Te Whaea

Teaching me to die. Some lightness will come later
When the heart has lost its unjust hope

For special treatment. Today I go with a bucket
Over the paddocks of young grass,

So delicate like fronds of maidenhair,
Looking for mushrooms. I find twelve of them,

Most of them little, and some eaten by maggots,
But they'll do to add to the soup. It's a long time now

Since the great ikons fell down,
God, Mary, home, sex, poetry,

Whatever one uses as a bridge
To cross the river that only has one beach,

And even one's name is a way of saying –
'This gap inside a coat' – the darkness I call God,

The darkness I call Te Whaea, how can they translate
The blue calm evening sky that a plane tunnels through

Like a little wasp, or the bucket in my hand,
Into something else? I go on looking

For mushrooms in the field, and the fist of longing
Punches my heart, until it is too dark to see.

JAMES K. BAXTER

Veni Creator

Come, Holy Spirit,
bending or not bending the grasses,
appearing or not above our heads in a tongue of flame,
at hay harvest or when they plough in the orchards or when snow
covers crippled firs in the Sierra Nevada.
I am only a man: I need visible signs.
I tire easily, building the stairway of abstraction.
Many a time I asked, you know it well, that the statue in church
lift its hand, only once, just once, for me.
But I understand that signs must be human,
therefore call one man, anywhere on earth,
not me – after all I have some decency –
and allow me, when I look at him, to marvel at you.

CZESLAW MILOSZ
translated from the Polish by Czeslaw Milosz & Robert Pinsky

Prayers of Steel

Lay me on an anvil, O God.
Beat me and hammer me into a crowbar.
Let me pry loose old walls.
Let me lift and loosen old foundations.

Lay me on an anvil, O God.
Beat me and hammer me into a steel spike.
Drive me into the girders that hold a skyscraper together.
Take red-hot rivets and fasten me into the central girders.
Let me be the great nail holding a skyscraper through blue nights
         into white stars.

CARL SANDBURG

'Last night while I was sleeping'

Last night while I was sleeping
I dreamed – blessed illusion! –
a fountain flowed
inside my heart.
Water, tell me by what hidden
channel you came to me
with a spring of new life
I never drank?

Last night while I was sleeping
I dreamed – blessed illusion! –
I had a beehive
inside my heart,
and from my old bitterness
the gold bees
were contriving white combs
and sweet honey.

Last night while I was sleeping
I dreamed – blessed illusion! –
a fiery sun glowed
inside my heart.
It was fiery, giving off heat
from a red fireplace.
It was the sun throwing out light
and made one weep.

Last night while I was sleeping
I dreamed – blessed illusion! –
that it was God I held
inside my heart.

ANTONIO MACHADO
translated from the Spanish by Willis Barnstone

Mission Impossible

He had been in paradise
Surrounded by a whole flotilla of angels
Each reflecting like mirrors
The warmth of the father;
We'll talk of this later. Well done,
My son. Stand back, to the angels
Their hot wings pressing like a feather
Mattress. Rest tonight and tomorrow
In the room next to mine
Tomorrow when you're feeling recovered
I have a proposition to put to you –
It involves going back. A spasm crossed
The wounds, a few drops of blood fell
On the floor. No, not that, my son
But to show there's no misunderstanding between us
Remember the last dark words and the sky.
The angels gagged me then by my orders in case
I intervened. Just to see a few friends
Walk round a bit like happier times
Be in their rooms without locks. Console them
Show yourself to the ones who seemed sorry.
The angels will take care of the stone.

Did he smile early on Sunday
Smelling the spices in his wounds
Tasting the white walls of the tomb
With his eyes, the fresh air of morning?

ELIZABETH SMITHER

from Counterpoint

To be alive then
was to be aware how necessary
prayer was and impossible.

The philosophers had done
their work well, demolishing
proofs we never believed in.

We were drifting in space-
time, in touch with what we had
left and could not return to.

We rehearsed the excuses
for the deficiencies of love's
kingdom, avoiding our eyebeams.

Beset, as we were,
with science's signposts, we whimpered
to no purpose that we were lost.

We are here still. What
is survival's relationship
with meaning? The answer once

was the bone's music at the lips
of time. We are incinerating
them both now in the mind's crematorium.

R.S THOMAS

Missing God

His grace is no longer called for
before meals: farmed fish multiply
without His intercession.
Bread production rises through
disease-resistant grains devised
scientifically to mitigate His faults.

Yet, though we rebelled against Him
like adolescents, uplifted to see
an oppressive father banished –
a bearded hermit – to the desert,
we confess to missing Him at times.

Miss Him during the civil wedding
when, at the blossomy altar
of the registrar's desk, we wait in vain
to be fed a line containing words
like 'everlasting' and 'divine'.

Miss Him when the TV scientist
explains the cosmos through equations,
leaving our planet to revolve on its axis
aimlessly, a wheel skidding in snow.

Miss Him when the radio catches a snatch
of plainchant from some echoey priory;
when the gospel choir raises its collective voice
to ask *Shall We Gather at the River?*
or the forces of the oratorio converge
on *I Know That My Redeemer Liveth*
and our contracted hearts lose a beat.

Miss Him when a choked voice at
the crematorium recites the poem
about fearing no more the heat of the sun.

Miss Him when we stand in judgement
on a lank Crucifixion in an art museum,
its stripe-like ribs testifying to rank.

Miss Him when the gamma-rays
recorded on the satellite graph
seem arranged into a celestial score,
the music of the spheres,
the *Ave Verum Corpus* of the observatory lab.

Miss Him when we stumble on the breast lump
for the first time and an involuntary prayer
escapes our lips; when a shadow crosses
our bodies on an x-ray screen; when we receive
a transfusion of foaming blood
sacrificed anonymously to save life.

Miss Him when we exclaim His name
spontaneously in awe or anger
as a woman in the birth ward
calls to her long-dead mother.

Miss Him when the linen-covered
dining-table holds warm bread rolls,
shiny glasses of red wine.

Miss Him when a dove swoops
from the orange grove in a tourist village
just as the monastery bell begins to take its toll.

Miss Him when our journey leads us
under leaves of Gothic tracery, an arch
of overlapping branches that meet
like hands in Michelangelo's *Creation*.

Miss Him when, trudging past a church,
we catch a residual blast of incense,
a perfume on par with the fresh-baked loaf
which Milosz compared to happiness.

Miss Him when our newly-fitted kitchen
comes in Shaker-style and we order
a matching set of Mother Ann Lee chairs.

Miss Him when we listen to the prophecy
of astronomers that the visible galaxies
will recede as the universe expands.

Miss Him when the sunset makes
its presence felt in the stained glass
window of the fake antique lounge bar.

Miss Him the way an uncoupled glider
riding the evening thermals misses its tug.

Miss Him, as the lovers shrugging
shoulders outside the cheap hotel
ponder what their next move should be.

Even feel nostalgic, odd days,
for His Second Coming,
like standing in the brick
dome of a dovecote
after the birds have flown.

DENNIS O'DRISCOLL

99

The Forest of Tangle

Deep in the Forest of Tangle
The King of the Makers sat
With a faggot of stripes for the tiger
And a flitter of wings for the bat.

He'd teeth and he'd claws for the cayman
And barks for the foxes and seals,
He'd a grindstone for sharpening swordfish
And electrical charges for eels.

He'd hundreds of kangaroo-pouches
On bushes and creepers and vines,
He'd hoots for the owls, and for glow-worms
He'd goodness knows how many shines.

He'd bellows for bullfrogs in dozens
And rattles for snakes by the score,
He'd hums for the humming-birds, buzzes for bees,
And elephant trumpets galore.

He'd pectoral fins for sea-fishes
With which they might glide through the air,
He'd porcupine quills and a bevy of bills
And various furs for the bear.

But O the old King of the Makers
With tears could have filled up a bay,
For no one had come to his warehouse
These many long years and a day.

And sadly the King of the Makers
His bits and his pieces he eyed
As he sat on a rock in the midst of his stock
And he cried and he cried and he cried.
He cried and he cried and he cried and he cried,
He cried and he cried and he cried.

CHARLES CAUSLEY

Credo

I believe in
the gingerbread man.
Who wouldn't run,
given the circumstances?

But not the Father,
not the Son.

I believe in
forgiveness.

But not in sin.

I believe in
communion:
bread wine
apples and us all
happy at table.

But not in saints.

I believe in
life. You have to,
don't you, being alive?

But not everlasting.

Those immortelles, petals
fallen like yellow teeth
in the tomb, bearing the
form of flowers.

But not the scent,
not the breath.

FIONA FARRELL

Retro Creation

Bungalows, God said, Day 1, and up they sprang like buttercups:
with lawns and railings, gate; three bedrooms off a hall; a phone that squats
on the hall-stand; back door, scullery, red formica countertops.

Day 2, God dollied in the stove, and rigged the central heating.
The oil-man came and fired her up; but God saw that a cold feeling
lingered, and called for back-boilers, slack, aeroboard on the ceiling.

Volkswagens, He said, Day 3, to get people out to do a run,
round the relatives, Armagh for butter, daytrips to Bundoran,
and once a year, two weeks down south, Courtown, Lahinch, Ballybunion –

where He made, Day 4, Strand Hotels, sandy beaches, buckets 'n' spades,
souvenir rock to strengthen teeth, a cliff walk, a straw hat, promenades,
donkey rides, pitch 'n' putt, a machine to roll pennies in arcades.

And God saw that all this was good, if thirsty, work; so God made fondness,
Day 5, and put a few pubs in every street. Next He made Guinness,
whiskey, gin, vodka, minerals. Then, nite-clubs to extend business

till all hours of Day 6: takeaways, coffee-shops, supermarkets,
99s, crispy pancakes, Tayto, Co-Op milk and custard yogurts,
squirty tomatoes, organic courgettes, kiwis, kitchen gadgets.

Day 7: Mass; said by Himself, and after that, *The Sunday Tribune*;
again, mostly about Himself, His enterprise – the good wine all gone,
His mangled talents rusting by slow rivers, His manna eaten,

and all His marvels dead, His oceans rising, hell-bent to Heaven.

AIDAN ROONEY-CÉSPEDES

God Says Yes To Me

I asked God if it was okay to be melodramatic
and she said yes
I asked her if it was okay to be short
and she said it sure is

I asked her if I could wear nail polish
or not wear nail polish
and she said honey
she calls me that sometimes
she said you can do just exactly
what you want to
Thanks God I said
And is it even okay if I don't paragraph
my letters
Sweetcakes God said
who knows where she picked that up
what I'm telling you is
Yes Yes Yes

KAYLIN HAUGHT

Sheep Fair Day

The real aim is not to see God in all things, it is that God,
through us, should see the things that we see.
SIMONE WEIL

I took God with me to the sheep fair. I said, 'Look
there's Liv, sitting on the wall, waiting;
these are pens, these are sheep,
this is their shit we are walking in, this is their fear.
See that man over there, stepping along the low walls
between pens, eyes always watching,
mouth always talking, he is the auctioneer.
That is wind in the ash trees above, that is sun
splashing us with running light and dark.
Those men over there, the ones with their faces sealed,
are buying or selling. Beyond in the ring
where the beasts pour in, huddle and rush,
the hoggets are auctioned in lots.
And that woman with the ruddy face and the home-cut hair
and a new child on her arm, that is how it is to be woman
with the milk running, sitting on wooden boards
in this shit-milky place of animals and birth and death
as the bidding rises and falls.'

103

Then I went back outside and found Fintan.
I showed God his hand as he sat on the rails,
how he let it trail down and his fingers played
in the curly back of a ewe. Fintan's a sheep-man
he's deep into sheep, though it's cattle he keeps now,
for sound commercial reasons.
                                        'Feel that,' I said,
'feel with my heart the force in that hand
that's twining her wool as he talks.'
Then I went with Fintan and Liv to Refreshments,
I let God sip tea, boiling hot, from a cup,
and I lent God my fingers to feel how they burned
when I tripped on a stone and it slopped.
'This is hurt,' I said, 'there'll be more.'
And the morning wore on and the sun climbed
and God felt how it is when I stand too long,
how the sickness rises, how the muscles burn.

Later, at the back end of the afternoon,
I went down to swim in the green slide of river,
I worked my way under the bridge, against the current,
then I showed how it is to turn onto your back
with, above you and a long way up, two gossiping pigeons,
and a clump of valerian, holding itself to the sky.
I remarked on the stone arch as I drifted through it,
how it dapples with sunlight from the water,
how the bridge hunkers down, crouching low in its track
and roars when a lorry drives over.

And later again, in the kitchen,
wrung out, at day's ending, and empty,
I showed how it feels
to undo yourself,
to dissolve, and grow age-old, nameless:

woman sweeping a floor, darkness growing.

KERRY HARDIE

Oh God, Fuck Me

Fuck me, oh God, with ordinary things,
    the things you love best in this world –

like trees in spring, exposing themselves,
    flashing leaf-buds so firm and swollen

I want to take them into my mouth.
    Speaking of trees, fuck me with birds,

say, an enormous raucous crow,
    proud as a man with his hand down his pants,

and then a sparrow, intimately brown,
    discreet and cautious as a concubine.

Fuck me with my kitchen faucet, dripping
    like a nymphomaniac,

all night slowly filling and filling,
    then overflowing the bowls in the sink –

and with the downstairs neighbor's vacuum,
    that great sucking noisy dragon

making the dirty come clean.
    Fuck me with breakfast, with English muffins,

the spirit of the dough aroused
    by browning, thrilled by buttering.

Fuck me with orange juice,
    its concentrated sweetness,

which makes the mouth as happy as summer,
    leaves sweet flecks of foam like spit

along the inside of the glass.
    Fuck me with coffee, strong and hot,

and then with cream poured into coffee,
   blossoming like mushroom clouds,

opening like parachutes.
   Fuck me with the ticking

clock, which is the ticking
   bomb, which is the ticking heart –

the heart we heard in the first months,
   in the original nakedness,

before we were squalling and born.
   Fuck me with the unwashed spoon

proud with its coffee stain –
   the faint swirl of a useful life

pooled into its center, round as a world.

RUTH L. SCHWARTZ

3

Family

I believe very strongly that a poem should be a disturbing unit;
that, when one goes into that force field, one will come out
the other end a changed person.

PAUL MULDOON

A good poem is almost always about something else,
which is why they are hard to write.

CHARLES CAUSLEY

THIS SECTION takes a journey through family life, beginning with conception and birth, and then tracing the lives of children and parents from infancy and adolescence through to leaving home and looking back. It extends the territory covered in section 5 of *Staying Alive* ('Growing up'). There are many more different kinds of poems here about mothers, fathers and children: tender poems as well as angry poems; poems celebrating good lives, nurturing, closeness and fearfulness for the child, but also others in which the family is dysfunctional and the child is anxious, afraid, and in some cases, abused.

The selection draws on the work of several poets who have written many thoughtful, moving poems about motherhood, fathers and children, notably Fleur Adcock, Kate Clanchy, Jeni Couzyn, Seamus Heaney, Kathleen Jamie, Sharon Olds and Anne Stevenson. If you like the poems here, you'll find their full collections even more rewarding. Both Kathleen Jamie (in *Jizzen*) and Kate Clanchy (in *Newborn*) have several poems on motherhood's surprises. Jamie's tender sequence 'Ultrasound' alternates between Scots and English (see *Staying Alive*, 174-77). Clanchy has also edited a lively anthology of poems on motherhood, *All the Poems You Need to Say Hello* (Picador).

Childhood has nurtured many of Seamus Heaney's most memorable poems, as he has acknowledged: 'My poems almost always start in some kind of memory ...like a little beeper going off in your mind. Some little thing wakens excitement, and it gets connected with some other things. Ideally, it's like an avalanche – a little pebble begins to move, gathers a lot of energy and multiplies itself.'

There are four poems by Gael Turnbull in *Being Alive* (174, 262, 275, 357), all of which I've titled 'Transmutation'. These are untitled prose poems from a series of 'transmutations' (continued through different books) in which the line-space is the pivot, a turning-point like the switch in an epic simile.

Smoke

My father kept a stove
with dog's legs
on a pink hearthstone.

One morning he climbed down the icy stairs
and spread his palms
on the blood-warm metal flanks.

He cranked open the iron doors,
like a black bank safe's,
but found no heat and ash heaped in its place.

He cracked grey whittled coals,
released brief blue flames,
and knocked downy soot through the bars of the grate.

The ash-pan, softly loaded
and almost as wide as a doorway,
he carried like dynamite through the dark house,

his bright face blown with smuts.
At the back door
he slid the ash into a tin dustbin,

then snapped sticks,
crumpled newspaper,
struck a match

and dipped it between the kindling.
Smoke unrolled, flames spread,
the rush of the stove eating air started up,

and my father would shake on rocks
from an old coal hod
and swing the doors shut.

But this time
he took a book, broke its spine
and slung that on instead:

his diaries,
year by year,
purred as their pages burned,

their leather boards shifted, popped
and fell apart.
Soon I would arrive,

pulled from under my mother's heart,
and grow to watch my father
break the charred crossbeam of a bird from the flue,

wondering if I too
had hung in darkness and smoke,
looking up at the light let down her throat
whenever my mother sang or spoke.

JACOB POLLEY

The watch

At this moment hundreds of women
a few miles from here are looking
for the same sign of reprieve, the red
splash of freedom. We run to check,
squirming through rituals of If I don't
look till two o'clock, if I skip lunch,
if I am good, if I am truly sorry,
probing, poking, hallucinating changes.
Flower, red lily, scarlet petunia
bloom for me. And some lesser number
of women in other bedrooms and bathrooms
see that red banner unfurl and mourn!
Another month, another chance missed.
Forty years of our lives, that flag
is shown or not and our immediate
and sometimes final fate determined,
red as tulips, red as poppies' satin,
red as taillights, red as a stoplight,
red as dying, our quick bright blood.

MARGE PIERCY

the lost baby poem

the time i dropped your almost body down
down to meet the waters under the city
and run one with the sewage into the sea
what did i know about waters rushing back
what did i know about drowning
or being drowned

you would have been born into winter
in the year of the disconnected gas
and no car   we would have made the thin
walk over Genesee hill into the Canada wind
to watch you slip like ice into strangers' hands
you would have fallen naked as snow into winter
if you were here i could tell you these
and some other things

if i am ever less than a mountain
for your definite brothers and sisters
let the rivers pour over my head
let the sea take me for a spiller
of seas   let black men call me stranger
always   for your never named sake

LUCILLE CLIFTON

Heartsong

I heard your heartbeat.
It flew out into the room, a startled bird
whirring high and wild.

I stopped breathing to listen
so high and fast it would surely race itself
down and fall

but it held strong, light
vibrant beside the slow deep booming
my old heart suddenly audible.

Out of the union that holds us separate
you've sent me a sound like a name.
Now I know you'll be born.

JENI COUZYN

Scan at 8 weeks

The white receiver
slides up my vagina,

I turn and you've come,
though I'm much too old for this
and you're much too young.

That's the baby
says the radiographer.
You are eight millimetres long
and pulsing,

bright in the centre of my much-used womb
which to my astonishment
still looks immaculate.

You are all heart,
I watch you tick and tick

and wonder
what you will come to,

will this be our only encounter
in the white gallery of ultrasound

or are you staying?
One day will we talk about this

moment when I first saw your spaceship
far off, heading for home?

HELEN DUNMORE

Ultrasound at 13 weeks

A child, I'd curl up small at night
in moonlight's brittle calm
and make believe I rested safe
within a giant palm.

This bell of muscle rings you round
as never fingers could
until the birthday when you come
to claim your personhood;

for now, this image speaks for you:
a snowflake hand outflung
proclaiming *human*, greeting us
in every human tongue.

KONA MACPHEE

The Sonogram

Only a few weeks ago, the sonogram of Jean's womb
resembled nothing so much
as a satellite-map of Ireland:

now the image
is so well-defined we can make out not only a hand
but a thumb;

on the road to Spiddal, a woman hitching a ride;
a gladiator in his net, passing judgement on the crowd.

PAUL MULDOON

The Ringing Chamber

I was four months gone –
my breasts already tender
against the bell-ropes;

we were ringing quarter-peals,
the sun flooding the bell-chamber,
the dust rippling between the joists

when the child quickened,
fluttered against the changes;
and suddenly through the clerestory

I saw that colder quickening –
random, reciprocal –
cloudshadow

and the flaxfield
like water under the wind.

PAULINE STAINER

Ninth Month

Already you are moving down.

Already your floating head
engaged in the inlet
from where you will head out.

Already the world, the world.

And you are slipping
down, away from my heart.

VICTORIA REDEL

An Unborn Child

(for Michael and Edna Longley)

I have already come to the verge of
Departure; a month or so and
I shall be vacating this familiar room.
Its fabric fits me almost like a glove
While leaving latitude for a free hand.
I begin to put on the manners of the world
Sensing the splitting light above
My head, where in the silence I lie curled.

Certain mysteries are relayed to me
Through the dark network of my mother's body
While she sits sewing the white shrouds
Of my apotheosis. I know the twisted
Kitten that lies there sunning itself
Under the bare bulb, the clouds
Of goldfish mooning around upon the shelf.
In me these data are already vested;

I know them in my bones – bones which embrace
Nothing, for I am completely egocentric.
The pandemonium of encumbrances
Which will absorb me, mind and senses,
Intricacies of the maze and the rat-race,
I imagine only. Though they linger and,
Like fingers, stretch until the knuckles crack,
They cannot dwarf the dimensions of my hand.

I must compose myself at the nerve centre
Of this metropolis, and not fidget –
Although sometimes at night, when the city
Has gone to sleep, I keep in touch with it,
Listening to the warm red water
Racing in the sewers of my mother's body;
Or the moths, soft as eyelids, or the rain
Wiping its wet wings on the window-pane.

And sometimes too, in the small hours of the morning
When the dead filament has ceased to ring,
After the goldfish are dissolved in darkness

114

And the kitten has gathered itself up into a ball
Between the groceries and the sewing,
I slip the trappings of my harness
To range these hollows in discreet rehearsal
And, battering at the concavity of my caul,

Produce in my mouth the words, 'I want to live!' –
This my first protest, and shall be my last.
As I am innocent, everything I do
Or say is couched in the affirmative.
I want to see, hear, touch and taste
These things with which I am to be encumbered.
Perhaps I needn't worry; give
Or take a day or two, my days are numbered.

DEREK MAHON

Prayer before birth

I am not yet born; O hear me.
Let not the bloodsucking bat or the rat or the stoat or the
    club-footed ghoul come near me.

I am not yet born, console me.
I fear that the human race may with tall walls wall me,
    with strong drugs dope me, with wise lies lure me,
        on black racks rack me, in blood-baths roll me.

I am not yet born; provide me
With water to dandle me, grass to grow for me, trees to talk
    to me, sky to sing to me, birds and a white light
        in the back of my mind to guide me.

I am not yet born; forgive me
For the sins that in me the world shall commit, my words
    when they speak me, my thoughts when they think me,
        my treason engendered by traitors beyond me,
            my life when they murder by means of my
                hands, my death when they live me.

I am not yet born; rehearse me
In the parts I must play and the cues I must take when
old men lecture me, bureaucrats hector me, mountains
frown at me, lovers laugh at me, the white
waves call me to folly and the desert calls
me to doom and the beggar refuses
my gift and my children curse me.

I am not yet born; O hear me,
Let not the man who is beast or who thinks he is God
come near me.

I am not yet born; O fill me
With strength against those who would freeze my
humanity, would dragoon me into a lethal automaton,
would make me a cog in a machine, a thing with
one face, a thing, and against all those
who would dissipate my entirety, would
blow me like thistledown hither and
thither or hither and thither
like water held in the
hands would spill me.

Let them not make me a stone and let them not spill me.
Otherwise kill me.

LOUIS MACNEICE

Births

We will never remember dying.

We were so patient
about being,
noting down
the numbers, the days,
the years and the months,
the hair, the mouths we kissed,
but that moment of dying:
we surrender it without a note,
we give it to others as remembrance

116

or we give it simply to water,
to water, to air, to time.
Nor do we keep
the memory of our birth,
though being born was important and fresh:
and now you don't even remember one detail,
you haven't kept even a branch
of the first light.

It's well known that we are born.

It's well known that in the room
or in the woods
or in the hut in the fishermen's district
or in the crackling canefields
there is a very unusual silence,
a moment solemn as wood,
and a woman gets ready to give birth.

It's well known that we were born.

But of the profound jolt
from not being to existing, to having hands,
to seeing, to having eyes,
to eating and crying and overflowing
and loving and loving and suffering and suffering,
of that transition or shudder
of the electric essence that takes on
one more body like a living cup,
and of that disinhabited woman,
the mother who is left there with her blood
and her torn fullness
and her end and beginning, and the disorder
that troubles the pulse, the floor, the blankets,
until everything gathers and adds
one more knot to the thread of life:
nothing, there is nothing left in your memory
of the fierce sea that lifted a wave
and knocked down a dark apple from the tree.

The only thing you remember is your life.

PABLO NERUDA
translated from the Spanish by Stephen Mitchell

The night before the last day of January

will be remembered by a random few
for having borne it out in sheeted snow
on no exceptional stretch of motorway,
rationing the engine's gas-and-air
to intervals of heat while still more snow
slipped down, unprecedented, otherworldly;

but I'll recall it as the unslept night
before that morning-after when you lay
against my heart on the white of ward-square sheets:
a little snowflake fallen into warmth,
fragile, precise, astoundingly unmelting.

KONA MACPHEE
(for Caitlin, b. 31.01.03)

Driving to the Hospital

We were low on petrol
so I said let's freewheel
when we get to the hill.
It was dawn and the city
was nursing its quiet
and I liked the idea
of arriving with barely
a crunch on the gravel.
You smiled kindly and
eased the clutch gently
and backed us out of
the driveway and patted
my knee with exactly
the gesture you used
when we were courting,
remember, on the way
to your brother's: *I like*

driving with my baby,
that's what you said. And
at the time I wondered
why my heart leapt and leapt.

KATE CLANCHY

The Harvest in March

The drive from Elgin to the hospital
had no tree felled across the way, no snow,
instead the March light opened our road east,
back from the blue beyond of Dennachie.
It cast itself across the stubbled parks,
and hours of sun seemed left in Aberdeen,
and so we walked out for the last time as
a couple. In the chipper you announced
'It's coming,' and you squatted, scaring both
me and the granite wifies serving me.

Twelve hours gave you your own geography:
a canal with a head stuck in it, so
they reached for forcing drugs, the opening knife,
and that domestic-looking suction plug
which pulled a girl out like a plum, still on
her stalk, since in the country inside you
it's always autumn. Wheeched her wheezing off
to thread her little nostrils with those tubes
that siphon out the faeces. Which looked like
she was being stitched onto our loud world.

And when I brought her back they'd stitched you too:
you chatted with the surgeon as he finished
your perineum like a trout fly, and
I handed you our daughter in a towel.

W.N. HERBERT

And let us say

(for Emma McKiernan, on her birth, 8.9.99)

That if the linen flapped too loud
The washing line was taken down

And if a shopdoor bell was rung
Its tongue was held with cotton thumbs

And if a milkfloat tattled by
It was flagged down and held aside

And should the rivers drown us out
We had them dammed at every mouth

And coughed our engines gently off
And wrapped our tyres in woollen socks

And sat awhile on silent roads
Or dawdled home in slippered shoes

And did not sound but held our tongues
And watched our watches stop, and startle on.

MATTHEW HOLLIS

Tempo

In the first month I think
it's a drop in a spider web's
necklace of dew

at the second a hazelnut; after,
a slim Black-eyed Susan demurely folded
asleep on a cloudy day

then a bushbaby silent as sap
in a jacaranda tree, but blinking
with mischief

at five months it's an almost-caught
flounder flapping back
to the glorious water

six, it's a song
with a chorus of basses: seven, five grapefruit
in a mesh bag that bounces on the hip
on a hot morning down at the shops

a watermelon next – green oval
of pink flesh and black seeds, ripe
waiting to be split by the knife

nine months it goes faster, it's a bicycle
pedalling for life over paddocks
of sun
no, a money-box filled with silver half-crowns
a sunflower following the clock
with its wide-open grin
a storm in the mountains, spinning rocks
down to the beech trees
three hundred feet below
– old outrageous Queen Bess's best dress
starched ruff and opulent tent of a skirt
packed with ruffles and lace
no no, I've remembered, it's a map
of intricate distinctions

purples for high ground burnt umber
for foothills green for the plains
and the staggering blue
of the ocean beyond
waiting and waiting and
aching
with waiting

no more alternatives! Suddenly now
you can see my small bag of eternity
pattern of power
my ace my adventure
my sweet-smelling atom
my planet, my grain of miraculous dust
my green leaf, my feather

my lily my lark
look at her, angels –
this is my daughter.

LAURIS EDMOND

Counting

You count the fingers first: it's traditional.
(You assume the doctor counted them too,
when he lifted up the slimy surprise
with its long dark pointed head and its father's nose
at 2.13 a.m. – 'Look at the clock!'
said Sister: 'Remember the time: 2.13.')

Next day the head's turned pink and round;
the nose is a blob. You fumble under the gown
your mother embroidered with a sprig of daisies,
as she embroidered your own Viyella gowns
when you were a baby. You fish out
curly triangular feet. You count the toes.

'There's just one little thing,' says Sister:
'His ears – they don't quite match. One
has an extra whorl in it. No one will notice.'
You notice like mad. You keep on noticing.
Then you hear a rumour: a woman in the next ward
has had a stillbirth. Or was it something worse?

You lie there, bleeding gratefully.
You've won the Nobel Prize, and the VC,
and the State Lottery, and gone to heaven.
Feed-time comes. They bring your bundle –
the right one: it's him all right.
You count his eyelashes: the ideal number.

You take him home. He learns to walk.
From time to time you eye him,
nonchalantly, from each side.
He has an admirable nose.

No one ever notices his ears. No one
ever stands on both sides of him at once.

He grows up. He has beautiful children.

FLEUR ADCOCK

Love

I hadn't met his kind before.
His misericord face – really
like a joke on his father – blurred
as if from years of polish;
his hands like curled dry leaves;

the profligate heat he gave
out, gave out, his shallow,
careful breaths: I thought
his filaments would blow,
I thought he was an emperor,

dying on silk cushions.
I didn't know how to keep
him wrapped, I didn't know
how to give him suck, I had
no idea about him. At night

I tried to remember the feel
of his head on my neck, the skull
small as a cat's, the soft spot
hot as a smelted coin,
and the hair, the down, fine

as the innermost, vellum layer
of some rare snowcreature's
aureole of fur, if you could meet
such a beast, if you could
get so near. I started there.

KATE CLANCHY

Morning Song

Love set you going like a fat gold watch.
The midwife slapped your footsoles, and your bald cry
Took its place among the elements.

Our voices echo, magnifying your arrival. New statue.
In a drafty museum, your nakedness
Shadows our safety. We stand round blankly as walls.

I'm no more your mother
Than the cloud that distils a mirror to reflect its own slow
Effacement at the wind's hand.

All night your moth-breath
Flickers among the flat pink roses. I wake to listen:
A far sea moves in my ear.

One cry, and I stumble from bed, cow-heavy and floral
In my Victorian nightgown.
Your mouth opens clean as a cat's. The window square

Whitens and swallows its dull stars. And now you try
Your handful of notes;
The clear vowels rise like balloons.

SYLVIA PLATH

Natural Son

Before the spectacled professor snipped
The cord, I heard your birth-cry flood the ward,
And lowered your mother's tortured head, and wept.
The house you'd left would need to be restored.

No worse pain could be borne, to bear the joy
Of seeing you come in a slow dive from the womb,
Pushed from your fluid home, pronounced 'a boy'.
You'll never find so well equipped a room.

No house we build could hope to satisfy
Every small need, now that you've made this move
To share our loneliness, much as we try
Our vocal skill to wall you round with love.

This day you crave so little, we so much
For you to live, who need our merest touch.

RICHARD MURPHY

Baby Song

From the private ease of Mother's womb
I fall into the lighted room.

Why don't they simply put me back,
Where it is warm and wet and black?

But one thing follows on another.
Things were different inside Mother.

Padded and jolly I would ride
The perfect comfort of her inside.

They tuck me in a rustling bed
– I lie there, raging, small, and red.

I may sleep soon, I may forget,
But I won't forget that I regret.

A rain of blood poured round her womb,
But all time roars outside this room.

THOM GUNN

Newly Born Twins

In separate incubators one of the twins was dying.
Against doctor's orders, a nurse put them together.

The strong twin, the one with nothing
pulling her back, she slung
her newly born arm over
the one who was wanting to leave,
and stabilised her heartbeat, made everything
regular in the body of the one who'd already
had enough.

The strong one, she will think
she is God, that she can pull back
life from where it was wanting to go.
It will be harder for her
than for the one who already knows
about separation, loneliness, where
they can make you want to go.

HELEN FARISH

My First Weeks

Sometimes, when I wonder what I'm like, underneath,
I think of my first two weeks, I was drenched
with happiness. The wall opened
like liquid, my head slid through, my legs, I
pushed off, from the side, soared
gently, turned, squeezed out
neatly into the cold illuminated
air and breathed it. Washed off, wrapped,
I slept, and when I woke there was the breast
the size of my head, hard and full,
the springy drupelets of the nipple. Sleep.
Milk. Heat. Every day
she held me up to the window and wagged
my fist at my sister, down in the street, who
waved her cone back at me so
hard the ice cream flew through the air like a
butter-brickle cannonball,

126

otherwise it was sleep and milk,
by day my mother's, by night the nurses
would prop me with a bottle. Paradise
had its laws – every four hours and not
a minute sooner I could drink, but every four
hours I could have the world in my mouth.
Two weeks, and then home, to the end of the hall,
where at night a nurse would give me four ounces of
water every four hours, and in the meantime I shrieked for it.
They knew it would build my character,
to learn to give up, and I learned it – dawn
and the satiny breast, the burp, the boiled
sheet to be placed on where my sister couldn't touch me,
I lay and moved my arms and legs like
feelers in the light. Glorious life!
And it would always be there, behind those nights
of tap water, the whole way back,
that fortnight of unlimited ration,
every four hours – clock of cream
and flame, I have known heaven.

SHARON OLDS

Nursling

Over there, a fly buzzed – bad.
All ours: the bra, the breast, the breeze.
Starlet of the reciprocal gaze.
Something about her rhymed like mad.

And ours the sigh, the suck, the sing.
We forgave everything we could.
Ravenous palmist. I'm gone for good.
At last I gauged the brash, brash spring.

The skin fiend folded like a fawn.
Torso Magellan. Time's own nub.
Here at the center of the dimmest bulb.
A mouth hovered before latching on.

KATHLEEN OSSIP

The Victory

I thought you were my victory
though you cut me like a knife
when I brought you out of my body
into your life.

Tiny antagonist, gory,
blue as a bruise. The stains
of your cloud of glory
bled from my veins.

How can you dare, blind thing,
blank insect eyes?
You barb the air. You sting
with bladed cries.

Snail. Scary knot of desires.
Hungry snarl. Small son.
Why do I have to love you?
How have you won?

ANNE STEVENSON

Stance

Now I sit my child on the jut
of my hip, and take
his weight with the curve
of my waist, like a tree
split at the fork,
like lovers leaning out of a waltz.

Nothing is lost. I was never
one of those girls
stood slim as a sapling.
I was often alone at the dance.

KATE CLANCHY

128

Red Onion, Cherries, Boiling Potatoes, Milk –

Here is a soul, accepting nothing.
Obstinate as a small child
refusing tapioca, peaches, toast.

The cheeks are streaked, but dry.
The mouth is firmly closed in both directions.

Ask, if you like,
if it is merely sulking, or holding out for better.
The soup grows cold in the question.
The ice cream pools in its dish.

Not this, is all it knows. Not this.
As certain cut flowers refuse to drink in the vase.

And the heart, from its great distance, watches, helpless.

JANE HIRSHFIELD

from Elizabeth Near and Far

Night Light

Only your plastic night light dusts its pink
on the backs and undersides of things; your mother,
head resting on the nightside of one arm,
floats a hand above your cradle
to feel the humid tendril of your breathing.
Outside, the night rocks, murmurs... Crouched
in this eggshell light, I feel my heart
slowing, opened to your tiny flame

as if your blue irises mirrored me
as if your smile breathed and warmed
and curled in your face which is only asleep.
There is space between me, I know,
and you. I hang above you like a planet –
you're a planet, too. One planet loves the other.

The Chair by the Window

Your rhythmic nursing slows. I feel
your smile before I see it: nipple pinched
in corner of mouth, your brimming, short, tuck-cornered
smile. I shake my head, my *no* vibrates
to you through ribs and arms. Your tapered ears
quiver, work faintly and still pinker, my
nipple spins right out and we
are two who sit and smile into each other's eyes.

Again, you frowning farmer, me your cow:
you flap one steadying palm against my breast,
thump down the other, chuckle, snort, and then
you're suddenly under, mouth moving steadily, eyes
drifting past mine abstracted, your familiar
blue remote and window-paned with light.

ANNE WINTERS

For Andrew

'Will I die?' you ask. And so I enter on
the dutiful exposition of that which you
would rather not know, and I rather not tell you.
To soften my 'Yes' I offer compensations –
age and fulfilment ('It's so far away;
you will have children and grandchildren by then')
and indifference ('By then you will not care').
No need: you cannot believe me, convinced
that if you always eat plenty of vegetables
and are careful crossing the street you will live for ever.
And so we close the subject, with much unsaid –
this, for instance: Though you and I may die
tomorrow or next year, and nothing remain
of our stock, of the unique, preciously-hoarded
inimitable genes we carry in us,
it is possible that for many generations
there will exist, sprung from whatever seeds,

children straight-limbed, with clear enquiring voices,
bright-eyed as you. Or so I like to think:
sharing in this your childish optimism.

FLEUR ADCOCK

Let Him Not Grow Up

May my little boy
stay just as he is.
He didn't suck my milk
in order to grow up.
A child's not an oak
or a ceiba tree.
Poplars, meadow grasses,
things like that grow tall.
My little boy
can stay a mallow-flower.

He has all he needs,
laughter, frowns, skills,
airs and graces.
He doesn't need to grow.

If he grows they'll all come
winking at him,
worthless women
making him shameless,
or all the big boys
that come by the house.
Let my little boy
see no monsters coming.

May his five summers
be all he knows.
Just as he is
he can dance and be happy.
May his birthdays fit
in the length of a yardstick,
all his Easters
and his Christmas Eves.

Silly women,
don't cry. Listen:
the Sun and the stones
are born and don't grow,
they never get older,
they last forever.
In the sheepfold
kids and lambs
grow up and die:
be damned to them!

O my Lord, stop him,
make him stop growing!
Stop him and save him
don't let my son die!

GABRIELA MISTRAL
translated from the Spanish by Ursula LeGuin

Daystar

She wanted a little room for thinking:
but she saw diapers steaming on the line,
a doll slumped behind the door.

So she lugged a chair behind the garage
to sit out the children's naps.

Sometimes there were things to watch –
the pinched armor of a vanished cricket,
a floating maple leaf. Other days
she stared until she was assured
when she closed her eyes
she'd see only her own vivid blood.

She had an hour, at best, before Liza appeared
pouting from the top of the stairs.
And just *what* was mother doing
out back with the field mice? Why,

building a palace. Later
that night when Thomas rolled over and
lurched into her, she would open her eyes
and think of the place that was hers
for an hour – where
she was nothing,
pure nothing, in the middle of the day.

RITA DOVE

The peacock of motherhood

This is the gift my son gave me,
strutting through my life, tail dragging,
perching on everything I do and as soon
as my back is turned, jumping down
with a thud and a cry, following me.

The pea-hen of girlhood
makes no sound now, sleeps
undisturbed. I can hardly remember
so brown a bird; if I try to think
up flashes the tail

of motherhood to distract me.
I remember she was as brown as thought.
But the peacock has found other cocks
to flash his tail at; the peacocks
of motherhood are strutting

at the school gates, the gifts
our sons gave us. The birds strut
and preen, flash their tails,
while the mothers smile
till the bell goes.

ANNA JACKSON

Single Parent

Because she shares the bedroom with the baby
she undresses in the dark
and tonight her underclothes flash

and crackle in the dry air, like
miniature lightning, like
silver fireworks. It reminds her

of strobe lights, and her old crowd.
She trips and cracks her head on the bedstead
but of course must not cry out.

CONNIE BENSLEY

Bearhug

Griffin calls to come and kiss him goodnight
I yell ok. Finish something I'm doing,
then something else, walk slowly round
the corner to my son's room.
He is standing arms outstretched
waiting for a bearhug. Grinning.

Why do I give my emotion an animal's name,
give it that dark squeeze of death?
This is the hug which collects
all his small bones and his warm neck against me.
The thin tough body under the pyjamas
locks to me like a magnet of blood.

How long was he standing there
like that, before I came?

MICHAEL ONDAATJE

Cartoon Physics, part 1

Children under, say, *ten*, shouldn't know
that the universe is ever-expanding,
inexorably pushing into the vacuum, galaxies

swallowed by galaxies, whole

solar systems collapsing, all of it
acted out in silence. At ten we are still learning

the rules of cartoon animation,

that if a man draws a door on a rock
only he can pass through it.
Anyone else who tries

will crash into the rock. Ten-year-olds
should stick with burning houses, car wrecks,
ships going down – earthbound, tangible

disasters, arenas

where they can be heroes. You can run
back into a burning house, sinking ships

have lifeboats, the trucks will come
with their ladders, if you jump

you will be saved. A child

places her hand on the roof of a schoolbus,
& drives across a city of sand. She knows

the exact spot it will skid, at which point
the bridge will give, who will swim to safety
& who will be pulled under by sharks. She will learn

that if a man runs off the edge of a cliff
he will not fall

until he notices his mistake.

NICK FLYNN

A Tray of Eggs

It's not the hens that matter,
scratching among the nettle
roots at the orchard's edge,
though much might be made of their red
foppish cockscombs, their speckled
feathers overlapping and the stutter
of their daft, deft pecking.

Nor is it the road pedalled
by heart to the farm, the known
fields never the same,
turning from a greenness to grain,
revolving, resolving into rows
of straight seedlings, stubble
burnt or interred under furrows.

Not even the ride shared
with my two-year-old child, astride
the crossbar, breathing the blown
scents he's making his own
unknowingly, being alive
to vibrations of place this admired
Ford tractor amplifies.

But what counts more than these small
pleasures are the eggs we bring home
in boxes and softly transpose
into the bevelled holes
in the cardboard tray, the domes
of these thirty shells
that will break like the days to come.

MICHAEL LASKEY

Skating with Heather Grace

Apart from the apparent values,
there are lessons in the circular:
paradigms for history,
time in a round world, turning,
love with another of your species –

To watch my only daughter
widening her circles is to ease
headlong into the traffic
of her upbringing.

Until nearly four she screamed
at my absence, mourned
my going out for any reason,
cried at scoldings,
agreed to common lies regarding
thunder, Christmas,
baby teeth. Last year

she started school
without incident;
this year ballet and new math. Soon

I think my love will seem
entirely deficient.

Later there's the hokey-pokey
and dim lights for the partners' dance.
She finds a shaky nine-year-old
to skate around
in counter-clockwise orbits,
laughing.

Is it more willingness than balance?
Is letting go the thing that keeps her steady?

I lean against the side-boards sipping
coffee. I keep a smile ready.

THOMAS LYNCH

Benevolence

When my father dies and comes back as a dog,
I already know what his favorite sound will be:
the soft, almost inaudible gasp
as the rubber lips of the refrigerator door
unstick, followed by that arctic

exhalation of cold air;
then the cracking of the ice-cube tray above the sink
and the quiet *ching* the cubes make
when dropped into a glass.

Unable to pronounce the name of his favorite drink, or to express
his preference for single malt,
he will utter one sharp bark
and point the wet black arrow of his nose
imperatively up
at the bottle on the shelf,

then seat himself before me,
trembling, expectant, water pouring
down the long pink dangle of his tongue
as the memory of pleasure from his former life
shakes him like a tail.

What I'll remember as I tower over him,
holding a dripping, whiskey-flavored cube
above his open mouth,
relishing the power rushing through my veins
the way it rushed through his,

what I'll remember as I stand there
is the hundred clever tricks
I taught myself to please him,
and for how long I mistakenly believed
that it was love he held concealed in his closed hand.

TONY HOAGLAND

Infancy

(to Abgar Renault)

My father got on his horse and went to the field.
My mother stayed sitting and sewing.
My little brother slept.
A small boy alone under the mango trees,
I read the story of Robinson Crusoe,
the long story that never comes to an end.

At noon, white with light, a voice that had learned
lullabies long ago in the slave-quarters — and never forgot —
called us for coffee.
Coffee blacker than the black old woman
delicious coffee
good coffee.

My mother stayed sitting and sewing
watching me:
Shh — don't wake the boy.
She stopped the cradle when a mosquito had lit
and gave a sigh...how deep!
Away off there my father went riding
through the farm's endless wastes.

And I didn't know that my story
was prettier than that of Robinson Crusoe.

CARLOS DRUMMOND DE ANDRADE
translated from the Portuguese by Elizabeth Bishop

The Mother

Of course I love them, they are my children.
That is my daughter and this my son.
And this is my life I give them to please them.
It has never been used. Keep it safe, pass it on.

ANNE STEVENSON

Sunlight

There was a sunlit absence.
The helmeted pump in the yard
heated its iron,
water honeyed

in the slung bucket
and the sun stood
like a griddle cooling
against the wall

of each long afternoon.
So, her hands scuffled
over the bakeboard,
the reddening stove

sent its plaque of heat
against her where she stood
in a floury apron
by the window.

Now she dusts the board
with a goose's wing,
now sits, broad-lapped,
with whitened nails

and measling shins:
here is a space
again, the scone rising
to the tick of two clocks.

And here is love
like a tinsmith's scoop
sunk past its gleam
in the meal-bin.

SEAMUS HEANEY

Starlight

My father stands in the warm evening
on the porch of my first house.
I am four years old and growing tired.
I see his head among the stars,
the glow of his cigarette, redder
than the summer moon riding
low over the old neighborhood. We
are alone, and he asks me if I am happy.
'Are you happy?' I cannot answer.
I do not really understand the word,
and the voice, my father's voice, is not
his voice, but somehow thick and choked,
a voice I have not heard before, but
heard often since. He bends and passes
a thumb beneath each of my eyes.
The cigarette is gone, but I can smell
the tiredness that hangs on his breath.
He has found nothing, and he smiles
and holds my head with both his hands.
Then he lifts me to his shoulder,
and now I too am there among the stars
as tall as he. Are you happy? I say.
He nods in answer, Yes! oh yes! oh yes!
And in that new voice he says nothing
holding my head tight against his head,
his eyes closed up against the starlight,
as though those tiny blinking eyes
of light might find a tall, gaunt child
holding his child against the promises
of autumn, until the boy slept
never to waken in that world again.

PHILIP LEVINE

from Clearances

(in memoriam M.K.H., 1911-1984)

When all the others were away at Mass
I was all hers as we peeled potatoes.
They broke the silence, let fall one by one
Like solder weeping off the soldering iron:
Cold comforts set between us, things to share
Gleaming in a bucket of clean water.
And again let fall. Little pleasant splashes
From each other's work would bring us to our senses.

So while the parish priest at her bedside
Went hammer and tongs at the prayers for the dying
And some were responding and some crying
I remembered her head bent towards my head,
Her breath in mine, our fluent dipping knives –
Never closer the whole rest of our lives.

SEAMUS HEANEY

My Father

The memory of my father is wrapped up in
white paper, like sandwiches taken for a day at work.

Just as a magician takes towers and rabbits
out of his hat, he drew love from his small body,

and the rivers of his hands
overflowed with good deeds.

YEHUDA AMICHAI
translated from the Hebrew by Azila Talit Reisenberger

Genetics

My father's in my fingers, but my mother's in my palms.
I lift them up and look at them with pleasure –
I know my parents made me by my hands.

They may have been repelled to separate lands,
to separate hemispheres, may sleep with other lovers,
but in me they touch where fingers link to palms.

With nothing left of their togetherness but friends
who quarry for their image by a river,
at least I know their marriage by my hands.

I shape a chapel where a steeple stands.
And when I turn it over,
my father's by my fingers, my mother's by my palms

demure before a priest reciting psalms.
My body is their marriage register.
I re-enact their wedding with my hands.

So take me with you, take up the skin's demands
for mirroring in bodies of the future.
I'll bequeath my fingers, if you bequeath your palms.
We know our parents make us by our hands.

SINÉAD MORRISSEY

Digging

Between my finger and my thumb
The squat pen rests; snug as a gun.

Under my window, a clean rasping sound
When the spade sinks into gravelly ground:
My father, digging. I look down

Till his straining rump among the flowerbeds
Bends low, comes up twenty years away
Stooping in rhythm through potato drills
Where he was digging.

The coarse boot nestled on the lug, the shaft
Against the inside knee was levered firmly.
He rooted out tall tops, buried the bright edge deep
To scatter new potatoes that we picked,
Loving their cool hardness in our hands.

By God, the old man could handle a spade.
Just like his old man.

My grandfather cut more turf in a day
Than any other man on Toner's bog.
Once I carried him milk in a bottle
Corked sloppily with paper. He straightened up
To drink it, then fell to right away
Nicking and slicing neatly, heaving sods
Over his shoulder, going down and down
For the good turf. Digging.

The cold smell of potato mould, the squelch and slap
Of soggy peat, the curt cuts of an edge
Through living roots awaken in my head.
But I've no spade to follow men like them.

Between my finger and my thumb
The squat pen rests.
I'll dig with it.

SEAMUS HEANEY

I See You Dancing, Father

No sooner downstairs after the night's rest
And in the door
Than you started to dance a step
In the middle of the kitchen floor.

And as you danced
You whistled.
You made your own music
Always in tune with yourself.

Well, nearly always, anyway.
You're buried now
In Lislaughtin Abbey
And whenever I think of you

I go back beyond the old man
Mind and body broken
To find the unbroken man.
It is the moment before the dance begins,

Your lips are enjoying themselves
Whistling an air.
Whatever happens or cannot happen
In the time I have to spare
I see you dancing, father.

BRENDAN KENNELLY

My Papa's Waltz

The whiskey on your breath
Could make a small boy dizzy;
But I hung on like death:
Such waltzing was not easy.

We romped until the pans
Slid from the kitchen shelf;
My mother's countenance
Could not unfrown itself.

The hand that held my wrist
Was battered on one knuckle;
At every step you missed
My right ear scraped a buckle.

You beat time on my head
With a palm caked hard by dirt,
Then waltzed me off to bed
Still clinging to your shirt.

THEODORE ROETHKE

My Father Is Shrinking

When we last hugged each other
in the garage,
our two heads were level.
Over his shoulder I could see
potato-sacks.

Another season
and in the dusty sunlight
I shall gather him to me,
smooth his collar,
bend to listen
for his precious breathing.

When he reaches
to my waist,
I shall no longer
detach his small hands
from my skirt,
escape his shrill voice
in the dawn garden.

When he comes to my knees,
I shall pick him up and rock him,
rub my face on the white
stubble of his cheek,
see his silver skull
gleam up at me
through thin combings.

SUSAN WICKS

Little Father

I buried my father
in the sky.
Since then, the birds
clean and comb him every morning
and pull the blanket up to his chin
every night.

I buried my father underground.
Since then, my ladders
only climb down,
and all the earth has become a house
whose rooms are the hours, whose doors
stand open at evening, receiving
guest after guest.
Sometimes I see past them
to the tables spread for a wedding feast.

I buried my father in my heart.
Now he grows in me, my strange son,
my little root who won't drink milk,
little pale foot sunk in unheard-of night,
little clock spring newly wet
in the fire, little grape, parent to the future
wine, a son the fruit of his own son,
little father I ransom with my life.

LI-YOUNG LEE

My Grandmother's Love Letters

There are no stars tonight
But those of memory.
Yet how much room for memory there is
In the loose girdle of soft rain.

There is even room enough
For the letters of my mother's mother,

Elizabeth,
That have been pressed so long
Into a corner of the roof
That they are brown and soft,
And liable to melt as snow.

Over the greatness of such space
Steps must be gentle.
It is all hung by an invisible white hair.
It trembles as birch limbs webbing the air.

And I ask myself:

'Are your fingers long enough to play
Old keys that are but echoes:
Is the silence strong enough
To carry back the music to its source
And back to you again
As though to her?'

Yet I would lead my grandmother by the hand
Through much of what she would not understand;
And so I stumble. And the rain continues on the roof
With such a sound of gently pitying laughter.

HART CRANE

Climbing My Grandfather

I decide to do it free, without a rope or net.
First, the old brogues, dusty and cracked;
an easy scramble onto his trousers,
pushing into the weave, trying to get a grip.
By the overhanging shirt I change
direction, traverse along his belt
to an earth-stained hand. The nails
are splintered and give good purchase,
the skin of his finger is smooth and thick
like warm ice. On his arm I discover
the glassy ridge of a scar, place my feet
gently in the old stitches and move on.

At his still firm shoulder, I rest for a while
in the shade, not looking down,
for climbing has its dangers, then pull
myself up the loose skin of his neck
to a smiling mouth to drink among teeth.
Refreshed, I cross the screed cheek,
to stare into his brown eyes, watch a pupil
slowly open and close. Then up over
the forehead, the wrinkles well-spaced
and easy, to his thick hair (soft and white
at this altitude), reaching for the summit,
where gasping for breath I can only lie
watching clouds and birds circle,
feeling his heat, knowing
the slow pulse of his good heart.

ANDREW WATERHOUSE

Custody

Every other weekend they go to their mother's
Some Tuesdays or Wednesdays they spend the night.
She takes them for two weeks in the summer.
We divvy up the holidays. Otherwise
they live here, with me. We agreed to this
after months of court-appointed enmity
during most of which we behaved like children.
In the end, I was 'awarded custody' –
a legalese to make it sound like winning –
pancakes and carpools and the dead of nights
with nightmares or earaches or wet bedlinen
Their mother got what's called her visitation rights –
a kind of catch-up-ball she plays with gifts
and fast-food dinners-out and talk of trips
to Disneyworld in the sparkling future.
They were ten, nine, six, and four when it happened.
I played their ages in the Lotto for awhile.
I never won. They were, of course, the prize.
They were, likewise, the ones, when we were through

with all that hateful paperwork and ballyhoo,
who seemed like prisoners of care and keeping
and settled into their perplexed routines
like criminals or parties to a grief –
accomplices in love and sundering.

THOMAS LYNCH

Second Home
(FROM *Oubliette*)

Where the long hall ended the living-room
began. What I mean is, I don't remember
a door before then. Today there's a door
and it's shut. My Daddy's visiting.
I dressed by firelight and nobody heard,
I did it so quietly. Now I'm outside:
a snowy landscape and a blur of red.
It's school-time and I'm in my wellingtons,
trying to stamp a path along the drive.
This time I make it to the dustbin, half
sunk in snow, when my heels skid and the sky
leaps over my head like that and smack...
This noiselessness, is it the sky or me?
When he got here it was in the night –
too late for me, yes, but he should have come
to wake me anyway. I would have liked it.
I tread back through my footprints, past the room
where he's asleep now and I want to peep
inside it but the curtains are shut tight,
and sounds of school are trickling down like poison
from the far end of the street. I edge
my way along the side-wall to a door
which opens and my mother's standing there.
I've tried three times to make it to the end
and now I'm crying, telling her I can't
do it – *please* – I want Daddy to take me.

JULIA COPUS

How Many Times

No matter how many times I try I can't stop my father
from walking into my sister's room

and I can't see any better, leaning from here to look
in his eyes. It's dark in the hall

and everyone's sleeping. This is the past
where everything is perfect already and nothing changes,

where the water glass falls to the bathroom floor
and bounces once before breaking.

Nothing. Not the small sound my sister makes, turning
over, not the thump of the dog's tail

when he opens one eye to see him stumbling back to bed
still drunk, a little bewildered.

This is exactly as I knew it would be.
And if I whisper her name, hissing a warning,

I've been doing that for years now, and still the dog
startles and growls until he sees

it's our father, and still the door opens, and she
makes that small *oh* turning over.

MARIE HOWE

No fairy story

I don't need to tell you what you've done;
I'm sure your memory opens at the thumb
to its favourite page, its pathetic glory:
the centrefold smuggled in a bedtime story.

You played Red King to my Unhappy Princess
and stowed your secrets beneath my mattress:
they kept me awake to the menace of your tread
and mocked the underpants I always wore to bed.

And what can Happy Ever Afters do
when every time I think I've banished you
your thumb slips in and prises me apart,
a staple through my abdomen, another through my heart?

KONA MACPHEE

House

She sleeps in late
as if the house were hers

but it is his.
She should have been more careful.

She should have been attentive
to his timing.

The fact that she was wrong
and he was right.

SELIMA HILL

The Cockfighter's Daughter

I found my father,
face down, in his homemade chili
and had to hit the bowl
with a hammer to get it off,
then scrape the pinto beans
and chunks of ground beef
off his face with a knife.
Once he was clean
I called the police,
described the dirt road
that snaked from the highway
to his trailer beside the river.

The rooster was in the bedroom,
tied to a table leg.
Nearby stood a tin of cloudy water
and a few seeds scattered on a piece of wax paper,
the cheap green carpet
stained by gobs of darker green shit.
I was careful not to get too close,
because, though his beak was tied shut,
he could still jump for me and claw me
as he had my father.
The scars ran down his arms to a hole
where the rooster had torn the flesh
and run with it,
finally spitting it out.
When the old man stopped the bleeding,
the rooster was waiting on top of the pickup,
his red eyes like Pentecostal flames.
That's when Father named him Preacher.
He lured him down with a hen
he kept penned in a coop,
fortified with the kind of grille
you find in those New York taxicabs.
It had slots for food and water
and a trap door on top,
so he could reach in and pull her out by the neck.
One morning he found her stiff and glassy-eyed
and stood watching
as the rooster attacked her carcass
until she was ripped
to bits of bloody flesh and feathers.
I cursed and screamed, but he told me to shut up,
stay inside, what did a girl know about it?
Then he looked at me with desire and disdain.
Later, he loaded the truck and left.
I was sixteen and I had a mean streak,
carried a knife
for the truckers and the bar clowns
that hung around night after night,
fighting sometimes
just for the sheer pleasure of it.
I'd quit high school, but I could write my name
and add two plus two without a calculator.
And this time, I got to thinking,

I got to planning, and one morning
I hitched a ride
on a semi that was headed for California
in the blaze of a west Texas sunrise.
I remember how he'd sit reading
his schedules of bouts and planning his routes
to the heart of a country
he thought he could conquer with only one soldier,
the $1000 cockfight always further down the pike,
or balanced on the knife edge,
but he wanted to deny me even that,
wanted me silent and finally wife
to some other unfinished businessman,
but tonight, it's just me and this old rooster,
and when I'm ready, I untie him
and he runs through the trailer,
flapping his wings and crowing
like it's daybreak
and maybe it is.

Maybe we've both come our separate ways
to reconciliation,
or to placating the patron saint
of roosters and lost children,
and when I go outside, he strolls after me
until I kneel down and we stare at each other
from the cages we were born to,
both knowing what it's like
to fly at an enemy's face
and take him down for the final count.
Preacher, I say, I got my GED,
a AA degree in computer science,
a husband, and a son named Gerald, who's three.
I've been to L.A., Chicago,
and New York City on a dare, and know what? –
it's shitty everywhere, but at least it's not home.

After the coroner's gone, I clean up the trailer,
and later, smoke one of Father's
hand-rolled cigarettes
as I walk by the river,
a quivering way down in my guts,
while Preacher huddles in his cage.

A fat frog catches the lit cigarette
and swallows it.
I go back and look at the picture
of my husband and son,
reread the only letter I ever sent
and which he did not answer,
then tear it all to shreds.
I hitch the pickup to the trailer
and put Preacher's cage on the seat,
then I aim my car for the river, start it,
and jump out just before it hits.
I start the pickup and sit
bent over the steering wheel,
shaking and crying, until I hear Preacher
clawing at the wire,
my path clear,
my fear drained from me like blood from a cut
that's still not deep enough
to kill you off, Father,
to spill you out of me for good.
What was it that made us kin,
that sends daughters crawling after fathers
who abandon them at the womb's door?
What a great and liberating crowing
comes from your rooster
as another sunrise breaks the night apart
with bare hands
and the engine roars
as I press the pedal to the floor
and we shoot forward onto the road.
Your schedule of fights,
clipped above the dashboard,
flutters in the breeze.
Barstow, El Centro, then swing back
to Truth or Consequences, New Mexico,
and a twenty-minute soak in the hot springs
where Geronimo once bathed,
before we wind back again into Arizona,
then all the way to Idaho by way of Colorado,
the climb, then the slow, inevitable descent
toward the unknown
mine now. Mine.

AI

155

Daddy

You do not do, you do not do
Any more, black shoe
In which I have lived like a foot
For thirty years, poor and white,
Barely daring to breathe or Achoo.

Daddy, I have had to kill you.
You died before I had time –
Marble-heavy, a bag full of God,
Ghastly statue with one gray toe
Big as a Frisco seal

And a head in the freakish Atlantic
Where it pours bean green over blue
In the waters off beautiful Nauset.
I used to pray to recover you.
Ach, du.

In the German tongue, in the Polish town
Scraped flat by the roller
Of wars, wars, wars.
But the name of the town is common.
My Polack friend

Says there are a dozen or two.
So I never could tell where you
Put your foot, your root,
I never could talk to you.
The tongue stuck in my jaw.

It stuck in a barb wire snare.
Ich, ich, ich, ich,
I could hardly speak.
I thought every German was you.
And the language obscene

An engine, an engine
Chuffing me off like a Jew.
A Jew to Dachau, Auschwitz, Belsen.
I began to talk like a Jew.
I think I may well be a Jew.

The snows of the Tyrol, the dear beer of Vienna
Are not very pure or true.
With my gipsy ancestress and my weird luck
And my Taroc pack and my Taroc pad
I may be a bit of a Jew.

I have always been scared of *you*,
With your Luftwaffe, your gobbledygoo.
And your neat mustache
And your Aryan eye, bright blue.
Panzer-man, panzer-man, O You –

Not God but a swastika
So black no sky could squeak through.
Every woman adores a Fascist,
The boot in the face, the brute
Brute heart of a brute like you.

You stand at the blackboard, daddy,
In the picture I have of you,
A cleft in your chin instead of your foot
But no less a devil for that, no not
Any less the black man who

Bit my pretty red heart in two.
I was ten when they buried you.
At twenty I tried to die
And get back, back, back to you.
I thought even the bones would do.

But they pulled me out of the sack,
And they stuck me together with glue.
And then I knew what to do.
I made a model of you,
A man in black with a Meinkampf look

And a love of the rack and the screw.
And I said I do, I do.
So daddy, I'm finally through.
The black telephone's off at the root,
The voices just can't worm through.

If I've killed one man, I've killed two –
The vampire who said he was you
And drank my blood for a year,
Seven years, if you want to know.
Daddy, you can lie back now.

There's a stake in your fat black heart
And the villagers never liked you.
They are dancing and stamping on you.
They always *knew* it was you.
Daddy, daddy, you bastard, I'm through.

SYLVIA PLATH

Waste Sonata

I think at some point I looked at my father
and thought *He's full of shit.* How did I
know fathers talked to their children,
kissed them? I knew. I saw him and judged him.
Whatever he poured into my mother
she hated, her face rippled like a thin
wing, sometimes, when she happened to be near him,
and the liquor he knocked into his body
felled him, slew the living tree,
loops of its grain started to cube,
petrify, coprofy, he was a
shit, but I felt he hated being a shit,
he had never imagined it could happen, this drunken
sleep was a spell laid on him –
by my mother! Well, I left to them
the passion of who did what to whom, it was a
baby in their bed they were rolling over on,
but I could not live with hating him.
I did not see that I had to. I stood
in that living room and saw him drowse
like the prince, in slobbrous beauty, I began
to think he was a kind of chalice,

158

a grail, his love the goal of a quest,
yes! He was the god of love
and I was a shit. I looked down at my forearm –
whatever was inside there
was not good, it was white stink,
bad manna. I looked in the mirror
and as I looked at my face the blemishes
arose, like pigs up out of the ground
to the witch's call. It was strange to me
that my body smelled sweet, it was proof I was
demonic, but at least I breathed out,
from the sour dazed scum within,
my father's truth. Well it's fun talking about this,
I love the terms of foulness. I have learned
to get pleasure from speaking of pain.
But to die, like this. To grow old and die
a child, lying to herself.
My father was not a shit. He was a man
failing at life. He had little shits
travelling through him while he lay there unconscious –
sometimes I don't let myself say
I loved him, anymore, but I feel
I almost love those shits that move through him,
shapely, those waste foetuses,
my mother, my sister, my brother, and me
in that purgatory.

SHARON OLDS

The Survivors

I came at night to the dark house
where the father had taken the fuse
from the fuse-box and killed the lights.

I came at night when the weepy mother sat
doll-like in the front room, cross-legged on the carpet,
hands stinging from smacking the brats,

listening to crackly recordings of Glenn Miller,
her heels drumming on the well-worn floor:
the plane crash had wiped her mind out.

The thumb-sized father climbed the stairs
with a candle, searching for survivors.

TRACEY HERD

The Strait-Jackets

I lay the suitcase on Father's bed
and unzip it slowly, gently.
Inside, packed in cloth strait-jackets
lie forty live hummingbirds
tied down in rows, each tiny head
cushioned on a swaddled body.
I feed them from a flask of sugar water,
inserting every bill into the pipette,
then unwind their bindings
so Father can see their changing colours
as they dart around his room.
They hover inches from his face
as if he's a flower, their humming
just audible above the oxygen recycler.
For the first time since I've arrived
he's breathing easily, the cannula
attached to his nostrils almost slips out.
I don't know how long we sit there
but when I next glance at his face
he's asleep, lights from their feathers
still playing on his eyelids and cheeks.
It takes me hours to catch them all
and wrap them in their strait-jackets.
I work quietly, he's in such
a deep sleep he doesn't wake once.

PASCALE PETIT

160

Self-Portrait as a Warao Violin

When they say 'Go on, play your little girl'
he splashes rum on the walls and roof

of his house to get it drunk
and invites everyone.

Even the jaguar and monkey
stand on their hind legs

and dance together
as he rub-rubs my body.

He made me from a red cedar
in Delta Amacuro.

I'm half the size of civilised violins
but much more shapely.

The resonance chamber is my body,
the scroll my head.

I also have a waist and back.
When all the dancers have collapsed

he wraps me in an old shirt
and hangs me from the ridgepole.

No one but my father can touch me.
When he sleeps

the night breeze blows across my strings
and makes them hum.

PASCALE PETIT

But till that morning, ain't no one gonna harm you

The little boy's hand, his hand full of trust,
trustingly offered to the bigger boy
as, without looking back, he walked away
from his mother to be beaten to death. Almost
more than I could bear, seeing in that slight back
turned forever, leaving forever, yours
as you walk off innocently towards
some horror I will fail to expect
or, worse, anticipate but not forestall.
Whenever I'm not holding you I know
nothing's *childproof*: no house, school, shopping mall,
no car, no bicycle. Nowhere to go
on God's green earth where children cannot fall
from mothers' arms. No. Nowhere to go.

SUSAN GLICKMAN

Hollis Street Square, Halifax

Two kinds in the Saturday crowd:
first, the sharp-edged uneroded ones, single
or in fresh pairs, click by
briskly on assertive heels. Themselves
what they offer the world, a craft-fair of faces.

And then those with children at the ends
of their arms, small versions of themselves brightly
inflating as they drain down,
as though they'd opened a vein in their wrists and
out poured blood taking the shape of a child
pulling them by the hand:

those getting brighter and brisker and those
going invisible, sucked up the straws
of six-year-old arms, diving
inside small skins,
starting over again, small.

JOHN STEFFLER

Returning North

The car lurches on goat paths,
North on north,
You ask shepherds directions as you drive.
Above the Arctic Circle
Norway's sun rises all night
On you bringing your family on your search
To meet your background face to face.
Your mother left in 1895,
A four-year-old Norwegian, steerage class,
Clutching a copper teapot in the hold,
Her one possession.
At forty-six
You come back as a dead sister's only son.

Your aged aunt waits at a pasture gate,
Holding your letter, looking anxious, small,
Shy as the summer snow
In patches at her feet.
You see your dead mother,
Her hands, her face, her raven hair, her eyes,
You see her hesitate.
She backs away, half frightened of our car,
And beckons us to follow her
Through cold summer meadows to a barn.
One by one we scale
A ladder and pull ourselves
Up through a hole in the ceiling
Above the pigs and geese,
We have arrived,
And there, lying upon a bed of straw,

A man stares, fever-eyed, then turns away.
Out of respect
The scared, exhilarated family
Hides whispering behind the kitchen door,
Peeking in turns to see
These rich Americans. Two children
Push each other into the room,
Their dialect is difficult for you.

They offer us
A plate of fish, a plate of goat cheese, bread
Which we are meant to eat in front of them,
Among the coughing and the shining eyes.
This would have been your mother's home.
And we begin to eat
Moments before you realise
The little household is tubercular.

Almost at once, you say that we must go,
There in the mountains
Days and days away,
You say our family is expected
Somewhere else, somewhere immediately,
You ask them to believe
Our visit has been good,
We must go south. They do not understand.
They pull at us, they watch us drive away,
Slowly, painfully south, finding
The way as tears will find their way
Into a mouth, hundreds of miles
To Oslo, the city of clean air
And Lutheran chapels stark, narrow, and pure,
And small, and white,
So like your mother's face.

You said lightly, Forget this incident.
But, Father, here, tonight,
It comes to mind
Or my mind comes to it as one winding
Through passageways cut through
Snow-covered sculptured hedges
Comes upon
A waterfall suspended in white frost
And stands amazed and lost, so am I
Lost remembering
The fear crossing your face.

GJERTRUD SCHNACKENBERG

Time Out

Such is modern life
STEPHEN DOBYNS

The two young ones fed, bathèd, zippered, read to and sung to.
    Asleep.
Time now to stretch on the sofa. Time for a cigarette.
When he realises he's out. Clean out of smokes.
He grabs a fistful of coins, hesitates to listen before
Pulling the door softly to. Then sprints for the cornershop.

When he trips on a shoelace, head first into the path of a
    U-turning cab.
The screech of brakes is coterminous with his scream.
The Somalian shopkeeper, who summons the ambulance, knows
    the face,
But the name or address? No – just someone he remembers
Popping in, always with kids (this he doesn't say).

Casualty is at full stretch and the white thirtyish male,
Unshaven, with broken runners, is going nowhere. Is cleanly dead.
Around midnight an orderly rummages his pockets: £2.50 in change,
A latchkey, two chestnuts, one mitten, scraps of paper,
Some written on, but no wallet, cards, licence, or address book.

Around 2 a.m. he's put on ice, with a numbered tag.
Around 3 a.m. a child wakes, cries, then wails for attention.
But after ten minutes, unusually, goes back to sleep.
Unusually his twin sleeps on undisturbed till six o'clock,
When they both wake together, kicking, calling out *dada, dada*

Happily: well slept, still dry, crooning and pretend-reading in the
    half-light.
Then one slides to the floor, toddles to the master bedroom
And, seeing the empty (unmade) bed, toddles towards the stairs,
Now followed by the other, less stable, who stumbles halfway down
And both roll the last five steps to the bottom, screaming.

To be distracted by the post plopping onto the mat: all junk,
Therefore bulky, colourful, glossy, illicit. Time slips.
Nine o'clock: hungry, soiled, sensing oddness and absence,
Edgy together and whimpering now, when they discover the TV
Still on, its 17-channel console alive to their touch.

The Italian Parliament, sumo wrestling, the Austrian Grand Prix,
Opera, the Parcel Force ad, see them through to half past nine
When distress takes hold and the solid stereophonic screaming begins,
Relentless and shrill enough to penetrate the attention
Of the retired French pharmacist next door

Who at, say ten o'clock, pokes a broomstick through her rear window
To rattle theirs: magical silencing effect, lasting just so long
As it takes for the elderly woman to draw up her shopping list,
To retrieve two tenners from the ice-compartment, deadlock her
        front doors,
Shake her head at the sunning milk, and make it to the bus.

Let us jump then to 10 p.m., to the nightmare dénouement...
No, let us duck right now out of this story, for such it is:
An idle, day-bed, Hitchcockian fantasy (though prompted by a news item,
A clockwork scenario: it was five days before that three-year-old
Was discovered beside the corpse of his Irish dad in Northolt).

Let us get *this* dad in and out of the shop, safely across the street,
Safely indoors again, less a couple of quid, plus the listings mags
And ten Silk Cut, back on board the sofa: reprieved, released, relaxed,
Thinking it's time for new sneakers, for a beard trim, for an overall
Rethink in the hair department. Time maybe to move on from the fags.

MAURICE RIORDAN

The blessing

The halls are thronged, the grand staircase murmurous.
There's a smell of close-packed bodies, lilac,
hair-gel and sweat. Handprints on the brass railings
fade like breath on a cold window.
Outside the city is stunned with snow.

There he is, just where he should be
by that leather-topped, deeply-scored table
where fortunes are lost and made. He explains,
and those at the back lean closer
to catch the ripple of laughter.

A joke, and the group dissolves
to stare, study, and point a finger.
He waits for them to catch up with him.
You need a guide, with so many rooms
and between them, so many turnings.

I am there too, but not speaking.
I wait while the paint peels,
alone with the pulse of a Matisse
and the sunlight beating full on us.
But perhaps I say this

as I see him hasten down another staircase:
'You always had a blessing with you,
and you still have a blessing with you.
Keep moving. Go as fast as you can
and whatever I say, don't listen '

HELEN DUNMORE

Walking Away
(for Sean)

It is eighteen years ago, almost to the day –
A sunny day with the leaves just turning,
The touch-lines new-ruled – since I watched you play
Your first game of football, then, like a satellite
Wrenched from its orbit, go drifting away

Behind a scatter of boys. I can see
You walking away from me towards the school
With the pathos of a half-fledged thing set free
Into a wilderness, the gait of one
Who finds no path where the path should be.

That hesitant figure, eddying away
Like a winged seed loosened from its parent stem,
Has something I never quite grasp to convey
About nature's give-and-take – the small, the scorching
Ordeals which fire one's irresolute clay.

I have had worse partings, but none that so
Gnaws at my mind still. Perhaps it is roughly
Saying what God alone could perfectly show –
How selfhood begins with a walking away,
And love is proved in the letting go.

C. DAY LEWIS

Mother-May-I

Mother-May-I
go down the bottom of the lane,
to the yellow-headed piss-the-beds,
and hunker at the may-hedge, skirts
fanned out
            in the dirt and see the dump
where we're not allowed –
twisty trees, the burn, and say:
    all hushed sweetie-breath:
    they are the woods
where men
            lift up your skirt
and take down your pants
even although you're crying.
Mother may I
            leave these lasses' games
            and play at Man-hunt, just
in the scheme Mother
may I
    tell small lies: *we were sot*
in the lane, sat on garage ramps,
picking harling
with bitten nails, as myths
rose thick as swamp mist
from the woods behind the dump
                        where hitch-hikers rot
in the curling roots of trees,
and men
leave tight rolled-up
dirty magazines.

168

Mother may we

                   pull our soft backsides
through the jagged may's
white blossom, run across the stinky dump
and muck about
at the woods and burn
                         dead pleased
to see the white dye
of our gym-rubbers seep downstream?

KATHLEEN JAMIE

Kid

Batman, big shot, when you gave the order
to grow up, then let me loose to wander
leeward, freely through the wild blue yonder
as you liked to say, or ditched me, rather,
in the gutter...well, I turned the corner.
Now I've scotched that 'he was like a father
to me' rumour, sacked it, blown the cover
on that 'he was like an elder brother'
story, let the cat out on that caper
with the married woman, how you took her
downtown on expenses in the motor.
Holy robin-redbreast-nest-egg-shocker!
Holy roll-me-over-in-the-clover,
I'm not playing ball boy any longer
Batman, now I've doffed that off-the-shoulder
Sherwood-Forest-green and scarlet number
for a pair of jeans and crew-neck jumper;
now I'm taller, harder, stronger, older.
Batman, it makes a marvellous picture:
you without a shadow, stewing over
chicken giblets in the pressure cooker,
next to nothing in the walk-in larder,
punching the palm of your hand all winter,
you baby, now I'm the real boy wonder.

SIMON ARMITAGE

Guests

Awe at the first arrival,
they turned up with wet plastered hair
faces flattened by travel,

journey's end the heart centre.
They stayed, settled in
grew familiar, departed.

Years of living together
concentrate down to a weekend visit
lit by anticipation,

the most honoured guests
for whom dishes, towels, sheets
are embellished with love.

Visit over
a phone call sets them
safe in their grown up lives.

Silence has changed into
absence of voices,
the small house too spacious,

washing and folding,
to pack love away again
hard to find room on the shelf.

CYNTHIA FULLER

from Book of Matches

Mother, any distance greater than a single span
requires a second pair of hands.
You come to help me measure windows, pelmets, doors,
the acres of the walls, the prairies of the floors.

You at the zero-end, me with the spool of tape, recording
length, reporting metres, centimetres back to base, then leaving
up the stairs, the line still feeding out, unreeling
years between us. Anchor. Kite.

I space-walk through the empty bedrooms, climb
the ladder to the loft, to breaking point, where something
has to give;
two floors below your fingertips still pinch
the last one-hundredth of an inch... I reach
towards a hatch that opens on an endless sky
to fall or fly.

SIMON ARMITAGE

Johnson Brothers Ltd

In those days when my father was still big,
dangerous tools in the bulging pockets
of his jacket, in his suits the odours
of teased out twine and lead,
behind his eyes the incomprehensible world
of a man, gas-fitter, first-class,
said mother, in those days how different
my feelings were, when he would shut the doors
on her and me.

Now he is dead and I am suddenly as old as he,
it turns out to my surprise that he too had
decay built into him. In his diary I see
appointments with persons unknown, on his wall
calendars with gas-pipe labyrinths,
on the mantelpiece the portrait of a woman
in Paris, his woman, the incomprehensible
world of a man.

Looking into the little hand-basin of porcelain
dating from the thirties, with its silly pair of lions,
Johnson Brothers Ltd, high up in the dead-still
house the shuffle of mother's slippers,

171

Jesus Christ, father, here come the tears
for now and for then – they flow together
into the lead of the swan-neck pipe,
no longer separable from the drops that come
from the little copper tap marked 'cold'.

RUTGER KOPLAND
translated from the Dutch by James Brockway

Laws of Gravity
(for Julian Turner)

I found a guidebook to the port he knew
intimately – its guano-coated ledges,
its weathervanes, his bird's-eye river view
of liner funnels, coal sloops and dredgers.
It helped me gain a foothold – how he felt
a hundred rungs above a fifties street,
and whether, being so high, he ever dwelt
on suicide, or flummoxed his feet
to last night's dance steps, still fresh in his head.
It's all here in his ledger's marginalia:
how he fell up the dark stairwell to bed
and projected right through to Australia;
and said a prayer for rainfall every night
so he could skip his first hungovered round.
The dates he's noted *chamois frozen tight
into bucket.* When he left the ground
a sense of purpose overtook and let
a different set of laws come into play:
like muezzins who ascend a minaret
to call the faithful of a town to pray.
Take one step at a time. Never look down.
He'd seen the hardest cases freeze halfway,
the arse-flap of their overalls turn brown.
As a rule, he writes, *your sense of angle
becomes acute at height.* A diagram
he's thumbnailed shows a drop through a triangle
if you miscalculated by a gram.

172

Sometimes, his senses still blunted from booze,
he'd drop his squeegee, watch it fall to earth
and cling onto the grim hypotenuse
of his own making for all he was worth.
He seems to have enjoyed working that hour
the low sun caught the glass and raised the ante
on every aerial, flue and cooling tower,
and gilded the lofts, the rooftop shanty
town, when everything was full of itself,
and for a while even the Latin plaques
ignited with the glow of squandered wealth.
At times like these I see what our world lacks,
the light of heaven on what we've produced
and here some words lost where his biro bled
then *clouds of dark birds zero in to roost.*
There's IOUs and debtors marked in red
and some description of the things he saw
beyond the pane – a hard-lit typing pool,
a room of faces on some vanished floor
closed off and absolute like a fixed rule.
His story of the boy butting a wall,
the secretary crying at her desk,
all happened in the air above a mall.
Each edifice, each gargoyle and grotesque,
is gone. The earliest thing I remember:
as our van dropped a gear up Brownlow Hill
I looked back at the panes of distemper
that sealed a world. We reached our overspill,
and this is where our stories overlap.
The coming of the cradle and sheet glass
was squeezing out the ladder and the slap
of leather into suds, and less and less
work came through the door. And anyway
you were getting too old for scaling heights.
Now, when I change a bulb or queue to pay
at fairs, or when I'm checking in for flights,
I feel our difference bit down to the quick.
There are no guidebooks to that town you knew
and this attempt to build it, brick by brick,
descends the page. I'll hold the foot for you.

PAUL FARLEY

Transmutation

(FROM *Might a Shape of Words*)

A boy is amazed to see his father home from work in the afternoon
with a bandaged finger. An accident, not serious. A week later, the
boy even sees the stitches, just before their removal. Then his father
is once more gone during the week.

But that scar, though fading over the years, persists. No one else
seems to remark on it: a narrowing streak, merely an absence of
pigment, eventually hardly more than a crease. Long after his father's
death, when that now grown boy tries to remember him, it is as if
nothing else were so eloquent of his father or so particular to himself.

GAEL TURNBULL

Family

My mother has gone and bought herself a piglet
because none of us comes to visit anymore.
George has good manners and is clean in his ways:
he is courtly, thoughtful, easy to amuse.
He goes to Mass with her, and sits sweetly
while she trots up to receive. He doesn't stray.
She has made a cot for him in the kitchen
where he turns in on our old clothes cut to size.

One Sunday I call on the way to somewhere else.
She props him up beside me in the high chair
and he fixes me with those dreary dark blue eyes.
When I tell him I'm glad he's there when I can't be,
he answers 'thank you' in a voice too like my own,
then bids me sit and make myself at home.

VONA GROARKE

174

Animals

When I come out of the bathroom
animals are waiting in the hall
and when I settle down to read
an animal comes between me
and my book and when I put on
a fancy dinner, a few animals
are under the table staring at the guests,
and when I mail a letter
or go to the Safeway there's always
an animal tagging along –
or crying left at home and when I get
home from work animals leap joyously
around my old red car so I feel like
an avatar with flowers & presents all over
her body, and when I dance around
the kitchen at night wild & feeling
lovely as Margie Gillis, the animals
try to dance too, they stagger on
back legs and open their mouths, pink
and black and fanged, and I take their paws
in my hands and bend toward them,
happy and full of love.

SHARON THESEN

Animals

I think the death of domestic animals
marks the sea changes in our lives.
Think how things were, when things were different.
There was an animal then, a dog or a cat,
not the one you have now, another one.
Think when things were different before that.
There was another one then. You had almost forgotten.

MILLER WILLIAMS

Forty-one, Alone, No Gerbil

In the strange quiet, I realise
there's no one else in the house. No bucktooth
mouth pulls at a stainless-steel teat, no
hairy mammal runs on a treadmill –
Charlie is dead, the last of our children's half-children.
When our daughter found him lying in the shavings, trans-
mogrified backwards from a living body
into a bolt of rodent bread
she turned her back on early motherhood
and went on single, with nothing. Crackers,
Fluffy, Pretzel, Biscuit, Charlie,
buried on the old farm we bought
where she could know nature. Well, now she knows it
and it sucks. Creatures she loved, mobile and
needy, have gone down stiff and indifferent,
she will not adopt again though she cannot
have children yet, her body like a blueprint
of the understructure for a woman's body,
so now everything stops for a while,
now I must wait many years
to hear in this house again the faint
powerful call of a young animal.

SHARON OLDS

Putting Down the Cat

The assistant holds her on the table,
the fur hanging limp from her tiny skeleton,
and the veterinarian raises the needle of fluid
which will put the line through her ninth life.

'Painless,' he reassures me, 'like counting
backwards from a hundred,' but I want to tell him
that our poor cat cannot count at all,
much less to a hundred, much less backwards.

BILLY COLLINS

On the euthanasia of a pet dog

Lightly she fell where the vets' hands held her
the two vets who came with shaver and syringe
two young blonde girls just out of vet school
and she died between them, surrounded by petting.

It was three o'clock. All day we sat with her
singly or together, making our farewells
while she sniffed the bright day, heart heaving
and lifted her muzzle to the faint breeze.

And when it was over we each wept copiously
the vets departed, we gave in to grief
as though we were rushing to basins to bend over
hands held to faces, we stumbled and stooped.

She lay on the carpet so soft and plumped-out
all dehydration gone, all clenching of sinews
she stayed there for hours so we could caress her
and talk to her finally, and bless her.

ELIZABETH SMITHER

'Noticing a man unable...'

Noticing a man unable
to gather the softness of a pup
up in his arms, I looked again
at the animal, at the curve of
its slinking away, slinked-back
ears. From this slow retreat a single
forepaw inched skywards. Immediately
the pup was swept up. Cuddled, loved
beyond love, reason; held above
the rig of buildings to the sun. So small,
it fitted in to the high country, the high
pocket of a short-sleeved summer shirt.

From there, shivering, it chased the nodding
world, this world, and the next and the next,
scenting each and every grass blade, as if
shaken by its origins on the homeward road,
shaken to its root.

GERRY McGRATH

Walking the Dog

Two universes mosey down the street
Connected by love and a leash and nothing else.
Mostly I look at lamplight through the leaves
While he mooches along with tail up and snout down,
Getting a secret knowledge through the nose
Almost entirely hidden from my sight.

We stand while he's enraptured by a bush
Till I can't stand our standing any more
And haul him off; for our relationship
Is patience balancing to this side tug
And that side drag; a pair of symbionts
Contented not to think each other's thoughts.

What else we have in common's what he taught,
Our interest in shit. We know its every state
From steaming fresh through stink to nature's way
Of sluicing it downstreet dissolved in rain
Or drying it to dust that blows away.
We move along the street inspecting it.

His sense of it is keener far than mine,
And only when he finds the place precise
He signifies by sniffing urgently
And circles thrice about, and squats, and shits,
Whereon we both with dignity walk home
And just to show who's master I write the poem.

HOWARD NEMEROV

4

Love Life

People in love or in mourning do feel that they must rise to
a big occasion, when they must use the best language there is.
Ordinary prose, which is used for instructions on how
to clean the cooker and so forth, won't do.

U.A. FANTHORPE

A naive reader always assumes that a love poem is necessarily
addressed to a person (either openly, or in secret). Yet this
is rarely the case, even when the poet says it is: it is love that
the poem loves, not the seeming object of that love...

JOHN BURNSIDE

THE LOVE POEMS in *Staying Alive* are combined in a section called 'In and out of love' with poems about desertion, betrayal and regret. In choosing poems for *Being Alive*, I found there were not only numerous celebrations of love, passion and sex, but even more poems extolling and berating both sexes. I've organised these poems into two sections: 'Love Life' for poems on the nature of love and 'Men and Women' for poems on gender and the nature of relationships.

Where the next section will focus on differences, the poems in 'Love Life' explore closeness, falling in love and staying in love, as well as staying alive to the world through love, as in Deryn Rees-Jones's 'What It's Like To Be Alive' (191) and Hayden Carruth's 'Alive' (191). In several poems, a sense of oneness between two people goes hand in hand with a sense of inner peace and communion with the world, children and other people, including three poems by leading American poets: Robert Hass's 'Misery and Splendor' (192), Sharon Olds' 'This Hour' (193) and Galway Kinnell's 'After Making Love We Hear Footsteps' (194).

Little-known outside America, Jack Gilbert is a latterday metaphysical poet whose work replays the myth of Orpheus and Eurydice, recurrent figures in his books. In poems such as 'The Great Fires' (195), he returns from the fire of passion to sing of love and loss. Gilbert's poetry bears witness to what he calls 'the craft of the invisible', that is, form in the service of his explosive content. James Dickey calls him 'a necessary poet': 'He takes himself away to a place more inward than it is safe to go; from that awful silence and tightening, he returns to us poems of savage compassion'. There are more poems by this extraordinary writer in other sections (76, 265, 325).

179

Love at First Sight

They're both convinced
that a sudden passion joined them.
Such certainty is beautiful,
but uncertainty is more beautiful still.

Since they'd never met before, they're sure
that there'd been nothing between them.
But what's the word from the streets, staircases, hallways –
perhaps they've passed by each other a million times?

I want to ask them
if they don't remember –
a moment face to face
in some revolving door?
perhaps a 'sorry' muttered in a crowd?
a curt 'wrong number' caught in the receiver?
but I know the answer.
No, they don't remember.

They'd be amazed to hear
that Chance has been toying with them
now for years.

Not quite ready yet
to become their Destiny,
it pushed them close, drove them apart,
it barred their path,
stifling a laugh,
and then leaped aside.

There were signs and signals,
even if they couldn't read them yet.
Perhaps three years ago
or just last Tuesday
a certain leaf fluttered
from one shoulder to another?
Something was dropped and then picked up.
Who knows, maybe the ball that vanished
into childhood's thicket?

There were doorknobs and doorbells
where one touch had covered another
beforehand.
Suitcases checked and standing side by side.
One night, perhaps, the same dream,
grown hazy by morning.

Every beginning
is only a sequel, after all,
and the book of events
is always open halfway through.

WISLAWA SZYMBORSKA
translated from the Polish by Stanislaw Baranczak and Clare Cavanagh

Story of a Hotel Room

Thinking we were safe – insanity!
We went in to make love. All the same
Idiots to trust the little hotel bedroom.
Then in the gloom...
...And who does not know that pair of shutters
With the awkward hook on them
All screeching whispers? Very well then, in the gloom
We set about acquiring one another
Urgently! But on a temporary basis
Only as guests – just guests of one another's senses.

But idiots to feel so safe you hold back nothing
Because the bed of cold, electric linen
Happens to be illicit...
To make love as well as that is ruinous.
Londoner, Parisian, someone should have warned us
That without permanent intentions
You have absolutely no protection
– If the act is clean, authentic, sumptuous,
The concurring deep love of the heart
Follows the naked work, profoundly moved by it.

ROSEMARY TONKS

Tryst

Night slips, trailing behind it
a suddenly innocent darkness.
Am I safe, now, to slip home?

My fists tighten your collar, your fingers
lock in my hair and we hover
between discretion and advertised purpose.

Dawn traffic in both directions,
taxis, milk floats, builders' vans.
Each proposes a service or poses a threat

like the police, slumped couples in cars
left to patrol each other, to converge
at a red light that stops little else.

Each separation is outweighed
by more faith, more sadness;
accumulated static, the shock in every step.

I go to sleep where my life is sleeping
and wake late to a fused morning,
a blistered mouth.

LAVINIA GREENLAW

Love after Love

The time will come
when, with elation,
you will greet yourself arriving
at your own door, in your own mirror
and each will smile at the other's welcome,

and say, sit here. Eat.
You will love again the stranger who was your self.

Give wine. Give bread, Give back your heart
to itself, to the stranger who has loved you

all your life, whom you ignored
for another, who knows you by heart.
Take down the love letters from the bookshelf,

the photographs, the desperate notes,
peel your own image from the mirror.
Sit. Feast on your life.

DEREK WALCOTT

Love, Like Water

Tumbling from some far-flung cloud
into your bathroom alone, to sleeve
a toe, five toes, a metatarsal arch,
it does its best to feign indifference
to the body, but will go on creeping
up to the neck till it's reading the skin
like braille, though you're certain it sees
under the surface of things and knows
the routes your nerves take as they branch
from the mind, which lately has been curling
in on itself like the spine of a dog
as it circles a patch of ground to sleep.
Now through the dappled window,
propped open slightly for the heat,
a light rain is composing
the lake it falls into, the way a lover's hand
composes the body it touches – Love,
like water! How it gives and gives,
wearing the deepest of grooves in our sides
and filling them up again, ever so gently
wounding us, making us whole.

JULIA COPUS

To My Love, Combing Her Hair

To my love, combing her hair
without a mirror, facing me,

a psalm: you've shampooed your hair, an entire
forest of pine trees is filled with yearning on your head.

Calmness inside and calmness outside
have hammered your face between them to a tranquil copper.

The pillow on your bed is your spare brain,
tucked under your neck for remembering and dreaming.

The earth is trembling beneath us, love.
Let's lie fastened together, a double safety-lock.

YEHUDA AMICHAI
translated from the Hebrew by Chana Bloch & Stephen Mitchell

The White Porch

I wrap the blue towel
after washing,
around the damp
weight of hair, bulky
as a sleeping cat,
and sit out on the porch.
Still dripping water,
it'll be dry by supper,
by the time the dust
settles off your shoes,
though it's only five
past noon. Think
of the luxury: how to use
the afternoon like the stretch
of lawn spread before me.
There's the laundry,

sun-warm clothes at twilight,
and the mountain of beans
in my lap. Each one.
I'll break and snap
thoughtfully in half.

But there is this slow arousal.
The small buttons
of my cotton blouse
are pulling away from my body.
I feel the strain of threads,
the swollen magnolias
heavy as a flock of birds
in the tree. Already,
the orange sponge cake
is rising in the oven.

I know you'll say it makes
your mouth dry
and I'll watch you
drench your slice of it
in canned peaches
and lick the plate clean.

So much hair, my mother
used to say, grabbing
the thick braided rope
in her hands while we washed
the breakfast dishes, discussing
dresses and pastries.
My mind often elsewhere
as we did the morning chores together.
Sometimes, a few strands
would catch in her gold ring.
I worked hard then,
anticipating the hour
when I would let the rope down
at night, strips of sheets,
knotted and tied,
while she slept in tight blankets.
My hair, freshly washed
like a measure of wealth,
like a bridal veil.

Crouching in the grass,
you would wait for the signal,
for the movement of curtains
before releasing yourself
from the shadow of moths.
Cloth, hair and hands,
smuggling you in.

CATHY SONG

Rosy Ear

I thought
but I know her so well
we have been living together so many years

I know
her bird-like head
white arms
and belly

until one time
on a winter evening
she sat down beside me
and in the lamplight
falling from behind us
I saw a rosy ear

a comic petal of skin
a conch with living blood
inside it

I didn't say anything then –

it would be good to write
a poem about a rosy ear
but not so that people would say
what a subject he chose
he's trying to be eccentric

so that nobody even would smile

so that they would understand that I proclaim
a mystery
I didn't say anything then
but that night when we were in bed together
delicately I essayed
the exotic taste
of a rosy ear

ZBIGNIEW HERBERT
translated from the Polish by Czeslaw Milosz

Variation on the Word *Sleep*

I would like to watch you sleeping,
which may not happen.
I would like to watch you,
sleeping. I would like to sleep
with you, to enter
your sleep as its smooth dark wave
slides over my head

and walk with you through that lucent
wavering forest of bluegreen leaves
with its watery sun & three moons
towards the cave where you must descend,
towards your worst fear

I would like to give you the silver
branch, the small white flower, the one
word that will protect you
from the grief at the center
of your dream, from the grief
at the center. I would like to follow
you up the long stairway
again & become
the boat that would row you back
carefully, a flame
in two cupped hands
to where your body lies
beside me, and you enter
it as easily as breathing in

I would like to be the air
that inhabits you for a moment
only. I would like to be that unnoticed
& that necessary

MARGARET ATWOOD

The Blindfold

Once in a room in Blackpool we had to make do
with the grubby band that held aside the curtain.
I perched on the edge of the bed while he
tied the knot once then (ouch) twice
sending me in that pretend dark back
to knicker-wetting games of Blind Man's Buff,
arms flailing down a hall of coats,
seeking ever greater dark in cellars,
deep in wardrobes, cornered in the arms of –

In that brief blindness you are bereft
but alert to the senses left to you
like the game-show hopeful conjuring out of his dark
a sofa, fridge, a week in the sun, or the night nurse
at noon, the nose-job patient counting the days
– all that dreaming under wraps! Even the hostage
inhaling oil-smeared cloth maps the cadence
of road and the condemned in his limbo
interprets every sound through the gauze of memory.

But who wouldn't seize the chance left
open by someone's careless hand as I did
that last dirty weekend when I lied to his
how many fingers? but did at least close my eyes
to lend a kind of authenticity to my guess.
And though I usually craved the not knowing
where or how his touch would next alight
now I could peek, like a thief through a letterbox, at him
still faithful to the rules of a game we'd made up

that I'd just dropped and it struck me then that in all
our time together, my tally of infidelities,
this was the closest I'd come to betrayal;
and when my keeper reached forward I flinched
knowing my time had come to confess, naked
as the day, babbling, and dazzled by the light.

GRETA STODDART

Silk of a Soul

Never
did I speak with her
either about love
or about death

only blind taste
and mute touch
used to run between us
when absorbed in ourselves
we lay close

I must
peek inside her
to see what she wears
at her centre

when she slept
with her lips open
I peeked

and what
and what
would you think
I caught sight of

I was expecting
branches
I was expecting
a bird

I was expecting
a house
by a lake great and silent

but there
on a glass counter
I caught sight of a pair
of silk stockings

my God
I'll buy her those stockings
I'll buy them

but what will appear then
on the glass counter
of the little soul

will it be something
which cannot be touched
even with one finger of a dream

ZBIGNIEW HERBERT
translated from the Polish by Peter Dale Scott

The Fist

The fist clenched round my heart
loosens a little, and I gasp
brightness; but it tightens
again. When have I ever not loved
the pain of love? But this has moved

past love to mania. This has the strong
clench of the madman, this is
gripping the ledge of unreason, before
plunging howling into the abyss.

Hold hard then, heart. This way at least you live.

DEREK WALCOTT

What It's Like To Be Alive
(after Django Bates)

I remember the nights, and the sounds of the nights,
and the moon, and the clouds, then the clear sky

and the stars and angels on the Rye,
and I remember the way we knelt on the bed, how the bedclothes

were a tide, and the sunlight was a tide, and how everything pulled,
and I remember the trains, leaving and arriving,
and I remember the tears, your tears, and my tears

and how we were children, not lovers,
how the angels cried,

and I remember your face and you coming in my hands,
and the clouds, and the stars, and how, for a moment,
with our eyes tight closed how the planets lurched

and the angels smiled,
and I remember how I did not know if this was grief or love,

this hot pool,
and the sounds,
and then nothing.

A watermark held up to the light.
A boat rowed off the edge of the world.

DERYN REES-JONES

Alive

I used to imagine we were a fine two-headed
    Animal, unison's two-tongued praise
Of fastened sex. But no, though singly bedded
    We went separately always.

When you burned your finger and mine smarted
    We had neither one body nor one soul,
But two in bright free being, consorted
    To play the romance of the whole.

It was good, else I had surely perished.
    In change may a changeless part survive?
As it is, crippled in the sex I cherished,
    I am full of love, and alive!

HAYDEN CARRUTH

Misery and Splendor

Summoned by conscious recollection, she
would be smiling, they might be in a kitchen talking,
before or after dinner. But they are in this other room,
The window has many small panes, and they are on a couch
embracing. He holds her as tightly
as he can, she buries herself in his body.
Morning, maybe it is evening, light
is flowing through the room. Outside,
the day is slowly succeeded by night,
succeeded by day. The process wobbles wildly
and accelerates: weeks, months, years. The light in the room
does not change, so it is plain what is happening.
They are trying to become one creature,
and something will not have it. They are tender
with each other, afraid
their brief, sharp cries will reconcile them to the moment
when they fall away again. So they rub against each other,
their mouths dry, then wet, then dry.
They feel themselves at the center of a powerful
and baffled will. They feel
they are an almost animal,
washed up on the shore of a world –
or huddled up against the gate of a garden –
to which they can't admit they can never be admitted.

ROBERT HASS

This Hour

We could never really say what it is like,
this hour of drinking wine together
on a hot summer night, in the living-room
with the windows open, in our underwear,
my pants with pale-gold gibbon monkeys on them
gleaming in the heat. We talk about our son
disappearing between the pine boughs,
we could not tell what was chrysalis or
bough and what was him. The wine
is powerful, each mouthful holds
for a moment its amber agate shape,
I think of the sweat I sipped from my father's
forehead the hour before his death. We talk about
those last days   that I was waiting for him to die.
You are lying on the couch, your underpants
a luminous white, your hand resting
relaxed, alongside your penis,
we talk about your father's illness,
your nipple like a pure circle of
something risen to the surface of your chest.
Even if we wanted to,
we could not describe it,
the end of the second glass when I sometimes
weep and you start to get sleepy – I love
to drink and cry with you, and end up
sobbing to a sleeping man, your
long body filling the couch and
draped slightly over the ends, the
untrained soft singing of your snore, it cannot be given.
Yes, we know we will make love, but we're
not getting ready to make love,
nor are we getting over making love,
love is simply our element,
it is the summer night, we are in it.

SHARON OLDS

After Making Love We Hear Footsteps

For I can snore like a bullhorn
or play loud music
or sit up talking with any reasonably sober Irishman
and Fergus will only sink deeper
into his dreamless sleep, which goes by all in one flash,
but let there be that heavy breathing
or a stifled come-cry anywhere in the house
and he will wrench himself awake
and make for it on the run – as now, we lie together,
after making love, quiet, touching along the length of our bodies,
familiar touch of the long-married,
and he appears – in his baseball pajamas, it happens,
the neck opening so small he has to screw them on –
and flops down between us and hugs us and snuggles himself to
        sleep,
his face gleaming with satisfaction at being this very child.

In the half darkness we look at each other
and smile
and touch arms across this little, startlingly muscled body –
this one whom habit of memory propels to the ground of his
        making,
sleeper only the mortal sounds can sing awake,
this blessing love gives again into our arms.

GALWAY KINNELL

Love
(from 'The World')

Love means to learn to look at yourself
The way one looks at distant things
For you are only one thing among many.
And whoever sees that way heals his heart,
Without knowing it, from various ills –
A bird and a tree say to him: Friend.

Then he wants to use himself and things
So that they stand in the glow of ripeness.
It doesn't matter whether he knows what he serves:
Who serves best doesn't always understand.

CZESLAW MILOSZ
translated from the Polish by the author

The Great Fires

Love is apart from all things
Desire and excitement are nothing beside it.
It is not the body that finds love.
What leads us there is the body.
What is not love provokes it.
What is not love quenches it.
Love lays hold of everything we know.
The passions which are called love
also change everything to a newness
at first. Passion is clearly the path
but does not bring us to love.
It opens the castle of our spirit
so that we might find the love which is
a mystery hidden there.
Love is one of many great fires.
Passion is a fire made of many woods,
each of which gives off its special odor
so we can know the many kinds
that are not love. Passion is the paper
and twigs that kindle the flames
but cannot sustain them. Desire perishes
because it tries to be love.
Love is eaten away by appetite.
Love does not last, but it is different
from the passions that do not last.
Love lasts by not lasting.
Isaiah said each man walks in his own fire
for his sins. Love allows us to walk
in the sweet music of our particular heart.

JACK GILBERT

Knowing Nothing

Love is not the reason.
Love is the lure,
the thin goat staked out in the clearing.

The lion has stalked
the village for a long time.
It does not want the goat,
who stands thin and bleating,
tied to its bit of wood.

The goat is not the reason.
The reason is the lion,
whose one desire is to enter –
Not the goat, which is
only the lure, only excuse,
but the one burning life
it has hunted for a long time
disguised as hunger. Disguised as love.
Which is not the reason.

Or would you think
that the bones of a lion reason?
Would you think that the tongue?
The lion does not want the goat,
it wants only to live. Alone if it must.
In pain if it must. Knowing nothing.
Like the goat, it wants only to live.
Like love. Or would you think that the heart?

JANE HIRSHFIELD

Warming Her Pearls

Next to my own skin, her pearls. My mistress
bids me wear them, warm them, until evening
when I'll brush her hair. At six, I place them
round her cool, white throat. All day I think of her,

resting in the Yellow Room, contemplating silk
or taffeta, which gown tonight? She fans herself
whilst I work willingly, my slow heat entering
each pearl. Slack on my neck, her rope.

She's beautiful. I dream about her
in my attic bed; picture her dancing
with tall men, puzzled by my faint, persistent scent
beneath her French perfume, her milky stones.

I dust her shoulders with a rabbit's foot,
watch the soft blush seep through her skin
like an indolent sigh. In her looking-glass
my red lips part as though I want to speak.

Full moon. Her carriage brings her home. I see
her every movement in my head...Undressing,
taking off her jewels, her slim hand reaching
for the case, slipping naked into bed, the way

she always does...And I lie here awake,
knowing the pearls are cooling even now
in the room where my mistress sleeps. All night
I feel their absence and I burn.

CAROL ANN DUFFY

Look at These

Seeing you makes me want to lift up my top,
breathe in and say *Look! Look at these!*
I've kept them hidden till now
under loose shirts, Dad's jumpers.

Suddenly I'm offering them
like a women ready to mate.
I'm holding my breath.
Don't tell me not to.

HELEN FARISH

I Wouldn't Thank You for a Valentine

(rap)

I wouldn't thank you for a Valentine.
I won't wake up early wondering if the postman's been.
Should 10 red-padded satin hearts arrive with sticky sickly saccharine
Sentiments in very vulgar verses I wouldn't wonder if you meant them.
Two dozen anonymous Interflora roses?
I'd not bother to swither over who sent them!
I wouldn't thank you for a Valentine.

Scrawl SWALK across the envelope
I'd just say 'Same Auld Story
I canny be bothered deciphering it –
I'm up to here with Amore!
The whole Valentine's Day Thing is trivial and commercial,
A cue for unleasing clichés and candyheart motifs to which I
        personally am not partial.'
Take more than singing Telegrams, or pints of Chanel Five or sweets –
To get me ordering oysters or ironing my black satin sheets.
I wouldn't thank you for a Valentine.

If you sent me a solitaire and promises solemn,
Took out an ad in the *Guardian* Personal Column
Saying something very soppy such as 'Who Loves Ya, Poo?
I'll tell you, I do, Fozzy Bear, that's who!'
You'd entirely fail to charm me, in fact I'd detest it
I wouldn't be eighteen again for anything, I'm glad I'm past it.
I wouldn't thank you for a Valentine.

If you sent me a single orchid, or a pair of Janet Reger's in a heart-
        shaped box and declared your Love Eternal
I'd say I'd not be caught dead in them they were politically suspect
        and I'd rather something thermal.
If you hired a plane and blazed our love in a banner across the skies;
If you bought me something flimsy in a flatteringly wrong size;
If you sent me a postcard with three Xs and told me how you felt
I wouldn't thank you, I'd melt.

LIZ LOCHHEAD

Valentine

Not a red rose or a satin heart.

I give you an onion.
It is a moon wrapped in brown paper.
It promises light
like the careful undressing of love.

Here.
It will blind you with tears
like a lover.
It will make your reflection
a wobbling photo of grief.

I am trying to be truthful.

Not a cute card or a kissogram.

I give you an onion.
Its fierce kiss will stay on your lips,
possessive and faithful
as we are,
for as long as we are.

Take it.
Its platinum loops shrink to a wedding-ring,
if you like.
Lethal.
Its scent will cling to your fingers,
cling to your knife.

CAROL ANN DUFFY

Ode to the Onion

Onion,
luminous flask,
your beauty formed
petal by petal,
crystal scales expanded you
and in the secrecy of the dark earth
your belly grew round with dew.
Under the earth
the miracle
happened
and when your clumsy
green stem appeared,
and your leaves were born
like swords
in the garden,
the earth heaped up her power
showing your naked transparency,
and as the remote sea
in lifting the breasts of Aphrodite
duplicated the magnolia,
so did the earth
make you,
onion,
clear as a planet,
and destined
to shine,
constant constellation,
round rose of water,
upon
the table
of the poor.

Generously
you undo
your globe of freshness
in the fervent consummation
of the cooking pot,
and the crystal shred
in the flaming heat of the oil
is transformed into a curled golden feather.

Then, too, I will recall how fertile
is your influence on the love of the salad,
and it seems that the sky contributes
by giving you the shape of hailstones
to celebrate your chopped brightness
on the hemispheres of a tomato.
But within reach
of the hands of the common people,
sprinkled with oil,
dusted
with a bit of salt,
you kill the hunger
of the day-laborer on his hard path.

Star of the poor,
fairy godmother
wrapped
in delicate
paper, you rise from the ground
eternal, whole, pure
like an astral seed,
and when the kitchen knife
cuts you, there arises
the only tear
without sorrow.

You make us cry without hurting us,
I have praised everything that exists,
but to me, onion, you are
more beautiful than a bird
of dazzling feathers,
you are to my eyes
a heavenly globe, a platinum goblet,
an unmoving dance
of the snowy anemone

and the fragrance of the earth lives
in your crystalline nature.

PABLO NERUDA
translated from the Spanish by Stephen Mitchell

If Love Was Jazz

If love was jazz,
I'd be dazzled
By its razzmatazz.

If love was a sax
I'd melt in its brassy flame
Like wax.

If love was a guitar,
I'd pluck its six strings,
Eight to the bar.

If love was a trombone,
I'd feel its slow
Slide, right down my backbone.

If love was a drum,
I'd be caught in its snare,
Kept under its thumb.

If love was a trumpet,
I'd blow it.

If love was jazz,
I'd sing its praises,
Like Larkin has.

But love isn't jazz.
It's an organ recital.
Eminently worthy,
Not nearly as vital.

If love was jazz,
I'd always want more.
I'd be a regular
On that smoky dance-floor.

LINDA FRANCE

Litany

You are the bread and the knife,
The crystal goblet and the wine...
JACQUES CRICKILLON

You are the bread and the knife,
the crystal goblet and the wine.
You are the dew on the morning grass
and the burning wheel of the sun.
You are the white apron of the baker,
and the marsh birds suddenly in flight.

However, you are not the wind in the orchard,
the plums on the counter,
or the house of cards.
And you are certainly not the pine-scented air.
There is just no way that you are the pine-scented air.

It is possible that you are the fish under the bridge,
maybe even the pigeon on the general's head,
but you are not even close
to being the field of cornflowers at dusk.

And a quick look in the mirror will show
that you are neither the boots in the corner
nor the boat asleep in its boathouse.

It might interest you to know,
speaking of the plentiful imagery of the world,
that I am the sound of rain on the roof.

I also happen to be the shooting star,
the evening paper blowing down an alley
and the basket of chestnuts on the kitchen-table.

I am also the moon in the trees
and the blind woman's tea cup.
But don't worry, I'm not the bread and the knife.
You are still the bread and the knife.
You will always be the bread and the knife,
not to mention the crystal goblet and – somehow – the wine.

BILLY COLLINS

203

from 100 Love Sonnets

XVII

I do not love you as if you were salt-rose, or topaz,
or the arrow of carnations the fire shoots off.
I love you as certain dark things are to be loved,
in secret, between the shadow and the soul.

I love you as the plant that never blooms
but carries in itself the light of hidden flowers;
thanks to your love a certain solid fragrance,
risen from the earth, lives darkly in my body.

I love you without knowing how, or when, or from where.
I love you straightforwardly, without complexities or pride;
so I love you because I know no other way

than this: where *I* does not exist, nor *you*,
so close that your hand on my chest is my hand,
so close that your eyes close as I fall asleep.

LXXXIX

When I die, I want your hands on my eyes:
I want the light and wheat of your beloved hands
to pass their freshness over me once more:
I want to feel the softness that changed my destiny.

I want you to live while I wait for you, asleep.
I want your ears still to hear the wind, I want you
to sniff the sea's aroma that we loved together,
to continue to walk on the sand we walk on.

I want what I love to continue to live,
and you whom I love and sang above everything else
to continue to nourish, full-flowered:

so that you can reach everything my love directs you to,
so that my shadow can travel along in your hair,
so that everything can learn the reason for my song.

PABLO NERUDA
translated from the Spanish by Stephen Tapscott

On Raglan Road

(AIR: *The Dawning of the Day*)

On Raglan Road on an autumn day I met her first and knew
That her dark hair would weave a snare that I might one day rue;
I saw the danger, yet I walked along the enchanted way,
And I said, let grief be a fallen leaf at the dawning of the day.

On Grafton Street in November we tripped lightly along the ledge
Of the deep ravine where can be seen the worth of passion's pledge,
The Queen of Hearts still making tarts and I not making hay –
O I loved too much and by such by such is happiness thrown away.

I gave her gifts of the mind I gave her the secret sign that's known
To the artists who have known the true gods of sound and stone
And word and tint. I did not stint for I gave her poems to say.
With her own name there and her own dark hair like clouds over
        fields of May.

On a quiet street where old ghosts meet I see her walking now
Away from me so hurriedly my reason must allow
That I had wooed not as I should a creature made of clay –
When the angel wooes the clay he'd lose his wings at the dawn of day.

PATRICK KAVANAGH

Raglan Lane

(after Patrick Kavanagh)

In Raglan Lane, in the gentle rain, I saw dark love again,
Beyond belief, beyond all grief, I felt the ancient pain,
The joyful thrust of holy lust, I stretched on heaven's floor,
One moment burned what the years had learned and I was wild
        once more.

The years' deep cries in her sad eyes became a source of light,
The heavy gloom and sense of doom changed to pure delight.
And as we walked in joy and talked we knew one thing for sure,
That love is blessed togetherness and loneliness is poor.

Then I grew rich with every touch, we loved the whole night long,
Her midnight hair on the pillow there became an angel's song,
Her happy skin, beyond all sin, was heaven opened wide
But as the dawn came shyly on, I slept, and she left my side.

Why did she go? I'll never know, nor will the gentle rain,
Her up and go was a cruel blow, and yet I felt no pain
For I had known her body and soul in my own loving way,
So I lay and thanked the God of love at the dawning of the day.

BRENDAN KENNELLY

Touch Me

Summer is late, my heart.
Words plucked out of the air
some forty years ago
when I was wild with love
and torn almost in two
scatter like leaves this night
of whistling wind and rain.
It is my heart that's late,
it is my song that's flown.
Outdoors all afternoon
under a gunmetal sky
staking my garden down,
I kneeled to the crickets trilling
underfoot as if about
to burst from their crusty shells;
and like a child again
marveled to hear so clear
and brave a music pour
from such a small machine.
What makes the engine go?
Desire, desire, desire.
The longing for the dance
stirs in the buried life.
One season only,
                    and it's done.

So let the battered old willow
thrash against the windowpanes
and the house timbers creak.
Darling, do you remember
the man you married? Touch me,
remind me who I am.

STANLEY KUNITZ

Misgivings

'Perhaps you'll tire of me,' muses
my love, although she's like a great city
to me, or a park that finds new
ways to wear each flounce of light
and investiture of weather.
Soil doesn't tire of rain, I think,

but I know what she fears: plans warp,
planes explode, topsoil gets peeled away
by floods. And worse than what we can't
control is what we could; those drab,
scuttled marriages we shed so
gratefully may augur we're on our owns

for good reasons. 'Hi, honey,' chirps Dread
when I come through the door, 'you're home.'
Experience is a great teacher
of the value of experience,
its claustrophobic prudence,
its gloomy name-the-disasters-

in-advance charisma. Listen,
my wary one, it's far too late
to unlove each other. Instead let's cook
something elaborate and not
invite anyone to share it but eat it
all up very very slowly.

WILLIAM MATTHEWS

The Hunter Home from the Hill

Quiet by the window of the train
watching the blanched skies, the bleaching stubble,
a breaking down of colour
to something matte and porous and not at the heart of vision –

watching the winter lying down in the fields
as a horse lies – bone following bone –
the long ridge, the sheep, the blue note of the beet fields,

the bungalows on rutted patches starting awake
out of wild dreams in which they are gardens,

Carlow, the ugly here and there of it, the damp-stained houses,
the sky over the beet plant sausaged with fat round smoke,

all as it is,

like watching him in the kitchen in the morning,
his vest, his thinning slept-in hair, the way he is in your life,
and you content that he be there.

KERRY HARDIE

The Waterfall

If you were to read my poems, all of them, I mean,
My life's work, at the one sitting, in the one place,
Let it be here by this half-hearted waterfall
That allows each pebbly basin its separate say,
Damp stones and syllables, then, as it grows dark
And you go home past overgrown vineyards and
Chestnut trees, suppliers once of crossbeams, moon-
Shaped nuts, flour, and crackly stuffing for mattresses,
Leave them here, on the page, in your mind's eye, lit
Like the fireflies at the waterfall, a wall of stars.

MICHAEL LONGLEY

Atlas

There is a kind of love called maintenance,
Which stores the WD40 and knows when to use it;

Which checks the insurance, and doesn't forget
The milkman; which remembers to plant bulbs;

Which answers letters; which knows the way
The money goes; which deals with dentists

And Road Fund Tax and meeting trains,
And postcards to the lonely; which upholds

The permanently ricketty elaborate
Structures of living; which is Atlas.

And maintenance is the sensible side of love,
Which knows what time and weather are doing
To my brickwork; insulates my faulty wiring;
Laughs at my dryrotten jokes; remembers
My need for gloss and grouting; which keeps
My suspect edifice upright in air,
As Atlas did the sky.

U.A. FANTHORPE

An Arundel Tomb

Side by side, their faces blurred,
The earl and countess lie in stone,
Their proper habits vaguely shown
As jointed armour, stiffened pleat,
And that faint hint of the absurd –
The little dogs under their feet.

Such plainness of the pre-baroque
Hardly involves the eye, until
It meets his left-hand gauntlet, still

Clasped empty in the other; and
One sees, with a sharp tender shock,
His hand withdrawn, holding her hand.

They would not think to lie so long.
Such faithfulness in effigy
Was just a detail friends would see:
A sculptor's sweet commissioned grace
Thrown off in helping to prolong
The Latin names around the base.

They would not guess how early in
Their supine stationary voyage
The air would change to soundless damage,
Turn the old tenantry away;
How soon succeeding eyes begin
To look, not read. Rigidly they

Persisted, linked, through lengths and breadths
Of time. Snow fell, undated. Light
Each summer thronged the glass. A bright
Litter of birdcalls strewed the same
Bone-riddled ground. And up the paths
The endless altered people came,

Washing at their identity.
Now, helpless in the hollow of
An unarmorial age, a trough
Of smoke in slow suspended skeins
Above their scrap of history,
Only an attitude remains:

Time has transfigured them into
Untruth. The stone fidelity
They hardly meant has come to be
Their final blazon, and to prove
Our almost-instinct almost true:
What will survive of us is love.

PHILIP LARKIN

5

Men and Women

A poem is an approach towards a truth. But poems can
be funny, witty, quirky and sly. They can be mischievous,
tricksterish. Their truths don't sound like the truths
of the courtroom or inquest. Does this, then, show us
something about the nature of truth? Can we say there
are many truths, or, rather, many aspects of Truth?
That truth itself is a shape-shifter?

KATHLEEN JAMIE

AFTER THE CELEBRATIONS of 'Love Life' (see 179), this section on 'Men and Women' brings us down to earth. Here are poems on the differences between the sexes, on gender, relationships, marriage and what happens when it all goes pear-shaped. But there is also much wit in the sparring and delineation of character. Some poems show people in aggressive positions while others have great fun at the expense of either sex.

The level of Sylvia Plath's anger and sense of grievance in 'The Applicant' (245) is evident not just from the poem itself but from its place in her *Collected Poems*, where it is dated 11 October 1962, the day before she wrote 'Daddy' (156), in that autumn leading up to her death when she went on a writing jag in a state of extreme agitation. That October she wrote 25 of her finest poems, including the bee poems, 'Lady Lazarus', 'Fever 103°', 'Cut', 'Ariel' and 'Poppies in October' (*Staying Alive*, 48).

Carol Ann Duffy's 'Mrs Midas' (224), from *The World's Wife*, and Liz Lochhead's 'Rapunzstiltskin' (234), from *The Grimm Sisters*, are feminist reinventions which turn myths and men upside down. Duffy has also written her *Feminine Gospels*, while Liz Lochhead has many other poems in which she takes liberties with man and myth.

Motorbikes feature in many of Frederick Seidel's extravagantly hip poems, and in 'Men and Women' (212), he hymns the gleaming phallic symbol only to conclude 'Women have won'. His cultured machismo is an uneasily ironic pose in poems which take even more emotional risks than his mentor, Robert Lowell. Brazenly forging public poetry out of private confession, Seidel treads a razor's edge of moral ambiguity, wearing his heart on a sleeve cut from the most expensive cloth. His dinner-party circle of New York friends in one poem are like 'the last Romanovs' as they relish their pressed duck in brandy: 'Why do we need anybody else,' says one, 'We're the world.'

211

Men and Woman

Her name I may or may not have made up,
But not the memory,
Sandy Moon with her lion's mane astride
A powerful motorcycle waiting to roar away, blipping
The throttle, a roar, years before such a sight
Was a commonplace,
And women had won,

And before a helmet law, or
Wearing their hair long, had made all riders one
Sex till you looked again; not that her chest
Wasn't decisive – breasts of Ajanta, big blue-sky clouds
Of marble, springing free of her unhooked bra
Unreal as a butterfly-strewn sweet-smelling mountainside
Of opium poppies in bloom.

It was Union Square. I remember. Turn a corner
And in a light year
She'd have arrived
At the nearby inky, thinky offices of *Partisan Review*.
Was she off to see my rival Lief,
Boyfriend of girls and men, who cruised
In a Rolls convertible?

The car was the *caca* color a certain
Very grand envoy of Franco favored for daytime wear –
But one shouldn't mock the innocent machinery
Of life, nor the machines we treasure. For instance,
Motorcycles. What definition of beauty can exclude
The MV Agusta racing 500-3,
From the land of Donatello, with blatting megaphones?

To see Giacomo Agostini lay the MV over
Smoothly as a swan curves its neck down to feed,
At ninety miles an hour – entering a turn with Hailwood
On the Honda, wheel to wheel, a foot apart –
The tromboning furor of the exhaust notes as they
Downshifted, heard even in the photographs!
Heroes glittering on the summit before extinction

Of the air-cooled four-strokes in GP.
Agostini – Agusta! Hailwood – Honda!
I saw Agostini, in the Finnish Grand Prix at Imatra,
When Hailwood was already a legend who'd moved on
To cars. How small and pretty Ago was,
But heavily muscled like an acrobat. He smiled
And posed, enjoying his own charming looks,

While a jumpsuited mechanic pushed his silent
Racer out of the garage, and with a graceful
Sidesaddle run-and-bump started its engine.
A lion on a leash being walked in neutral
Back and forth to warm it up, it roared and roared;
Then was shut off; releasing a rather heady perfume
Of hot castor oil, as it docilely returned to the garage.

Before a race, how would Hailwood behave?
Racers get killed racing.
The roped-off crowd hushed outside the open door.
I stood in awe of Ago's ease –
In his leathers, like an animal in nature –
Inhumanly unintrospective, now smiling less
Brilliantly, but by far the brightest being in the room.

I feared finding his fear,
And looked for it,
And looked away so as not to mar the perfect.
There was an extraordinary girl there to study
Instead; and the altar-piece, the lily
Painted the dried blood MV racing red,
Slender and pure – one hundred eighty miles an hour.

A lion which is a lily,
From the land of Donatello: where else could they design
Streamlined severe elegance in a toy color?
A phallus which was musical when it roared? By contrast,
Hailwood's Honda had been an unsteerable monster,
Only a genius could have won on it,
All engine and no art.

A lily that's a lion: handmade with love
By the largest helicopter manufacturer in Europe,

Whose troop carriers shielded junta and emir from harm,
And cicatriced presidents clutching
A golden ceremonial fly whisk and CIA dollars.
How storybook that a poor country boy
Should ride the Stradivarius of a Count –

The aristocrat industrialist Agusta – against
The middle-class son of a nicely well-off businessman;
English; and weekly wallowing near death
On the nearly ungovernable Japanese horsepower.
A clone of Detroit, Honda Company, in going for power,
Empire-building
In peacetime displaced to motorcycle sales.

Honda raced no more. No need to
Sell Hondas now. The empire nourished elsewhere
Than glory. I swooned in the gray even indoor air
Of a garage in Finland, as racetime neared.
Daylight blinded the doorway – the day beyond,
The crowd outside, were far away. I studied
The amazing beauty, whom Ago seemed determined to ignore,

Seated like Agostini in skintight racing leathers.
Her suit looked sweet, like Dr Denton's on a child;
Until – as she stood up – the infant's-wear blue-innocence
Swelled violently to express
The breasts and buttocks of a totem, Magna Mater,
Overwhelming and almost ridiculous,
Venus in a racing suit,

Built big as Juno – out of place but filling up
The room, if you looked at her, which no one else did;
Though I still couldn't tell
Who she was, whose friend she was, if she was anyone's;
Whose girl, the one woman in the room.
The meaning of the enormous quiet split
Into men and woman around the motorcycle.

I thought of Sandy Moon,
Advancing toward me through the years to find me there,
Moving toward me through the years across the room
I'd rented, to hide and work,

Near Foley Square; where I wrote, and didn't write –
Through the sky-filled tall windows
Staring out for hours

At the State Supreme Court building with its steps
And columns, and the Federal Courthouse with its,
And that implacably unadorned low solid, the Department
Of Motor Vehicles. I'd leaf
Through one of my old motorcycle mags
And think of Sandy Moon – and here she was,
Naked and without a word walking slowly toward me.

Women have won. The theme is
Only for a cello, is the lurking glow
Pooled in the folds of a rich velvet, darkly phosphorescent.
Summer thunder rumbled over Brooklyn, a far-off sadness.
Naked power and a mane of glory
Shall inherit the earth. Outside the garage,
The engine caught and roared – time to go.

FREDERICK SEIDEL

The Dress

In those days, those days which exist for me only as the most
        elusive memory now,
when often the first sound you'd hear in the morning would be a
        storm of birdsong,
then the soft clop of the hooves of the horse hauling a milk wagon
        down your block

and the last sound at night as likely as not would be your father
        pulling up in his car,
having worked late again, always late, and going heavily down to
        the cellar, to the furnace,
to shake out the ashes and damp the draft before he came upstairs
        to fall into bed;

in those long-ago days, women, my mother, my friends' mothers,
     our neighbors,
all the women I knew, wore, often much of the day, what were
     called "housedresses,"
cheap, printed, pulpy, seemingly purposefully shapeless light cotton
     shifts,

that you wore over your nightgown, and, when you had to go to
     look for a child,
hang wash on the line, or run down to the grocery store on the
     corner, under a coat,
the twisted hem of the nightgown, always lank and yellowed, dangling
     beneath.

More than the curlers some of the women seemed constantly to
     have in their hair,
in preparation for some great event, a ball, one would think, that
     never came to pass;
more than the way most women's faces not only were never made
     up during the day,

but seemed scraped, bleached, and, with their plucked eyebrows,
     scarily mask-like;
more than all that it was those dresses that made women so unknow-
     able and forbidding,
adepts of enigmas to which men could have no access, and boys
     no conception.

Only later would I see the dresses also as a proclamation: that in
     your dim kitchen,
your laundry, your bleak concrete yard, what you revealed of your-
     self was a fabulation;
your real sensual nature, veiled in those sexless vestments, was utterly
     your dominion.

In those days, one hid much else, as well: grown men didn't embrace
     one another,
unless someone had died, and not always then; you shook hands,
     or, at a ball game,
thumped your friend's back and exchanged blows meant to be codes
     for affection;

once out of childhood you'd never again know the shock of your
father's whiskers
on your cheek, not until mores at last had evolved, and you could
hug another man,
then hold on for a moment, then even kiss (your father's bristles
white and stiff now).

What release finally, the embrace: though we were wary – it seemed
so audacious –
how much unspoken joy there was in that affirmation of equality
and communion,
no matter how much misunderstanding and pain had passed between
you by then.

We knew so little in those days, as little as now, I suppose, about
healing those hurts:
even the women, in their best dresses, with beads and sequins sewn
on the bodices,
even in lipstick and mascara, their hair aflow, could only stand
wringing their hands,

begging for peace, while father and son, like thugs, like thieves,
like Romans,
simmered and hissed and hated, inflicting sorrows that endured,
the worst anyway,
through the kiss and embrace, bleeding from brother to brother
into the generations.

In those days there was still countryside close to the city, farms,
cornfields, cows;
even not far from our building with its blurred brick and long
shadowy hallway
you could find tracts with hills and trees you could pretend were
mountains and forests.

Or you could go out by yourself even to a half-block-long empty
lot, into the bushes:
like a creature of leaves you'd lurk, crouched, crawling, simplified,
savage, alone;
already there was wanting to be simpler, wanting when they called
you, never to go back.

C.K. WILLIAMS

The Mutes

Those groans men use
passing a woman on the street
or on the steps of the subway

to tell her she is a female
and their flesh knows it,

are they a sort of tune,
an ugly enough song, sung
by a bird with a slit tongue
but meant for music?

Or are they the muffled roaring
of deafmutes trapped in a building that is
slowly filling with smoke?

Perhaps both.

Such men most often
look as if groan were all they could do,
yet a woman, in spite of herself,

knows it's a tribute:
if she were lacking all grace
they'd pass her in silence:

so it's not only to say she's
a warm hole. It's a word

in grief-language, nothing to do with
primitive, not an ur-language;
language stricken, sickened, cast down

in decrepitude. She wants to
throw the tribute away, dis-
gusted, and can't,

it goes on buzzing in her ear,
it changes the pace of her walk,
the torn posters in echoing corridors

spell it out, it
quakes and gnashes as the train comes in.
Her pulse sullenly

had picked up speed,
but the cars slow down and
jar to a stop while her understanding

keeps on translating:
'Life after life after life goes by

without poetry,
without seemliness,
without love.'

DENISE LEVERTOV

The Inspection

Whenever a good-looking secretary walks down the aisle at
Goodstone Aircraft Company,
the machinists make a point of staring at her
from the moment they spot her.
They move around their machines
to keep her tits and ass and thighs
in view,
making sure that it is obvious
they are watching her.
They drift away from their machines,
sticking their necks out into the aisle
to keep her in view
until she is out the door of the building.
Then they let out with shrill whistles,
shaking their heads and hands
and going limp all over as if they were about to collapse,
making sure that everyone knows
how much their lustful minds sucked in
every inch of every curve on her body,
competing with each other
to see who
can stagger and whistle and maintain

their open-mouthed blank-eyed look
the longest,
glancing about at each other
to take stock of the results.
Finally, when it is safe to quit whistling and moaning
tributes to her body,
they return to their machines,
reassured that they have once again passed
the test.

FRED VOSS

In the men's room(s)

When I was young I believed in intellectual conversation:
I thought the patterns we wove on stale smoke
floated off to the heaven of ideas.
To be certified worthy of high masculine discourse
like a potato on a grater I would rub on contempt,
suck snubs, wade proudly through the brown stuff on the floor.
They were talking of integrity and existential ennui
while the women ran out for six-packs and had abortions
in the kitchen and fed the children and were auctioned off.

Eventually of course I learned how their eyes perceived me:
when I bore to them cupped in my hands a new poem to nibble,
when I brought my aerial maps of Sartre or Marx,
they said, she is trying to attract our attention,
she is offering up her breasts and thighs.
I walked on eggs, their tremulous equal:
they saw a fish peddler hawking in the street.

Now I get coarse when the abstract nouns start flashing.
I go out to the kitchen to talk cabbages and habits.
I try hard to remember to watch what people do.
Yes, keep your eyes on the hands, let the voice go buzzing.
Economy is the bone, politics is the flesh,
watch who they beat and who they eat,
watch who they relieve themselves on, watch who they own.
The rest is decoration.

MARGE PIERCY

220

A Simple Story

A visiting conductor
   when I was seventeen,
took me back to his hotel room
   to cover the music scene.

I'd written a composition.
   Would wonders never cease –
here was a real musician
   prepared to hold my piece.

He spread my score on the counterpane
   with classic casualness,
and put one hand on the manuscript
   and the other down my dress.

It was hot as hell in the Windsor.
   I said I'd like a drink.
We talked across gin and grapefruit,
   and I heard the ice go clink

as I gazed at the lofty forehead
   of one who led the band,
and guessed at the hoarded sorrows
   no wife could understand.

I dreamed of a soaring passion
   as an egg might dream of flight,
while he read my crude sonata.
   If he'd said, 'That bar's not right,'

or, 'Have you thought of a coda?'
   or, 'Watch that first repeat,'
or, 'Modulate to the dominant,'
   he'd have had me at his feet.

But he shuffled it all together,
   and said, 'That's *lovely*, dear,'
as he put it down on the washstand
   in a way that made it clear

that I was no composer.
  And I being young and vain,
removed my lovely body
  from one who'd scorned my brain.

I swept off like Miss Virtue
  down dusty Roma Street,
and heard the goods trains whistle
  WHO? WHOOOOOO? in aching heat.

GWEN HARWOOD

The Change

The season turned like the page of a glossy fashion magazine.
In the park the daffodils came up
and in the parking lot, the new car models were on parade.

Sometimes I think that nothing really changes –

The young girls show the latest crop of tummies,
    and the new president proves that he's a dummy.

But remember the tennis match we watched that year?
Right before our eyes

some tough little European blonde
pitted against that big black girl from Alabama,
cornrowed hair and Zulu bangles on her arms,
some outrageous name like Vondella Aphrodite –

We were just walking past the lounge
    and got sucked in by the screen above the bar,
and pretty soon
we started to care about who won,

putting ourselves into each whacked return
as the volleys went back and forth and back
like some contest between
the old world and the new,

and you loved her complicated hair
and her to-hell-with-everybody stare,

222

and I,
     I couldn't help wanting
the white girl to come out on top,

because she was one of my kind, my tribe,
with her pale eyes and thin lips

and because the black girl was so big
and so black,
          so unintimidated,

hitting the ball like she was driving the Emancipation Proclamation
down Abraham Lincoln's throat,
like she wasn't asking anyone's permission.

There are moments when history
passes you so close
        you can smell its breath,
you can reach your hand out
            and touch it on its flank,

and I don't watch all that much *Masterpiece Theatre*,
but I could feel the end of an era there

in front of those bleachers full of people
in their Sunday tennis-watching clothes

as that black girl wore down her opponent
then kicked her ass good
then thumped her once more for good measure

and stood up on the red clay court
holding her racket over her head like a guitar.

And the little pink judge
        had to climb up on a box
to put the ribbon on her neck,

still managing to smile into the camera flash,
even though everything was changing

and in fact, everything had already changed –

Poof, remember? It was the twentieth century almost gone,
we were there,

and when we went to put it back where it belonged,
it was past us
and we were changed.

TONY HOAGLAND

Mrs Midas

It was late September. I'd just poured a glass of wine, begun
to unwind, while the vegetables cooked. The kitchen
filled with the smell of itself, relaxed, its steamy breath
gently blanching the windows. So I opened one,
then with my fingers wiped the other's glass like a brow.
He was standing under the pear tree snapping a twig.

Now the garden was long and the visibility poor, the way
the dark of the ground seems to drink the light of the sky,
but that twig in his hand was gold. And then he plucked
a pear from a branch – we grew Fondante d'Automne –
and it sat in his palm like a light bulb. On.
I thought to myself, Is he putting fairy lights in the tree?

He came into the house. The doorknobs gleamed.
He drew the blinds. You know the mind; I thought of
the Field of the Cloth of Gold and of Miss Macready.
He sat in that chair like a king on a burnished throne.
The look on his face was strange, wild, vain. I said,
What in the name of God is going on? He started to laugh.

I served up the meal. For starters, corn on the cob.
Within seconds he was spitting out the teeth of the rich.
He toyed with his spoon, then mine, then with the knives, the forks.
He asked where was the wine. I poured with a shaking hand,
a fragrant, bone-dry white from Italy, then watched
as he picked up the glass, goblet, golden chalice, drank.

It was then that I started to scream. He sank to his knees.
After we'd both calmed down, I finished the wine
on my own, hearing him out. I made him sit
on the other side of the room and keep his hands to himself.
I locked the cat in the cellar. I moved the phone.
The toilet I didn't mind. I couldn't believe my ears:

how he'd had a wish. Look, we all have wishes; granted.
But who has wishes granted? Him. Do you know about gold?
It feeds no one; aurum, soft, untarnishable; slakes
no thirst. He tried to light a cigarette; I gazed, entranced,
as the blue flame played on its luteous stem. At least,
I said, you'll be able to give up smoking for good.

Separate beds. In fact, I put a chair against my door,
near petrified. He was below, turning the spare room
into the tomb of Tutankhamun. You see, we were passionate then,
in those halcyon days; unwrapping each other, rapidly,
like presents, fast food. But now I feared his honeyed embrace,
the kiss that would turn my lips to a work of art.

And who, when it comes to the crunch, can live
with a heart of gold? That night, I dreamt I bore
his child, its perfect ore limbs, its little tongue
like a precious latch, its amber eyes
holding their pupils like flies. My dream-milk
burned in my breasts. I woke to the streaming sun.

So he had to move out. We'd a caravan
in the wilds, in a glade of its own. I drove him up
under cover of dark. He sat in the back.
And then I came home, the woman who married the fool
who wished for gold. At first I visited, odd times,
parking the car a good way off, then walking.

You knew you were getting close. Golden trout
on the grass. One day, a hare hung from a larch,
a beautiful lemon mistake. And then his footprints,
glistening next to the river's path. He was thin,
delirious; hearing, he said, the music of Pan
from the woods. Listen. That was the last straw.

What gets me now is not the idiocy or greed
but lack of thought for me. Pure selfishness. I sold
the contents of the house and came down here.
I think of him in certain lights, dawn, late afternoon,
and once a bowl of apples stopped me dead. I miss most,
even now, his hands, his warm hands on my skin, his touch.

CAROL ANN DUFFY

Spunk Talking

When men are belligerent or crude,
it's spunk talking, it's come come up for a verbal interlude:
in your face Jack, get shagged, get screwed, get your tits out,
get him, lads, bugger that, hands off, just you try it,
you're nicked, left hook, nice one Eric, hammer hard,
shaft him, stitch that, do you want to get laid or not, red card.
Spunk speaks in gutturals, with verbs. No parentheses.
Spunk's a young con crazy to break from Alcatraz.
Sonny, you'll go feet first. So spunk has to sing,
hoarsely, *The Song of the Volga Boatmen, I am an Anarchist,*
the Troggs' *Wild Thing.*
Cynthia Payne said, after her researches, not to be debunked,
that men are appreciably nicer when de-spunked.
Before time began the void revolved, as smooth and bored
as an egg, when a tiny ragged crack appeared,
and the world exploded like an umpire's shout,
as the primal spunk of the cosmos bellowed OUT!

ANNE ROUSE

Four of the Belt

Jenkins, all too clearly it is time
for some ritual physical humiliation;
and if you cry, boy, you will prove
what I suspect – you are not a man.

As they say, Jenkins, this hurts me
more than it hurts you. But I show you
I am a man, by doing this, to you.

When *you* are a man, Jenkins, you may hear
that physical humiliation and ritual
are concerned with strange adult matters
– like rape, or masochistic fantasies.

226

You will not accept such stories.
Rather, you will recall with pride,
perhaps even affection, that day when I,
Mr Johnstone, summoned you before me,
and gave you four of the belt

like this. And this. And this. And this.

TOM LEONARD

A Man in the Valley of Women

He was captured in the Valley of Women.
They manacled his ankles and chained his wrists.
His captors pinioned him. One held his head.
Another picked up a needle and thread.

'What are you going to do?' he asked.
She played the needle over a candle flame.
'Sew your lips together!' she laughed,
trailing a finger between his shoulder-blades.

She teased the needle through his upper lip,
and drew the flesh together with silk-twine.
He felt the pressure of her fingertips
as her nails dug deep into his spine.

Slowly they broke all the bones in his feet.
The blood was used to rouge his cheeks.
His testes made an executive toy,
his glans a novelty cork for the wine.

Seized by the throes of change, he was aware
of a contending self, radically other;
an abrupt warping, a cruel deflection
of his sex from masculine to feminine.

The next few months, they fed him on jasmine
which stirred the female wings inside his breasts.
His ankles grew slimmer. His hair shone.
His vagina fermented like yeast.

A musk clung to his body. Unmistakable.
His clitoris thickened like a tonsil.
Buttermilk and aloe dissolved his Adam's apple.
His voice modulated to a falsetto.

They plucked every dark hair from his face
and pencilled his eyebrows until they were perfect.
They painted his lips in arresting shades,
and squeezed him into a whalebone corset.

Finally, he was ready for the Queen's birthday.
His hips swivelled pertly, his backside swayed.
'*Tsk tsk!*' went the other courtiers slyly.
'That's a frisky one,' he heard them say.

He burst from the cake, high-kicking through the icing,
swanking bridally from the marzipan.
Later, the Queen bid him kiss her ring.
She sighed: 'To think that once you were a man...'

CHRIS GREENHALGH

Prayer To Be with Mercurial Women

Let me never have her father
call me, saying how's about
a round of golf? Instead I'll take
the grim, forbidding monster
who inspects me for a crooked
trouser crease. And spare me too
from palmy evenings which sail by
in restaurants, on barstools,
without a storming off or two.
'Darling, you were made for me.'
I pray I'll never hear those words.
I need to feel I'm stealing
love another man would kill for.
When in sleep she curls herself
around me, may she whisper names

that are not mine. I'd prefer
to be the second best she's had.
A curse on mouths which dovetail
as if there'd been a blueprint made:
I'd rather blush and slobber.
And once a month, please let me be
a punchbag. I'll take the blame
for everything: I want to taste
the stinging of a good slap.
I hope I'll find my begging notes
crumpled, torn in half, unread,
and when I phone, I want to hear
an endless sound of ringing.
Help me avoid the kind of girl
who means things when she says them,
unless she's screeching, telling me
exactly what I am. Amen.

RODDY LUMSDEN

Bloody Men

Bloody men are like bloody buses –
You wait for about a year
And as soon as one approaches your stop
Two or three others appear.

You look at them flashing their indicators,
Offering you a ride.
You're trying to read the destinations,
You haven't much time to decide.

If you make a mistake, there is no turning back.
Jump off, and you'll stand there and gaze
While the cars and the taxis and lorries go by
And the minutes, the hours, the days.

WENDY COPE

And Another Bloody Thing...
(after Wendy Cope)

Bloody men are like bloody cigarettes –
A habit you swear you'll crack,
Then you find you've snuck out of the office
To suck one off round the back.

CLARE POLLARD

sexpot

'you know,' she said, 'you were at
the bar so you didn't see
but I danced with this guy.
we danced and we danced
close.
but I didn't go home with him
because he knew I was with
you.'

'thanks a bunch,' I
said.

she was always thinking of sex.
she carried it around with her
like something in a paper
bag.
such energy.
she never forgot.
she stared at every man available
in morning cafés
over bacon and eggs
or later
over a noon sandwich or
a steak dinner.

'I've modeled myself after
Marilyn Monroe,' she told
me.

'she's always running off
to some local disco to dance
with a baboon,' a friend once told
me, 'I'm amazed that you've
stood for it as long as you have.'

she'd vanish at racetracks
then come back and say,
'three men offered to buy me
a drink.'

or I'd lose her in the parking
lot and I'd look up and she'd
be walking along with a strange man.
'well, he came from this direction
and I came from that and we
kind of walked together. I
didn't want to hurt his
feelings.'

she said that I was a very
jealous man.

one day she just
fell down
inside of her sexual organs
and vanished.

it was like an alarm clock
dropping into the
Grand Canyon.
it banged and rattled and
rang and rang
but I could no longer
see or hear it.

I'm feeling much better
now.
I've taken up tap-dancing
and I wear a black felt
hat pulled down low
over my right
eye.

CHARLES BUKOWSKI

I'll Be a Wicked Old Woman

I'll be a wicked old woman
Thin as a rail,
The way I am now.
Not one of those big-assed ones
With buttocks churning behind them,
As Celine said.
Not one of the good-natured grandmas and aunties
Against whose soft and plump arms
It is nice to lay one's cheek.
I'm more like a scarecrow
In our gardens full of rosy tomatoes
Like children's cheeks.
There are some old crones
Who are both vivacious and angry as a bee
With eyes on top of their heads
Who see everything, hear everything and have an opinion –
Grumblers since birth.
I'll squawk and chatter all day,
Cackle like a hen over her chicks
About the days when I was
A young, good-looking girl,
When I led boys by the nose.
Colts and stallions I tamed
With the flash in my eye, the flash of my skirt,
Passing over infidelities and miseries
The way a general passes over his lost battles.
I'll be free to do anything as an old woman,
Among things I still can and want to do
Like playing bridge or dancing
The light-footed dances of my days.
I'll spin and trip on my sticklike legs,
Attached to my body like toothpicks to a kabob.
That old hag sure can boogie!
The young smarties gathered around me
Will shout and applaud.
An old woman like a well-baked bun with sesame seeds,
That's what I'm going to be like.
I'll stick between everyone's teeth, as I did before
While with a wide hat and dresses down to the ground

232

I stroll through the landscapes of my past life.
Smelling the furze, admiring the heather,
On every thistle catching my undergarment – my soul.

RADMILA LAZIĆ
translated from the Serbian by Charles Simic

Ballygrand Widow

So, you have gone my erstwhile glad boy,
Whose body, I remember, stained my big cream bed,
And didn't we mix the day and the night in our play,
We never got up for a week.

If I must set my alarm again,
And feed the hungry hens in the yard,
And draw the milk from my cow on time,
And skulk my shame down Ballygrand Street
To get a drink,
It'll not be for you I think,
But my next husband,
A fine cock he shall be.

So, you are no more in this town
My lovely schoolboy, and how the floss
Of your chin tickled me.
And you swam your hands all over,
You shouted for joy, the first time.
Ah, my darling!

I wear your mother's spit on my shoes,
The black crow priest has been to beat me.
But you gave me a belly full, the best,
And they shan't take it.
The days are unkind after you, they are empty.
I lie in the sheets, the very same sheets;
You smelled sweeter than meadow hay.
My beautiful boy you have killed me.

DEBORAH RANDALL

233

'What Do Women Want?'

I want a red dress.
I want it flimsy and cheap,
I want it too tight, I want to wear it
until someone tears it off me.
I want it sleeveless and backless,
this dress, so no one has to guess
what's underneath. I want to walk down
the street past Thrifty's and the hardware store
with all those keys glittering in the window,
past Mr and Mrs Wong selling day-old
donuts in their café, past the Guerra brothers
slinging pigs from the truck and onto the dolly,
hoisting the slick snouts over their shoulders.
I want to walk like I'm the only
woman on earth and I can have my pick.
I want that red dress bad.
I want it to confirm
your worst fears about me,
to show you how little I care about you
or anything except what
I want. When I find it, I'll pull that garment
from its hanger like I'm choosing a body
to carry me into this world, through
the birth-cries and love-cries too,
and I'll wear it like bones, like skin,
it'll be the goddamned
dress they bury me in.

KIM ADDONIZIO

Rapunzstiltskin

& just when our maiden had got
good & used to her isolation,
stopped daily expecting to be rescued,
had come to almost love her tower,
along comes This Prince

with absolutely
all the wrong answers.
Of course she had not been brought up to look for
originality or gingerbread
so at first she was quite undaunted
by his tendency to talk in strung-together cliché.
'Just hang on and we'll get you out of there,'
he hollered like a fireman in some soap opera
when she confided her plight (the old
hag inside etc & how trapped she was);
well, it was corny but
he did look sort of gorgeous
axe and all.
So there she was, humming & pulling
all the pins out of her chignon,
throwing him all the usual lifelines
till, soon, he was shimmying in & out
every other day as though
he owned the place, bringing her
the sex manuals & skeins of silk
from which she was meant, eventually,
to weave the means of her own escape.
'All very well & good,' she prompted,
'but when exactly?'
She gave him till
well past the bell on the timeclock.
She mouthed at him, hinted,
she was keener than a TV quizmaster
that he should get it right.
'I'll do everything in my power,' he intoned, 'but
the impossible (she groaned) might
take a little longer.' He grinned.
She pulled her glasses off.
'All the better
to see you with my dear?' he hazarded.
She screamed, cut off her hair.
'Why, you're beautiful?' he guessed tentatively.
'No, No, No!' she
shrieked & stamped her foot so
hard it sank six cubits through the floorboards.
'I love you?' he came up with
as she finally tore herself in two.

LIZ LOCHHEAD

English Girl Eats Her First Mango

If I did tell she
hold this gold
of sundizzy
tonguelicking juicy
mouthwater flow
ripe with love
from the tropics

she woulda tell me
trust you to be
melodramatic

so I just say
taste this mango

and I watch she hold
the smooth cheeks
of the mango
blushing yellow
and a glow
rush to she own cheeks

and she ask me
what do I do now
just bite into it?

and I was temptede
to tell she
why not be a devil
and eat of the skin
of original sin

but she woulda tell me
trust you to be
mysterious

so I just say
it's up to you
if you want to peel it

and I watch she feel it
as something precious

then she smile and say
looks delicious

and I tell she
don't waste sweet words
when sweetness
in you hand

just bite it man
peel it with the teeth
that God give you

or better yet
do like me mother
used to do
and squeeze
till the flesh
turn syrup
nibble a hole
then suck the gold.
like bubby
in child mouth
squeeze and tease out
every drop of spice

sounds nice
me friend tell me

and I remind she
that this ain't
apple core
so don't forget
the seed
suck that too
the sweetest part
the juice does run
down to you heart

236

man if you see
the English rose
she face was bliss
down to the pink
of she toes

and when she finish
she smile
and turn to me

lend me your hanky
my fingers
are all sticky
with mango juice

and I had to tell she
what hanky
you talking bout

you don't know
when you eat mango
you hanky
is you tongue

man just lick
you finger
you call that
culture
lick you finger
you call that
culture

unless you prefer
to call it
colonisation
in reverse

JOHN AGARD

Pleasure

A poem, like the clitoris, is there
For pleasure and although some experts say
It can't be only pleasure it is there for
But must do something else to pay its way
But what that something else is can't agree
We leave them to their wrangling and say
The pleasure principle will do for you and me:
End in itself, servant to nothing other
Than what it carries (love). Take, for example,
A wanted realisation's long postponement
Over caesurae and line-endings, torment
Of let and rallentando and reversal,
Word upon word, staccato then eliding,
A gathering rising final overriding...
They ask what the syntax of our pleasure does?
Makes with a rush of sense something that *is*.

DAVID CONSTANTINE

Done

When you're gone out of town, the way I get you back is
I masturbate. If you're away this week, next week, no matter.
I raise one hand. In a second it's your tongue on my clitoris,
your head's weight on my lap in the striped pink armchair,
your jaw opening like a thought between my thighs, lower,
your tongue a delicate knifeblade licking stone. My wetness
eases your work. My blood satisfies the heat with a tremor.
You lift your head. Done, my hands lift.
Under my ass there is a cold damp like saliva. Nothing else left.

Back, at 2 a.m., you're more than the sharp memory I angled
between my legs, sensation after the day's numb headlines.
Your hand sweats and dreams on my stomach, not your imagined
hand in my jeans in the backyard dark, no clandestine
act while above us a neighbor's cigarette shines red.
In the garden a moonflower is stretching its jaws in the cold,
its smell of my mother's face powder, its skin like your skin.
I drowse. Everything outside this room is alone.
I move. You say my name. Your hip backs me like warm stone.

MINNIE BRUCE PRATT

Please Can I Have a Man

Please can I have a man who wears corduroy.
Please can I have a man
who knows the names of 100 different roses;
who doesn't mind my absent-minded rabbits
wandering in and out
as if they own the place,
who makes me creamy curries from fresh lemon-grass,
who walks like Belmondo in *A Bout de Souffle*;
who sticks all my carefully-selected postcards –
sent from exotic cities
he doesn't expect to come with me to,
but would if I asked, which I will do –

with nobody else's, up on his bedroom wall,
starting with Ivy, the Famous Diving Pig,
whose picture, in action, I bought ten copies of;
who talks like Belmondo too, with lips as smooth
and tightly-packed as chocolate-coated
(*melting* chocolate) peony buds;
who knows that piling himself stubbornly on top of me
like a duvet stuffed with library books and shopping-bags
is all too easy: please can I have a man
who is not prepared to do that.
Who is not prepared to say I'm 'pretty' either.
Who, when I come trotting in from the bathroom
like a squealing freshly-scrubbed piglet
that likes nothing better than a binge
of being affectionate and undisciplined and uncomplicated,
opens his arms like a trough for me to dive into.

SELIMA HILL

Man in Space

All you have to do is listen to the way a man
sometimes talks to his wife at a table of people
and notice how intent he is on making his point
even though her lower lip is beginning to quiver,

and you will know why the women in science
fiction movies who inhabit a planet of their own
are not pictured making a salad or reading a magazine
when the men from earth arrive in their rocket,

why they are always standing in a semicircle
with their arms folded, their bare legs set apart,
their breasts protected by hard metal disks.

BILLY COLLINS

Wedding

From time to time our love is like a sail
and when the sail begins to alternate
from tack to tack, it's like a swallowtail
and when the swallow flies it's like a coat;
and if the coat is yours, it has a tear
like a wide mouth and when the mouth begins
to draw the wind, it's like a trumpeter
and when the trumpet blows, it blows like millions
and this, my love, when millions come and go
beyond the need of us, is like a trick;
and when the trick begins, it's like a toe
tiptoeing on a rope, which is like luck;
and when the luck begins, it's like a wedding,
which is like love, which is like everything.

ALICE OSWALD

The Tightrope Wedding

We can't take our eyes off the young
couple walking to meet one another
on this cable strung between twin
towers of the castle. Fifty feet

up in the air and no net. Arms
wide, they're holding out matching
aluminium balancing poles
that are light but so long they bow slightly.

We can see how the slim, dark-haired
and suited groom bends his knees
as he leans forward shifting his weight
onto the front foot to take

his next step. The bride, we assume,
must be doing the same, somehow
holding sway over her stiff
petticoats, the satin and lace;

and, adjusting to any gust
tugging at her train, she comes on
steadily, one white shoe showing,
its soft sole curved over the rope.

They're wired up, they counterbalance
each other, but they're not one flesh yet.
We bite our lips, can't bear to look,
are glad to be distracted

by this tubby, game, down-to-earth priest
about to climb into the picture
up the fire appliance's steep
but not impossible ladder.

MICHAEL LASKEY

The Whitsun Weddings

That Whitsun, I was late getting away:
    Not till about
One-twenty on the sunlit Saturday
Did my three-quarters-empty train pull out,
All windows down, all cushions hot, all sense
Of being in a hurry gone. We ran
Behind the backs of houses, crossed a street
Of blinding windscreens, smelt the fish-dock; thence
The river's level drifting breadth began,
Where sky and Lincolnshire and water meet.

All afternoon, through the tall heat that slept
    For miles inland,
A slow and stopping curve southwards we kept.
Wide farms went by, short-shadowed cattle, and
Canals with floatings of industrial froth;
A hothouse flashed uniquely: hedges dipped
And rose: and now and then a smell of grass
Displaced the reek of buttoned carriage-cloth
Until the next town, new and nondescript,
Approached with acres of dismantled cars.

At first, I didn't notice what a noise
   The weddings made
Each station that we stopped at: sun destroys
The interest of what's happening in the shade,
And down the long cool platforms whoops and skirls
I took for porters larking with the mails,
And went on reading. Once we started, though,
We passed them, grinning and pomaded, girls
In parodies of fashion, heels and veils,
All posed irresolutely, watching us go,

As if out on the end of an event
   Waving goodbye
To something that survived it. Struck, I leant
More promptly out next time, more curiously,
And saw it all again in different terms:
The fathers with broad belts under their suits
And seamy foreheads; mothers loud and fat;
An uncle shouting smut; and then the perms,
The nylon gloves and jewellery-substitutes,
The lemons, mauves, and olive-ochres that

Marked off the girls unreally from the rest.
   Yes, from cafés
And banquet-halls up yards, and bunting-dressed
Coach-party annexes, the wedding-days
Were coming to an end. All down the line
Fresh couples climbed aboard: the rest stood round;
The last confetti and advice were thrown,
And, as we moved, each face seemed to define
Just what it saw departing: children frowned
At something dull; fathers had never known

Success so huge and wholly farcical;
   The women shared
The secret like a happy funeral;
While girls, gripping their handbags tighter, stared
At a religious wounding. Free at last,
And loaded with the sum of all they saw,
We hurried towards London, shuffling gouts of steam.
Now fields were building-plots, and poplars cast
Long shadows over major roads, and for
Some fifty minutes, that in time would seem

Just long enough to settle hats and say
   I nearly died,
A dozen marriages got under way.
They watched the landscape, sitting side by side
– An Odeon went past, a cooling tower,
And someone running up to bowl – and none
Thought of the others they would never meet
Or how their lives would all contain this hour.
I thought of London spread out in the sun,
Its postal districts packed like squares of wheat:

There we were aimed. And as we raced across
   Bright knots of rail
Past standing Pullmans, walls of blackened moss
Came close, and it was nearly done, this frail
Travelling coincidence; and what it held
Stood ready to be loosed with all the power
That being changed can give. We slowed again,
And as the tightened brakes took hold, there swelled
A sense of falling, like an arrow-shower
Sent out of sight, somewhere becoming rain.

PHILIP LARKIN

The Pattern

Thirty-six years, to the day, after our wedding
When a cold figure-revealing wind blew against you
And lifted your veil, I find in its fat envelope
The six-shilling *Vogue* pattern for your bride's dress,
Complicated instructions for stitching bodice
And skirt, box pleats and hems, tissue-paper outlines,
Semblances of skin which I nervously unfold
And hold up in snow light, for snow has been falling
On this windless day, and I glimpse your wedding dress
And white shoes outside in the transformed garden
Where the clothesline and every twig have been covered.

MICHAEL LONGLEY

243

Les Grands Seigneurs

Men were my buttresses, my castellated towers,
the bowers where I took my rest. The best and worst
of times were men: the peacocks and the cockatoos,
the nightingales, the strutting pink flamingos.

Men were my dolphins, my performing seals; my sailing-ships,
the ballast in my hold. They were the rocking-horses
prancing down the promenade, the bandstand
where the music played. My hurdy-gurdy monkey-men.

I was their queen. I sat enthroned before them.
out of reach. We played at courtly love:
the troubadour, the damsel and the peach.

But after I was wedded, bedded, I became
(yes, overnight) a toy, a plaything, little woman,
wife, a bit of fluff. My husband clicked
his fingers, called my bluff.

DOROTHY MOLLOY

Being a Wife

So this is what it's like being a wife.
The body I remember feeling as big as America in,
the thighs so far away
his hand had to ride in an aeroplane to get there;
the giggles I heard adults giggling with
I was puzzled about,
and felt much too solemn to try;
buttons unbuttoned by somebody else, not me;
the record-player
neither of us were able to stop what we were doing
to turn off;
the smell of fish
I dreaded I'd never get used to,

the peculiar, leering, antediluvian taste
I preferred not to taste;
the feeling of being on the edge of something
everyone older than us,
had wasted,
and not understood,
as we were about to do;
his pink hand gripping my breast
as if his life depended on it;
the shame of the thought of the mirror
reflecting all this,
seem long ago,
yet somehow authentic and right.
Being a wife is like acting being a wife,
and the me that was her with him in the past is still me.

SELIMA HILL

The Ache of Marriage

The ache of marriage:

thigh and tongue, beloved,
are heavy with it,
it throbs in the teeth

We look for communion
and are turned away, beloved,
each and each

It is leviathan and we
in its belly
looking for joy, some joy
not to be known outside it

two by two in the ark of
the ache of it.

DENISE LEVERTOV

The Applicant

First, are you our sort of a person?
Do you wear
A glass eye, false teeth or a crutch,
A brace or a hook,
Rubber breasts or a rubber crotch,

Stitches to show something's missing? No, no? Then
How can we give you a thing?
Stop crying.
Open your hand.
Empty? Empty. Here is a hand

To fill it and willing
To bring teacups and roll away headaches
And do whatever you tell it.
Will you marry it?
It is guaranteed

To thumb shut your eyes at the end
And dissolve of sorrow.
We make new stock from the salt.
I notice you are stark naked.
How about this suit –

Black and stiff, but not a bad fit.
Will you marry it?
It is waterproof, shatterproof, proof
Against fire and bombs through the roof.
Believe me, they'll bury you in it.

Now your head, excuse me, is empty.
I have the ticket for that.
Come here, sweetie, out of the closet.
Well, what do you think of *that*?
Naked as paper to start

But in twenty-five years she'll be silver,
In fifty, gold.
A living doll, everywhere you look.

It can sew, it can cook,
It can talk, talk, talk.

It works, there is nothing wrong with it.
You have a hole, it's a poultice.
You have an eye, it's an image.
My boy, it's your last resort.
Will you marry it, marry it, marry it.

SYLVIA PLATH

Good Gifts

He gives her a black lace bra:
her heart swells. She fills the C-cup.

He gives her a bottle of champagne
costing £24.50. He has got a bargain.

He gives her a basket of strawberries.
Open wide! he says, gently. She opens.

He gives her a smooth round bloodstone
to wear round her neck. So cold.

He gives her a little house. All day long
she cleans his fingerprints from the paintwork.

He gives her five gold rings, one in her ear,
one in her nose, one in her nipple,

one in her navel, one in her finger. He takes
a fine gold wire and threads it between

ear, nose, nipple, navel and finger.
He twitches the end. She dances.

DOROTHY NIMMO

Breakfast

He put the coffee
In the cup
He put the milk
In the cup of coffee
He put the sugar
In the *café au lait*
With the coffee spoon
He stirred
He drank the *café au lait*
And he set down the cup
Without a word to me
He lit
A cigarette
He made smoke-rings
With the smoke
He put the ashes
In the ash-tray
Without a word to me
Without a look at me
He got up
He put
His hat upon his head
He put his raincoat on
Because it was raining
And he left
In the rain
Without a word
Without a look at me
And I   I took
My head in my hand
And I cried.

JACQUES PRÉVERT
translated from the French by Lawrence Ferlinghetti

Ill-Wishing Him

I'm going to have to leave you, he said,
very politely. *Sorry*.

I stood up to riddle the Aga,
to draw the red curtains I'd bought
ready-made, marked down, to put out
the cat and I said, *Oh really? When
were you thinking of going?*

As if I might offer to take him
to the station. As if I didn't want
to make him angry in case he left me.

I wish I'd said, Get out. Now.
In his pyjamas. In the rain.
Scrabbling in the gravel for his toothbrush.
Begging for a change of underpants.

I wish he'd had to rent a room
in Peterborough, to take his washing
to the launderette, watch his shirts turn pink.
I wish he'd lived on pork-pie and pizza
and it had made him sick.

I wish he'd gone senile and forgotten
who he was and what he'd done
and every day I could remind him. I wish
he'd died and left my name
as next of kin. They'd ring me
and I'd say, *Never heard of him.*

DOROTHY NIMMO

My Way

I only did it for a laugh
I did it because I'm a fool for love
I did it because push had come to shove
I did it because – my age – I've got nothing to prove

But I did it
I did it
I did it
Yes I did

I did it to settle an argument with a friend
I did it to drive our Hazel round the bend
I did it to get one over on our kid
I did it to nip it in the bud
I did it that way because I couldn't stand the sight of blood

But I did it
I did it
I did it
Yes I did

I did it to bury the hatchet and get a night's sleep
I did it to get out before I was in too deep
I did it to piss on his chips and put his gas at a peep

But I did it
I did it
I did it
Mea absolutely culpa, me!

I did it to go out in a blaze of glory
I did it to make them listen to my side of the story
I only did it to get attention
I did it to get an honourable mention
I did it to put an end to it all
I did it for no reason at all

But I did it
I did it
I did it
Yes I did

LIZ LOCHHEAD

Love Rats

Bored with cards, chess or novel
    on a long afternoon?
        Lock all the doors,
           push back your hair and sleeves,
      lash on your apron,
try your hand at Love Rat Casserole!

Firstly take a good dose of love rats
    black to the bitter core –
        as many as you want
           or care to round up and count
      and soak for an hour
to soften up their foul exteriors.

Remove any black seeds, pips or stones
    also known as lies,
        shams, frauds, fibs and fiction,
           deceit and malicious-invention.
      These don't smell too nice –
scrub your hands after these vital extractions.

Now let's progress to the chopping-block –
    slam unwanted *extras*.
        Take hold of a sharp knife
           and squeezing tightly slice
      tongues, cocks and fingers –
leave nothing waggling, unfit for the pot.

Run a sharp blade over their backs
    right down to the bone –
        a good, clean, deep cut,
           then stuff the slits with coarse salt
      rubbed right in,
stuff the gobs with lumps of fat.

Now for the pièce-de-résistance, master flourish –
    a good strong stuffing
        of raspberries or radishes
           stuffed up their tight arses
      for a real tang!
A talking-point of any supper dish.

No need to bind the ankles and necks,
    but feel free to do so.
        A good length of twine or string
        stops them slipping and sloshing –
    and nice and tight now,
you're not taking grandma's dog for a walk.

Place the little buggers top-to-tail
    face down in a dish
        no less than choked on boozy gravy.
        They'll cook best that way –
    sweating the sticky stuff
from every little orifice and hole.

What you serve them with is up to you –
    anything from cabbage to cream
        and although the chef's no appetite
        (she really couldn't take a bite)
    she's wildly waving her spoon
to serve. Who wants a portion? Form a queue.

CHERYL FOLLON

Recension Day

Unburn the boat, rebuild the bridge,
Reconsecrate the sacrilege,
Unspill the milk, decry the tears,
Turn back the clock, relive the years,
Replace the smoke inside the fire,
Unite fulfilment with desire,
Undo the done, gainsay the said,
Revitalise the buried dead,
Revoke the penalty and clause,
Reconstitute unwritten laws,
Repair the heart, untie the tongue,
Change faithless old to hopeful young,
Inure the body to disease
And help me to forget you please.

DUNCAN FORBES

Before That

Distinction was never yours
and now you are nothing.
Before that you were still a young man
breathing monoxides
in a car with your lover.
Before that you were
the overweight younger man,
still single, playing darts
in a pub back home.
Before that you were the schoolboy
with a round flat face
like a plate of battered steel,
dodging the ball at rugby.
Before that you were
a boy in short trousers
afraid of the bully
at the end of the alley.
Before that you were a baby
and your mother loved you.
Before that you were
a movement without a face
in the comfort of warm waters.
Before that you were nothing.
And before that.

MICHAEL BLACKBURN

The New Bride

Dying, darling, is the easy bit. Fifty paracetamol,
bride-white and sticking in the throat, ten shots
of Johnnie Walker, and the deed is done.
A twilight day of drowsing, then the breathing
slows to a whisper, like a sinner in Confession.

Death is dead easy. No, what happens next
is the difficulty. You bastard, howling in public,
snivelling over photos, ringing round for consolation.
And you have me burnt, like a dinner gone wrong,
you keep the charred remains of me on show

at the Wake, inviting everyone I hate. Oh God,
they come in packs, sleek as rats with platitudes
and an eye on my half of the bed, hoping to find
leftover skin, a hint of fetid breath. I leave them
no hairs on the pillow; there are none to leave.

And a year to the day since I shrug off the yoke
of life, you meet the new bride. In group therapy.
You head straight for a weeper and wailer,
telling strangers all her little tragedies. You love
the way she languishes, her tears sliming your neck,

you give into her on vile pink Austrian blinds.
The Wedding is a riot of white nylon. Everybody
drinks your health and hers, the simpering bitch.
She and Delia Smith keep you fat and happy
as a pig in shit. I want her cells to go beserk.

Some nights I slip between you. The new bride
sleeps buttoned up, slug-smug in polyester. You,
my faithless husband, turn over in your dreams,
and I'm there, ice-cold and seeking out your eyes
and for a moment you brush my lips, and freeze.

CATHERINE SMITH

Sleeping with the Fishes

When I was a goldfish you never noticed me.
Every day I would watch you eat breakfast.
I knew your favourite cereal, how many times
you would chew before you swallowed each spoonful.

On Tuesdays and Thursdays you worked late.
You bought Chinese food and ate in front of the TV.
This invariably gave you indigestion.
I did worry about you – you always looked so tired.

At night I would circle round while you could not sleep.
I would sing you lullabies that you could not hear.
Sweet tunes to drift you away to a place I would never go,
until the light of morning broke through the dirty window.

When one night you didn't come back from work,
I watched the mail pile up for days, alone in your empty house.
The phone rang once, but I couldn't reach it.
Was it you? Did you phone me? Did you?

I dreamt you chose to swim with me.
You liked the patterns light makes on the surface
How the world distorts with each turning tide
as icy water soothed your tired eyes.

HELEN IVORY

Let's Go Over It All Again

Some people are like that
They split up and then they think;
Hey, maybe we haven't hurt each other to the uttermost.
Let's meet up and have a drink

Let's go over it all again
Let's rake over the dirt.
Let me pick that scab of yours
Does it hurt?

Let's go over what went wrong –
How and why and when.
Let's go over what went wrong
Again and again.

We hurt each other badly once.
We said a lot of nasty stuff
But lately I've been thinking how
I didn't hurt you enough.

Maybe there's more where that came from,
Something more malign.
Let me damage you again
For the sake of auld lang syne.

Yes, let me see you bleed again
For the sake of auld lang syne.

JAMES FENTON

Sonnet
(FROM *50 Sonnets*)

Not if you crawled from there to here, you hear?
Not if you *begged* me, on your bleeding knees.
Not if you lay exhausted at my door,
and *pleaded* with me for a second chance.
Not if you *wept* (am I making this clear?)
or found a thousand different words for 'Please',
ten thousand for 'I'm sorry'; I'd ignore
you so sublimely; every new advance
would meet with such complete indifference.
Not if you promised me fidelity.
Not if you *meant* it. What impertinence,
then, is this voice that murmurs, 'What if he
didn't? That isn't *his* line of attack.
What if he simply grinned, and said, I'm back?'

ELEANOR BROWN

6

Being and Loss

The poem that refuses to risk sentimentality, that refuses
to risk making a statement, is probably a poem that is going
to feel lukewarm. So I'm in favor of work that if it fails,
fails on the side of boldness, passion, intensity.

MARK DOTY

THIS SECTION draws upon poems about being and identity, and how these are
affected by loss and changes in our lives. It begins with Wallace Stevens's
enigmatic poem 'The Emperor of Ice-Cream' (258) which many readers love
for its language and panache even if the poem itself continues to baffle. But
the poet's letters are illuminating here: 'The words "concupiscent curds" have no
genealogy; they are merely expressive: at least, I hope they are expressive. They
express the concupiscence of life but by contrast with the things in relation in
the poem, they express or accentuate life's destitution, and it is this that gives
them something more than a cheap lustre...The true sense of "Let be be finale
of seem" is let being become the conclusion or dénouement of appearing to
be: in short, ice cream is an absolute good. The poem is obviously not about
ice cream, but about being as distinguished from seeming to be.'

In James Merrill's 'Mirror' (259), a mirror witnesses changes in a family.
Sylvia Plath wrote her own 'Mirror' (*Staying Alive*, 203) in 1961, and must
have known Merrill's poem (first published in 1959). Other poems explore
the differences between how we feel, how we seem and how we see ourselves
– and how these are affected by change and loss, such as disappointment in
love and life in Yeats's 'The Circus Animals' Desertion' (264); bereavement
in Jack Gilbert's 'Measuring the Tyger' (265); disempowerment, a recurrent
theme in poems by writers who have lived in totalitarian states, including the
two here by Aleksandar Ristovic and Marin Sorescu (263); and helplessness,
both in Esther Jansma's 'Descent' (278), her response to a child's death after
a heart operation, and in the three disturbing poems about murder (298-301).

Many of the poems in this section relate to illness – mental and physical – as
well as ageing, mortality and unfulfilled lives, extending the territory explored in
Staying Alive (sections 2, 3 & 4). Berryman's poem (266) is one of ten *Dream
Songs* haunted by the suicide of the poet Delmore Schwartz (*Staying Alive*,
54 & 67). Cavafy's Italian title 'Che Fece...Il Gran Rifiuto' (269) is borrowed
from Dante's *Inferno* (III, 60), and means 'Who made...the great refusal'; he
deliberately omitted the words 'per vilta' (i.e. 'because of cowardice').

The Emperor of Ice-Cream

Call the roller of big cigars
The muscular one, and bid him whip
In kitchen cups concupiscent curds.
Let the wenches dawdle in such dress
As they are used to wear, and let the boys
Bring flowers in last month's newspapers.
Let be be finale of seem.
The only emperor is the emperor of ice-cream.

Take from the dresser of deal,
Lacking the three glass knobs, that sheet
On which she embroidered fantails once
And spread it so as to cover her face.
If her horny feet protrude, they come
To show how cold she is, and dumb.
Let the lamp affix its beam.
The only emperor is the emperor of ice-cream.

WALLACE STEVENS

Somebody Else

If I was not myself, I would be somebody else.
But actually I am somebody else.
I have been somebody else all my life.

It's no laughing matter going about the place
all the time being somebody else:
people mistake you; you mistake yourself.

JACKIE KAY

Mirror

I grow old under an intensity
Of questioning looks. *Nonsense,*
I try to say, *I cannot teach you children*
How to live. – If not you, who will?
Cries one of them aloud, grasping my gilded
Frame till the world sways. *If not you, who will?*
Between their visits the table, its arrangement
Of Bible, fern and Paisley, all past change,
Does very nicely. If ever I feel curious
As to what others endure,
Across the parlor *you* provide examples,
Wide open, sunny, of everything I am
Not. You embrace a whole world without once caring
To set it in order. That takes thought. Out there
Something is being picked. The red-and-white bandannas
Go to my heart. A fine young man
Rides by on horseback. Now the door shuts. Hester
Confides in me her first unhappiness.
This much, you see, would never have been fitted
Together, but for me. Why then is it
They more and more neglect me? Late one sleepless
Midsummer night I strained to keep
Five tapers from your breathing. *No,* the widowed
Cousin said, *let them go out.* I did.
The room brimmed with gray sound, all the instreaming
Muslin of your dream...
Years later now, two of the grown grandchildren
Sit with novels face-down on the sill,
Content to muse upon your tall transparence,
Your clouds, brown fields, persimmon far
And cypress near. One speaks. *How superficial*
Appearances are! Since then, as if a fish
Had broken the perfect silver of my reflectiveness,
I have lapses. I suspect
Looks from behind, where nothing is, cool gazes
Through the blind flaws of my mind. As days,
As decades lengthen, this vision
Spreads and blackens. I do not know whose it is,
But I think it watches for my last silver

To blister, flake, float leaf by life, each milling-
Downward dumb conceit, to a standstill
From which not even you strike any brilliant
Chord in me, and to a faceless will,
Echo of mine, I am amenable.

JAMES MERRILL

The Mirror
(in memory of my father)

I

He was no longer my father
but I was still his son;
I would get to grips with that cold paradox,
the remote figure in his Sunday best
who was buried the next day.

A great day for tears, snifters of sherry,
whiskey, beef sandwiches, tea.
An old mate of his was recounting
their day excursion
to Youghal in the Thirties,
how he was his first partner
on the Cork/Skibbereen route
in the late Forties.
There was a splay of Mass cards
on the sitting-room mantelpiece
which formed a crescent round a glass vase,
his retirement present from C.I.E.

II

I didn't realise till two days later
it was the mirror took his breath away.

The monstrous old Victorian mirror
with the ornate gilt frame
we had found in the three-storey house
when we moved in from the country.
I was afraid that it would sneak
down from the wall and swallow me up
in one gulp in the middle of the night...

While he was decorating the bedroom
he had taken down the mirror
without asking for help;
soon he turned the colour of terracotta
and his heart broke that night.

III

There was nothing for it
but to set about finishing the job,
papering over the cracks,
painting the high window,
stripping the door, like the door of a crypt.
When I took hold of the mirror
I had a fright. I imagined him breathing through it.
I heard him say in a reassuring whisper:
I'll give you a hand, here.

And we lifted the mirror back in position
above the fireplace,
my father holding it steady
while I drove home
the two nails.

MICHAEL DAVITT
translated from the Irish by Paul Muldoon

Cat and Mirror

I'd like to turn my eyes
on the mirror's hard water
and not see myself,
not know myself to be me.
My young brown tiger-cat can do it –

he sniffs a little smear
where someone touched the glass,
happy to be on the bureau, so high up.
From there he can survey the entire
kingdom of the moment, and rule it.

CHASE TWICHELL

Transmutation

(FROM *Might a Shape of Words*)

It was as if she couldn't know herself. Only other persons could do that. When she searched for her image, there was always the reminder: one green eye, one brown. Her mother had tried to reassure that it made her attractive, interesting, that it was an asset, not a defect

which wasn't what troubled, or even the lack of symmetry, but that when she looked in the mirror, she was always reversed, with her green eye on the left, her brown on the right. Only others saw her as she was. Only others might make the affirmation, 'You are'. For her, it was always the reflection, 'Am I?'

GAEL TURNBULL

Original Face

Some mornings I wake up kicking like a frog.
My thighs ache from going nowhere all night.
I get up – tailless, smooth-skinned, eyes protruding –
and scrub around for my original face.
It is good I am dreaming, I say to myself.
The real characters and events would hurt me.
The real lying, shame and envy would turn
even a pleasure-loving man into a stone.
Instead, my plain human flesh wakes up
and gazes out at real sparrows skimming the luminous
wet rooftops at the base of a mountain.
No splayed breasts, no glaring teeth, appear before me.
Only the ivory hands of morning touching
the real face in the real mirror on my bureau.

HENRI COLE

The essential

I was not allowed to live my life,
so I pretended to be dead
and interested solely in things
a dead man could be interested in:
petrified reptiles,
museum bric-à-brac,
fake evidence passed off as truth.
I felt a great need to be really dead,
and so at all times I wore
a mask made of wood
on which someone occasionally drew,
with colored pencils,
the look of contentment,
impatience, desire, bliss,
or the look of someone who is thinking
about an entirely different matter.

ALEKSANDAR RISTOVIĆ
translated from the Serbian by Charles Simic

Pond

The pond was a deep pond once,
The baits hung down
Like fruit, like shining fruit, lanterns,
Attainable planets and we
Went busily choosing a heart's delight
For the size of our mouths and rose flapping
Like Angels. Now
Here we are in a crowd
In a muddy six inches gasping
For worms and the shadows
Of peering fisherman
Have quite put out the light.

MARIN SORESCU
translated from the Romanian by David Constantine & Ioana Russell-Gebbett

The Circus Animals' Desertion

I

I sought a theme and sought for it in vain,
I sought it daily for six weeks or so.
Maybe at last, being but a broken man,
I must be satisfied with my heart, although
Winter and summer till old age began
My circus animals were all on show,
Those stilted boys, that burnished chariot,
Lion and woman and the Lord knows what.

II

What can I but enumerate old themes,
First that sea-rider Oisin led by the nose
Through three enchanted islands, allegorical dreams,
Vain gaiety, vain battle, vain repose,
Themes of the embittered heart, or so it seems,
That might adorn old songs or courtly shows;
But what cared I that set him on to ride,
I, starved for the bosom of his fairy bride?

And then a counter-truth filled out its play,
The Countess Cathleen was the name I gave it;
She, pity-crazed, had given her soul away,
But masterful Heaven had intervened to save it.
I thought my dear must her own soul destroy,
So did fanaticism and hate enslave it,
And this brought forth a dream and soon enough
This dream itself had all my thought and love.

And when the Fool and Blind Man stole the bread
Cuchulain fought the ungovernable sea;
Heart-mysteries there, and yet when all is said
It was the dream itself enchanted me:
Character isolated by a deed
To engross the present and dominate memory.
Players and painted stage took all my love,
And not those things that they were emblems of.

III

Those masterful images because complete
Grew in pure mind but out of what began?
A mound of refuse or the sweepings of a street,
Old kettles, old bottles, and a broken can,
Old iron, old bones, old rags, that raving slut
Who keeps the till. Now that my ladder's gone,
I must lie down where all the ladders start,
In the foul rag-and-bone shop of the heart.

W.B. YEATS

Measuring the Tyger

Barrels of chains. Sides of beef stacked in vans.
Water buffalo dragging logs of teak in the river mud
outside Mandalay. Pantocrater in the Byzantium dome.
The mammoth overhead crane bringing slabs of steel
through the dingy light and roar to the giant shear
that cuts the adamantine three-quarter-inch plates
and they flop down. The weight of the mind fractures
the girders and piers of the spirit, spilling out
the heart's melt. Incandescent ingots big as cars
trundling out of titanic mills, red slag scaling off
the brighter metal in the dark. The Monongahela River
below, night's sheen on its belly. Silence except
for the machinery clanging deeper in us. You will
love again, people say. Give it time. Me with time
running out. Day after day of the everyday.
What they call real life, made of eighth-inch gauge.
Newness strutting around as if it were significant.
Irony, neatness and rhyme pretending to be poetry.
I want to go back to that time after Michiko's death
when I cried every day among the trees. To the real.
To the magnitude of pain, of being that much alive.

JACK GILBERT

The black heralds

There are knocks in life so hard... I don't know!
Knock's like God's hate; as if under them
the backwash of everything suffered
had stagnated in your soul... I don't know!

They are few; but they are... They open dark weals
in the keenest face, in the hardest back.
They could be the colts of wild Attilas;
or the black heralds death sends us.

They are the deep chutes of your soul Christs,
of some pretty faith Destiny blasphemes.
Those bloodied knocks are the crackling
of a loaf that burns up at the oven door.

And man... Poor man! He turns his eyes as
when a clap on the shoulder summons us;
he turns his mad eyes, and everything lived
stagnates like a guilt pond in his look.

There are knocks in life, so hard... I don't know!

CÉSAR VALLEJO
translated from the Spanish by Ed Dorn & Gordon Brotherston

from Dream Songs (155)

I can't get him out of my mind, out of my mind,
Hé was out of his own mind for years,
in police stations & Bellevue.
He drove up to my house in Providence
ho ho at 8 a.m. in a Cambridge taxi
and told it to wait.

He walked my living-room, & did not want breakfast
or even coffee, or even even a drink.
He paced, I'd say Sit down,
it makes me nervous, for a moment he'd sit down,
then pace. After an hour or so *I* had a drink.
He took it back to Cambridge,

we never learnt why he came, or what he wanted.
His mission was obscure. His mission was real,
but obscure.
I remember his electrical insight as the young man,
his wit & passion, gift, the whole young man
alive with surplus love.

JOHN BERRYMAN

The Death by Heroin of Sid Vicious

There – but for the clutch of luck – go I.

At daybreak – in the arctic fog of a February daybreak –
Shoulder-length helmets in the watchtowers of the concentration
        camp
Caught me out in the intersecting arcs of the swirling searchlights.

There were at least a zillion of us caught out there –
Like ladybirds under a boulder –
But under the microscope each of us was unique,

Unique and we broke for cover, crazily breasting
The barbed wire and some of us made it
To the forest edge, but many of us did not

Make it, although their unborn children did –
Such as you whom the camp commandant branded
Sid Vicious of the Sex Pistols. Jesus, break his fall:

There – but for the clutch of luck – go we all.

PAUL DURCAN

Otherwise

I got out of bed
on two strong legs.
It might have been
otherwise. I ate
cereal, sweet
milk, ripe, flawless
peach. It might
have been otherwise.
I took the dog uphill
to the birchwood.
All morning I did
the work I love.

At noon I lay down
with my mate. It might
have been otherwise.
We ate dinner together
at a table with silver
candlesticks. It might
have been otherwise.
I slept in a bed
in a room with paintings
on the walls, and
planned another day
just like this day.
But one day, I know,
it will be otherwise.

JANE KENYON

The Mistake

With the mistake your life goes in reverse.
Now you can see exactly what you did
Wrong yesterday and wrong the day before
And each mistake leads back to something worse

And every nuance of your hypocrisy
Towards yourself, and every excuse
Stands solidly on the perspective lines
And there is perfect visibility.

What an enlightenment. The colonnade
Rolls past on either side. You needn't move.
The statues of your errors brush your sleeve.
You watch the tale turn back – and you're dismayed.

And this dismay at this, this big mistake
Is made worse by the sight of all those who
Knew all along where these mistakes would lead –
Those frozen friends who watched the crisis break.

Why didn't they *say*? Oh, but they did indeed –
Said with a murmur when the time was wrong
Or by a mild refusal to assent
Or told you plainly but you would not heed.

Yes, you can hear them now. It hurts. It's worse
Than any sneer from any enemy.
Take this dismay. Lay claim to this mistake.
Look straight along the lines of this reverse.

JAMES FENTON

Che Fece... Il Gran Rifiuto

For some people the day comes
when they have to declare the great Yes
or the great No. It's clear at once who has the Yes
ready within him; and saying it,

he goes from honour to honour, strong in his conviction.
He who refuses does not repent. Asked again,
he'd still say no. Yet that no – the right no –
drags him down all his life.

C.P. CAVAFY
translated from the Greek by Edmund Keeley & Philip Sherrard

Speaking About My Cracked Sump

I tell her about the pool
under my car each morning,
its blackness, the successive
seven drips I must always
count; watching what should be held,
released. She nods. Go on. Go
on. But only if you want
to. Her encouraging smile.
I say that the oil is like
a shadow resting there. I
say that one day it will spread
from beneath my car and flow
down this road. Babies and pets
will skate over it. There may
be confusions. Then the oil
will turn right at the junction,
and swamp the small roundabout,
mount a kerb, soak towards the
edge of our fine promenade,
stop by the railings, listening
to the waves below and drip,
troubling the water. She has
a question for me. Are you
the oil or the water? I pause.
I am the skating baby
and I am the final drop.

ANDREW WATERHOUSE

Ophelia's Confession

Every day God pats my head and calls me
angel, his little broken woman
and gives me flowers as if I hadn't had enough of these
and I choke back my rage and he mistakes this
for distress as I stand there shaking
in my little sackcloth dress.

Had I ever had the choice
I'd have worn a very different dress,
slit from breast to navel and far too tight
and I'd have smoked and sworn and been
out of my head on drugs, not grief, and the flowers
would have been a tattoo around my ankle,
not an anchor to drag me down, and as for
being a virgin, I'd have slept with both men and women.

I would never recommend a shallow stream
and what was no more than a daisy chain
as being the ideal way to die.
It was far too pretty but I had to improvise
and I was a poet, far more so than him,
who threw out every word he ever thought
as if that might have kept his sorry life afloat.

I didn't drown by accident. I was a suicide.
At least let me call my mind my own
even when my heart was gone beyond recall.

Today, a car crash might have been my final scene,
a black Mercedes in a tunnel by the Seine,
with no last words, no poetry,
with flashbulbs tearing at my broken body
because broken was the way I felt inside,
the cameras lighting up the wreckage of a life.
That would, at least, have been an honest way to die.

TRACEY HERD

Hairbrush

Anyone who touched her would be sorry
and that's why they've put her away, because they were sorry,
and they've put her away
where no one will see her but nurses
who, seeing her sit here alone with nothing to do,
are standing behind her
ceaselessly brushing her hair –

the most beautiful hair the lodger had ever seen,
the hair of angels,
lovers –

till she panics.
She cannot bear their need to understand her,
she cannot bear their need to get so close,
to fondle her scar
and take off their gloves and explore it
and climb up her hair
and drill through her brain to the sorrow
that never stops trying to snatch at the hands on the brush
as they ceaselessly, ceaselessly brush
her desirable hair.

SELIMA HILL

Elvis the Performing Octopus

hangs in the tank like a ruined balloon,
an eight-armed suit sucked empty,

ushering the briefest whisper
across the surface, keeping

his slurred drift steady with an effort
massive as the ocean resisting the moon.

When the last technician,
whistling his own colourless tune,

splashes through the disinfectant tray,
one might see, had anyone been left to look,

Elvis changing from spilt milk to tumbling blue,
pulsing with colour like a forest in sunlight.

Elvis does the full range, even the spinning top
that never quite worked out, as the striplight fizzes

and the flylamp cracks like a firework.
Elvis has the water applauding,

and the brooms, the draped cloths, the dripping tap,
might say that a story that ends in the wrong place

always ends like this – completely
fabulous in an empty room,

unravelled by the tender men in white,
laid out softly in the morning.

POLLY CLARK

Flight

The mother blackbird I've been feeding
has flown in the open door of the kitchen,
where she flutters against the stuck window,
like a butterfly, finding no way through.

A startled eye stares. In the flap of a wing
it all comes back: my heart beating
so fast I thought it would explode,
my mind and body in overload,

running the corridors, fleeing nurses,
who seemed stranger than another species,
then trapped in a room with nowhere to go,
how I was cornered at a safety window,

which opened only far enough for air,
how I didn't know there was no cause to fear,
how they outnumbered me, fastened their grip,
laid me down and injected me, like rape.

I cup the bird gently in my hands, like water,
carry her out, as if a Section order
has been lifted, give her to the air,
then watch her spread her wings and soar.

SARAH WARDLE

Autumn Cancer
(i.m. Liz Suttle)

Each day, the autumn, eating a little further
into the bone.

A leaf falls on a stiller day, coloured a richer brown,
more glowing, more holding, like glazed bread or old apples;

and the lap of the lake gone smaller, a nibbling as of fishes
at feet in tidal pools. The heron stands longer.

Shoals of leaves float further on the water,
the low sun pulses, and light shafts pick more delicately

over woodland and the limbs of ash grown sensuous,
shapely, as a woman from a bath;

while on the alders, yellow, and here and there,
a round leaf hangs, spent coin in the stillness.

I have never known so exactly
this abacus of days. This withdrawal. This closing out.

KERRY HARDIE

Chemotherapy

I did not imagine being bald
at forty-four. I didn't have a plan.
Perhaps a scar or two from growing old,
hot flushes. I'd sit fluttering a fan.

But I am bald, and hardly ever walk
by day, I'm the invalid of these rooms,
stirring soups, awake in the half dark,
not answering the phone when it rings.

I never thought that life could get this small,
that I would care so much about a cup,
the taste of tea, the texture of a shawl,
and whether or not I should get up.

I'm not unhappy. I have learnt to drift
and sip. The smallest things are gifts.

JULIA DARLING

Transmutation
(FROM *Might a Shape of Words*)

Taken severely ill, he is conscious only at brief intervals, enough
to know that the diagnosis is as uncertain as the outcome, and well
beyond any treatment

until, one afternoon, he recovers enough to know that he is recovering,
would live and not die, which seems a matter of great indifference
except for the novelty. He finds himself weeping, in amazement at
the gift of it, as if no more related to him than the pattern of clouds
he can glimpse through a corner of the window.

GAEL TURNBULL

She Replies to Carmel's Letter

It was a mild Christmas, the small fine rain kept washing over,
so I coated myself in plastics,
walked further than I could manage.
Leave me now, I'd say, and when they had tramped ahead
I'd sit myself down on a stone or the side of a high grass ditch,
or anywhere – like a duck in a puddle –
I'd rest a bit, then I would muddle around
the winding boreens that crawled the headland.

Sometimes, water-proofed and not caring,
I'd sit in a road which was really a stream-bed,
being and seeing from down where the hare sees,
sitting in mud and in wetness,
the world rising hummocky round me,
the sudden grass on the skyline,
the fence-post, with the earth run from under it,
swinging like a hanged man.

Then I would want to praise
the ease of low wet things, the song of them, like a child's low drone,
and praising I'd watch how the water flowing the track
is clear, so I might not see it
but for the cross-hatched place where it runs on a scatter of grit,
the flat, swelled place where it slides itself over a stone.
So now, when you write that you labour to strip off the layers,
and there might not, under them, be anything at all,

I remember that time, and I wish you had sat there, with me,
your skin fever-hot, the lovely wet coldness of winter mud
on your red, uncovered hands,
knowing it's all in the layers,
the flesh on the bones, the patterns that the bones push
upwards onto the flesh. So, you will see how it is with me,
and that sometimes even sickness is generous
and takes you by the hand and sits you
beside things you would otherwise have passed over.

KERRY HARDIE

Caesura

Sometimes at night when the heart stumbles and stops
a full second endless the endless steps
that lead me on through this time terrain
without edges and beautiful terrible
are gone never to proceed again.

Here is a moment of enormous trouble
when the kaleidoscope sets unalterable
and at once without meaning without motion
like a stalled aeroplane in the middle sky
ready to fall down into a waiting ocean.

Blackness rises. Am I now to die
and feel the steps no more and not see day
break out its answering smile of hail all's well
from east full round to east and hear the bird
whistle all creatures that on earth do dwell?

Not now. Old heart has stopped to think of a word
as someone in a dream by far too weird
to be unlikely feels a kiss and stops
to praise all heaven stumbling in all his senses...
and suddenly hears again the endless steps.

KENNETH MACKENZIE

Heart

I thought of other significant hearts:
Christ's, which in the Greek
would throw itself out;
Shelley's saved from fire and water
brought back to Bournemouth.
Now this child's. The doctor's hand
went far either side of it.
The pink tubes of the stethoscope
divined an unfamiliar sluicing.
Something in nature was too tight.
Something in Greek had gone wrong,
and although it made the old phrases
new – 'take heart', 'with all my heart'
for three days we put them aside
until the valve, tough as tripe, came right.

DAVID SCOTT

Descent

We crossed the Styx.
The ferryman lay drunk in his boat.
I held the helm and we sank like stones.

Water like the earth consists of layers,
transparent ribbons, glistening strata
of ever less life, less warmth.

Bubbles blossomed in your hair,
the current tugged your head backwards
and stroked your throat.

Stones waved with arms made of algae and ferns,
gurgled softly, sang of 'peace'.
They sliced your clothes away.

Fish licked the blood from your legs.
I held your hand tight. I wanted to comfort you,
but we were falling too fast and there are no words

that exist without air; my love
stayed above, blue balloons, brief buoys,
marking the site of the accident,

before flowing on. Your mouth fell open,
your face turned red, your hands sought
for balance, sought my arms.

You tried to climb me.
You were a glass blower with a cloud of diamonds
at his mouth. I held you like a kitten.

I stroked your fingers.
You did not let go.
You slept and I stroked your fingers, let go.

ESTHER JANSMA
translated from the Dutch by James Brockway & Esther Jansma

Broken Moon

(for Emma)

Twelve, small as six,
strength, movement, hearing
all given in half measure,
my daughter,
child of genetic carelessness,
walks uphill, always.

I watch her morning face;
precocious patience as she hooks each sock,
creeps it up her foot,
aims her jersey like a quoit.
My fingers twitch;
her private frown deters

Her jokes can sting:
'My life is like dressed crab
– lot of effort, rather little meat.'
Yet she delights in seedlings taking root,
finding a fossil,
a surprise dessert.

Chopin will not yield to her stiff touch;
I hear her cursing.
She paces Bach exactly,
firm rounding of perfect cadences.
Somewhere inside
she is dancing a courante.

In dreams she skims the sand,
curls toes into the ooze of pools,
leaps on to stanchions.
Awake, her cousins take her hands;
they lean into the waves,
stick-child between curved sturdiness.

She turns away from stares,
laughs at the boy who asks
if she will find a midget husband.

Ten years ago, cradling her,
I showed her the slice of silver in the sky.
'Moon broken,' she said.

CAROLE SATYAMURTI

Names

She was Eliza for a few weeks
When she was a baby –
Eliza Lily. Soon it changed to Lil.

Later she was Miss Steward in the baker's shop
And then 'my love', 'my darling', Mother.

Widowed at thirty, she went back to work
As Mrs Hand. Her daughter grew up,
Married and gave birth.

Now she was Nanna. 'Everybody
Calls me Nanna,' she would say to visitors.
And so they did – friends, tradesmen, the doctor.

In the geriatric ward
They used the patients' Christian names.
'Lil,' we said, 'or Nanna,'
But it wasn't in her file
And for those last bewildered weeks
She was Eliza once again.

WENDY COPE

Alzheimer's

Chairs move by themselves, and books.
Grandchildren visit, stand
new and nameless, their faces' puzzles
missing pieces. She's like a fish

280

in deep ocean, its body made of light.
She floats through rooms, through
my eyes, an old woman bereft
of chronicle, the parable of her life.

And though she's almost a child
there's still blood between us:
I passed through her to arrive.
So I protect her from knives,

stairs, from the street that calls
as rivers do, a summons to walk away,
to follow. And dress her,
demonstrate how buttons work,

when she sometimes looks up
and says my name, the sound arriving
like the trill of a bird so rare
it's rumored no longer to exist.

BOB HICOK

Have We Had Easter Yet?

'Who are you?' asks my mother.
'If you're looking after me
I ought to know your name.'

I show her me when I was small,
A faded photograph.
'That's Bobbins,' she says instantly.

'I wonder where she is, she never comes to see me.'
I go away. To get my mother's lunch.
'How good it looks. Please thank the cook.'

Later I found it in the bin.
'I didn't know who'd cooked it,
So I had those custard creams.'

She smiles at me with faded, muddled eyes
And says my name,
Then struggles off on shaky legs,

Looks for her stick,
Opens the outside door,
Calls home dead dogs.

ALISON PRYDE

Lucky

If you are lucky in this life,
you will get to help your enemy
the way I got to help my mother
when she was weakened past the point of saying no.

Into the big enamel tub
half-filled with water
which I had made just right,
I lowered the childish skeleton
she had become.

Her eyelids fluttered as I soaped and rinsed
her belly and her chest,
the sorry ruin of her flanks
and the frayed gray cloud
between her legs.

Some nights, sitting by her bed
book open in my lap
while I listened to the air
move thickly in and out of her dark lungs,
my mind filled up with praise
as lush as music,

amazed at the symmetry and luck
that would offer me the chance to pay
my heavy debt of punishment and love
with love and punishment.

And once I held her dripping wet
in the uncomfortable air
between the wheelchair and the tub,
until she begged me like a child

to stop,
an act of cruelty which we both understood
was the ancient irresistible rejoicing
of power over weakness.

If you are lucky in this life,
you will get to raise the spoon
of pristine, frosty ice cream
to the trusting creature mouth
of your old enemy

because the tastebuds at least are not broken
because there is a bond between you
and sweet is sweet in any language.

TONY HOAGLAND

Brilliance

Maggie's taking care of a man
who's dying; he's attended to everything,
said goodbye to his parents,

paid off his credit card.
She says *Why don't you just
run it up to the limit?*

but he wants everything
squared away, no balance owed,
though he misses the pets

he's already found a home for
– he can't be around dogs or cats,
too much risk. He says,

I can't have anything.
She says, *A bowl of goldfish?*

He says he doesn't want to start

with anything and then describes
the kind he'd maybe like,
how their tails would fan

to a gold flaring. They talk
about hot jewel tones,
gold lacquer, say maybe

they'll go pick some out
though he can't go much of anywhere and then
abruptly he says *I can't love*

anything I can't finish.
He says it like he's had enough
of the whole scintillant world,

though what he means is
he'll never be satisfied and therefore
has established this discipline,

a kind of severe rehearsal.
That's where they leave it,
him looking out the window,

her knitting as she does because
she needs to do something.
Later he leaves a message:

Yes to the bowl of goldfish.
Meaning: let me go, if I have to,
in brilliance. In a story I read,

a Zen master who'd perfected
his detachment from the things of the world
remembered, at the moment of dying,

a deer he used to feed in the park,
and wondered who might care for it,
and at that instant was reborn

in the stunned flesh of a fawn.
So, Maggie's friend –
is he going out

into the last loved object
of his attention?
Fanning the veined translucence

of an opulent tail,
undulant in some uncapturable curve,
is he bronze chrysanthemums,

copper leaf, hurried darting,
doubloons, icon-colored fins
troubling the water?

MARK DOTY

Flames

A red setter leaping
constant up and down, up-and-down,
like a big, living flame
in a dark slum room
where an old poor woman lies in bed sick,
the heat cut off the light cut off,
her only light her only heat
the red-gold setter leaping
tireless up and down like a tall
sinuous brilliant almost healing flame.

Never such buoyancy, never!

A long skinnymalink with auburn hair
loose-limbed in his mid-thirties
immaculate in a flame-coloured suit,
leaping up and down, up-and-down,
like a loose-haired flame
in a bar at the head of the Zeedijk
at one in the morning as Justin
played planxties on the penny-whistle.
Such Amsterdancing! He couldn't get enough of it.
Vertical wavering, a grace, a flame.

Never such buoyancy, never!

PEARSE HUTCHINSON

The Very Rich Hours

(for Dave Royle, 1960-1996)

His window frames our pictured, distanced city:
people, traffic, countless other windows,
the very rich hours of the land of the living.

Inside the golden sun illuminates
four vases of flowers, a plastic water-jug,
dust motes in the vacancy, and Dave in a red chair.

I sit facing his level, absent gaze
the muscles of anger and pleasure have withered to;
he does not know me: I hardly know him.

Each morning he is cradled in a bath;
his cigarettes burn down to his finger-tips;
all I can do for him is tap the ash.

Pitched against the gym's weights and measures,
discovered in the fluencies of the showers,
his body seemed to me a worked perfection;

he used it for spare cash and for the stories;
up cranky Soho stairwells, in gas-fire rooms
he modelled for "amateur photographers"

who tested him up close with their light meters,
and composed him – athletic, classical –
held still, *'Poetry!'*, for their camera fire.

Between a bureau de change and a cigarette kiosk
he'd return to London's arcane A-Z
of night life, bars, punters, strangers and friends;

there were dark back-rooms and moonless midnight parks,
shadows in the margins, the casual glory of skin;
desire, not the sorrow of desire.

Now mortality has become familiar;
his friends are dying, or gathered here, or both,
in this book of hours and hours of smoking and waiting

to turn the page; and nothing to be done
except to stay, so simple and difficult. Leaving,
I picture him for the last time, for myself;

his window discloses a dark, deserted city;
the traffic lights are changing on their own;
the moon repeats itself in countless windows.

The silenced TV casts its blue and silver,
the world's text, irrelevantly across
the parchment of his dream-skin;

the tattoed swallow soars from his right arm
and his slight weight; may tomorrow's sunlight
shine right through to illuminate his heart:

a Proper of Time, a brief history, a love story.

NICK DRAKE

The Embrace

You weren't well or really ill yet either;
just a little tired, your handsomeness
tinged by grief or anticipation, which brought
to your face a thoughtful, deepening grace.

I didn't for a moment doubt you were dead.
I knew that to be true still, even in the dream.
You'd been out – at work maybe? –
having a good day, almost energetic.

We seemed to be moving from some old house
where we'd lived, boxes everywhere, things
in disarray: that was the *story* of my dream,
but even asleep I was shocked out of narrative

by your face, the physical fact of your face:
inches from mine, smooth-shaven, loving, alert.
Why so difficult, remembering the actual look
of you? Without a photograph, without strain?

So when I saw your unguarded, reliable face,
your unmistakable gaze opening all the warmth
and clarity of you – warm brown tea – we held
each other for the time the dream allowed.

Bless you. You came back so I could see you
once more, plainly, so I could rest against you
without thinking this happiness lessened anything,
without thinking you were alive again.

MARK DOTY

What's Left
(for Peter Hennessy)

I used to wait for the flowers,
my pleasure reposed on them.
Now I like plants before they get to the blossom.
Leafy ones – foxgloves, comfrey, delphiniums –
fleshy tiers of strong leaves pushing up
into air grown daily lighter and more sheened
with bright dust like the eyeshadow
that tall young woman in the bookshop wears,
its shimmer and crumble on her white lids.

The washing sways on the line, the sparrows pull
at the heaps of drying weeds that I've left around.
Perhaps this is middle age. Untidy, unfinished,
knowing there'll never be time now to finish,
liking the plants – their strong lives –
not caring about flowers, sitting in weeds
to write things down, look at things,
watching the sway of shirts on the line,
the cloth filtering light.

I know more or less
how to live through my life now.
But I want to know how to live what's left
with my eyes open and my hands open;
I want to stand at the door in the rain
listening, sniffing, gaping.
Fearful and joyous,
like an idiot before God.

KERRY HARDIE

poem to my uterus

you   uterus
you have been patient
as a sock
while i have slippered into you
my dead and living children
now
they want to cut you out
stocking i will not need
where i am going
where am i going
old girl
without you
uterus
my bloody print
my estrogen kitchen
my black bag of desire
where can i go
barefoot
without you
where can you go
without me

LUCILLE CLIFTON

to my last period

well girl, goodbye,
after thirty-eight years.
thirty-eight years and you
never arrived
splendid in your red dress
without trouble for me
somewhere, somehow.

now it is done,
and i feel just like
the grandmothers who,
after the hussy has gone,
sit holding her photograph
and sighing, *wasn't she*
beautiful? wasn't she beautiful?

LUCILLE CLIFTON

The Pruned Tree

As a torn paper might seal up its side,
Or a streak of water stitch itself to silk
And disappear, my wound has been my healing,
And I am made more beautiful by losses.
See the flat water in the distance nodding
Approval, the light that fell in love with statues
Seeing me alive, turn its motion toward me.
Shorn, I rejoice in what was taken from me.

What can the moonlight do with my new shape
But trace and retrace its miracle of order?
I stand, waiting for the strange reaction
Of insects who knew me in my larger self,
Unkempt, in a naturalness I did not love.
Even the dog's voice rings with a new echo,
And all the little leaves I shed are singing,
Singing to the moon of shapely newness.

Somewhere what I lost I hope is springing
To life again. The roofs, astonished by me,
Are taking new bearings in the night, the owl
Is crying for a further wisdom, the lilac
Putting forth its strongest scent to find me.
Butterflies, the sailboat's grooves, are winging
Out of the water to wash me, wash me.
Now, I am stirring like a seed in China.

HOWARD MOSS

Tomcat

This tomcat cuts across the
zones of the respectable
through fences, walls, following
other routes, his own. I see
the sad whiskered skull-mouth fall
wide, complainingly, asking

to be picked up and fed, when
I thump up the steps through bush
at 4 p.m. He has no
dignity, thank God! has grown
older, scruffier, the ash-
black coat sporting one or two

flowers like round stars, badges
of bouts and fights. The snake head
is seamed on top with rough scars:
old Samurai! He lodges
in cellars, and the tight furred
scrotum drives him into wars

as if mad, yet tumbling on
the rug looks female, Turkish-
trousered. His bagpipe shriek at
sluggish dawn dragged me out in
pyjamas to comb the bush
(he being under the vet

for septic bites): the old fool
stood, body hard as a board,
heart thudding, hair on end, at
the house corner, terrible,
yelling at something. They said,
'Get him doctored.' I think not.

JAMES K. BAXTER

The Hoist

The hoist was strange. Going up, the Nurse said,
First floor haberdashery. Stranger than that
Old word haberdashery, the way he dangled
Under the beak of it like a babe arriving,
Mute in a grim patience, his empty mouth
And his eyes tight shut as if he guarded
A fitter idea of himself in a sort of privacy.

A thing to look away from but we gawped
Like clownish witnesses of an ascension
And I thought of an old mad king still gripping
Tatters of divinity around his shoulders
Or one in a tumbril and the old folk crossing themselves
Or a pharaoh, or a lost god, when the Nurse said
Going down, and settled him in the chair and wheeled him off.

DAVID CONSTANTINE

Lore

Job Davies, eighty-five
Winters old, and still alive
After the slow poison
And treachery of the seasons.

Miserable? Kick my arse!
It needs more than the rain's hearse,
Wind-drawn, to pull me off
The great perch of my laugh.

What's living but courage?
Paunch full of hot porridge,
Nerves strengthened with tea,
Peat-black, dawn found me

Mowing where the grass grew,
Bearded with golden dew.
Rhythm of the long scythe
Kept this tall frame lithe.

What to do? Stay green.
Never mind the machine,
Whose fuel is human souls.
Live large, man, and dream small.

R.S. THOMAS

Here

Here I am in the garden laughing
an old woman with heavy breasts
and a nicely mapped face

how did this happen
well that's who I wanted to be

at last   a woman
in the old style   sitting
stout thighs apart under
a big skirt   grandchild sliding
on   off my lap   a pleasant
summer perspiration

that's my old man across the yard
he's talking to the meter reader
he's telling him the world's sad story
how electricity is oil or uranium
and so forth   I tell my grandson
run over to your grandpa   ask him
to sit beside me for a minute   I
am suddenly exhausted by my desire
to kiss his sweet explaining lips

GRACE PALEY

Who's Joking with the Photographer?
(Photographs of myself approaching seventy)

Not my final face, a map of how to get there.
Seven ages, seven irreversible layers, each
subtler and more supple than a snake's skin.
Nobody looks surprised when we slough off one
and begin to inhabit another.
Do we exchange them whole in our sleep, or
are they washed away in pieces, cheek by brow by chin,
in the steady abrasions of the solar shower?
Draw first breath, and time turns on its taps.
No wonder the newborn's tiny face crinkles and cries:
chill, then a sharp collision with light,
the mouth's desperation for the foreign nipple,
all the uses of eyes, ears, hands still to be learned
before the self pulls away in its skin-tight sphere
to endure on its own the tectonic geology of childhood.

Imagine in space-time irretrievable mothers viewing
the pensioners their babies have become.
'Well, that's life, nothing we can do about it now.'
They don't love us as much as they did, and
why should they? We have replaced them. Just as we're
being replaced by big sassy kids in school blazers.
Meanwhile, Federal Express has delivered my sixth face –
grandmother's, scraps of me grafted to her bones.

I don't believe it. Who made this mess,
this developer's sprawl of roads that can't be retaken,
high tension wires that run dangerously under the skin?
What is it the sceptical eyes are saying to the twisted lips:
ambition is a cliché, beauty a banality? In any case,
this face has given them up – old friends whose obituaries
it reads in the mirror with scarcely a regret.

So, who's joking with the photographer?
And what did she think she was doing,
taking pictures of the impossible? Was a radioscope
attached to her lens? Something teasing under the skull
has infiltrated the surface, something you can't see
until you look away, then it shoots out and tickles you.
You could call it soul or spirit, but that would be serious.
Look for a word that mixes affection with insurrection,
frivolity, child's play, rude curiosity,
a willingness to lift the seventh veil and welcome Yorick.
That's partly what the photo says. The rest is private,
guilt that rouses memory at four in the morning,
truths such as Hamlet used, torturing his mother,
all the dark half-tones of the sensuous unsayable
finding a whole woman there, in her one face.

ANNE STEVENSON

Weathering

Literally thin-skinned, I suppose, my face
catches the wind off the snow-line and flushes
with a flush that will never wholly settle. Well:
that was a metropolitan vanity,
wanting to look young for ever, to pass.

I was never a Pre-Raphaelite beauty,
nor anything but pretty enough to satisfy
men who need to be seen with passable women.
But now that I am in love with a place
which doesn't care how I look, or if I'm happy,

happy is how I look, and that's all.
My hair will turn grey in any case,
my nails chip and flake, my waist thicken,
and the years work all their usual changes.
If my face is to be weather-beaten as well

that's little enough lost, a fair bargain
for a year among lakes and fells, when simply
to look out of my window at the high pass
makes me indifferent to mirrors and to what
my soul may wear over its new complexion.

FLEUR ADCOCK

3 A.M.

I remember the last red rose
and that it darkened a little
every day, drawing into itself
almost black at the end in its
bright green bottle
on the white sill by the kitchen window,
and the winter weather waning
the garden greening, beyond –
I remember it died, months ago.

The last hard clasp of hands
and the standing together
in the blue winter twilight
with infinite gentleness talking
inconsequentially through
someone's silent weeping – that too
is over; we scattered long ago
to our afternoon houses
to work and to sleep.

But the night is querulous and full
of arrangements; composing
answers to letters, remembering
obligations, I am held as
at a dull meeting; dry-eyed,
tired-minded, I hear no voices

but the night wind
meddling at the silence.

In a great sorrow we are helpless:
children, we trust the pitiless stars
to lead us by the hand; this small
darkness is a shut room.
It is not pain we fear, but triviality.

LAURIS EDMOND

The Shade

A summer cold. No rash. No fever. Nothing. But a dozen times
    during the night I wake
to listen to my son whimpering in his sleep, trying to snort the
    sticky phlegm out of his nostrils.
The passage clears, silence, nothing. I cross the room, groping for
    the warm,
elusive creature of his breath and my heart lunges, stutters, tries
    to race away;
I don't know from what, from my imagination, from life itself, maybe
    from understanding too well
and being unable to do anything about how much of my anxiety
    is always for myself.
Whatever it was, I left it when the dawn came. There's a park near
    here
where everyone who's out of work in our neighborhood comes to
    line up in the morning.
The converted school buses shuttling hands to the cannery fields
    in Jersey were just rattling away when I got there
and the small-time contractors, hiring out cheap walls, cheap ditches,
    cheap everything,
were loading laborers onto the sacks of plaster and concrete in the
    backs of their pickups.
A few housewives drove by looking for someone to babysit or clean
    cellars for them,
then the gates of the local bar unlaced and whoever was left drifted
    in out of the wall of heat
already rolling in with the first fists of smoke from the city incin-
    erators.

It's so quiet now, I can hear the sparrows foraging scraps of garbage
    on the paths.
The stove husk chained as a sign to the store across the street creaks
    in the last breeze of darkness.
By noon, you'd have to be out of your mind to want to be here:
    the park will reek of urine,
bodies will be sprawled on the benches, men will wrestle through
    the surf of broken bottles,
but even now, watching the leaves of the elms softly lifting toward
    the day, softly falling back,
all I see is fear forgiving fear on every page I turn; all I know is every
    time I try to change it,
I say it again: my wife, my child...my home, my work, my sorrow.
If this were the last morning of the world, if time had finally moved
    inside us and erupted
and we were Agamemnon again, Helen again, back on that faint,
    beginning planet
where even the daily survivals were giants, filled with light, I think
    I'd still be here,
afraid or not enough afraid, silently howling the litanies of death
    over the grass and asphalt.
The morning goes on, the sun burning, the earth burning, and
    between them, part of me lifts and starts back,
past the wash of dead music from the bar, the drinker reeling on
    the curb, the cars coughing alive,
and part, buried in itself, stays, forever, blinking into the glare,
    freezing.

C.K. WILLIAMS

Dune Road, Southampton

The murderer has been injecting her remorselessly
With succinylcholine, which he mixes in her daily insulin.
She's too weak to give herself her shots. By the time she has
    figured it out,
She is helpless.

She can't move any part of her face.
She can't write a note.
She can't speak
To say she hasn't had a stroke.

It's terrifying that she's aware
That something terrible is being done to her.
One day he ups the dose. And gets scared.
She has to be rushed to the local hospital and intubated.

They know at the hospital who she is,
One of the richest women in the world.
The murderer hands the attending a faked M.R.I.
It flaunts the name of a world authority. Showing she has had a stroke.

The neurologist on call introduces herself to the murderer and concurs.
Locked-in Syndrome, just about the worst
Alive, with staring eyes.
The mind is unaffected.

And with the patient looking on expressionlessly,
Screaming don't let him take me home, without a sign or sound,
The doctor tells the murderer he can take her home,
If that's their wish.

Their little beach house has forty rooms.
Her elevator is carved mahogany.
The Great Gatsby swimming pool upstairs is kept full and never used.
Her tower bedroom flies out over the winter ocean, spreading its wings.

Mother, you're going to die,
He tells her, once they're alone.
You have the right to remain silent.
I'm making a joke.

I'll read you your rights.
He takes a syringe.
A woman has the right to bare arms. I particularly like them bare.
I might as well be talking to cement.

FREDERICK SEIDEL

The Box

79 years in a cast-iron box
in the basement of an old hotel
that was once the best in Donegal –
and only the porter could open the lock
to reveal what was in the box
and you wouldn't have guessed for a gillion
that a broken-up skeleton was in there
holding its skull in its hands,
with its legs folded beneath it,
and in the box alongside it
a yellowy scroll of pig's leather
sound as the day it was tanned.

It fell to the hotel manager
to read the scroll. A throat-clearing,
then a voice: *Here sits folded*
Magnus McLaughlin, who did
more skitterish deeds in his life
than an English blackguard,
and so I built this box myself
to keep him in, and I chopped him
with the cleaver I kept for pork
and you should have seen the blood.
She paused, and added *March 1913.*
And we all stared at the box.

MATTHEW SWEENEY

The Murderer Is a Cow

He killed in a cow mask.
Discovering tents in the forest at night

He cut through the canvas
Like ripping open a letter

To find the sleepy human
Contents which he knifed.

From her snug sleeping
Bag all the tourist could see

Were the twitching ears of a cow
And a blade as the murderer

Paddled on all fours
On the drenched groundsheet.

And when all the movement had stopped,
Still with his invented face

He blew warm steam from his
Slippery nostrils and licked

With the single muscle of his tongue
The gore.

And then moved off into the forest
Where real cows stepped quietly among

The trees, their careful feet now
And then cracking twigs until his

Shovelling nose came across the green
Membrane of another tent

Where, within, a half asleep hiker
Breathed a sigh of relief

That cows and not killers
Sniffed tents in the forest.

GERARD WOODWARD

Moving House

Bubble-wrap the chimney like a vase,
its bouquet of wilted smoke
tipped out, and pack the slates
the way you'd box a brittle set of books.
You'll find the attic can't be moved
once the sky floods in, though another will appear
when the last trickle's wrung from the new roof
and the dark takes place between the rafters.

Flat-pack each room, careful not to tear
the windows away from their views:
they must be eased on to their fresh prospects
to keep their perspectives true;
lead the bath out by the plug chain,
its tin legs squealing, and poke the electricity
from its hole with a forked stick,
pinning it to the ground by the throat.

Carry the doors on your backs,
for they've leant so heavily against the world
they deserve this one good turn;
the foundations will make their own way –
tap the ground gently when you arrive
and they'll rise to the surface like worms
after rain.
                    Should you not have time to memorise
these instructions, to squeeze all the air

out of the stairs;
should you be so utterly unprepared
as to leave your house behind,
rooms thrown around their walls
by the bare bulbs swinging in your wake;
should you have nowhere to set those thoughts,
fumbled at the beginning of the day
and caught again in a sunlit doorway,

nowhere for the table and chairs to stretch
their old shadows every afternoon

or the floorboards to query each footstep –
bury them, deep in the woods,
and fashion new ones by the glow
of your little camp fire, as wolves howl
high in the snow-covered hills
and the stars whistle over your head.

JACOB POLLEY

This room

This room is breaking out
of itself, cracking through
its own walls
in search of space, light,
empty air.

The bed is lifting out of
its nightmares.
From dark corners, chairs
are rising up to crash through clouds.

This is the time and place
to be alive:
when the daily furniture of our lives
stirs, when the improbable arrives.
Pots and pans bang together
in celebration, clang
past the crowd of garlic, onions, spices,
fly by the ceiling fan.
No one is looking for the door.

In all this excitement
I'm wondering where
I've left my feet, and why

my hands are outside, clapping.

IMTIAZ DHARKER

Kindness

Before you know what kindness really is
you must lose things,
feel the future dissolve in a moment
like salt in a weakened broth.
What you held in your hand,
what you counted and carefully saved,
all this must go so you know
how desolate the landscape can be
between the regions of kindness.
How you ride and ride
thinking the bus will never stop,
the passengers eating maize and chicken
will stare out the window forever.

Before you learn the tender gravity of kindness,
you must travel where the Indian in a white poncho
lies dead by the side of the road.
You must see how this could be you,
how he too was someone
who journeyed through the night with plans
and the simple breath that kept him alive.

Before you know kindness as the deepest thing inside,
you must know sorrow as the other deepest thing.
You must wake up with sorrow.
You must speak to it till your voice
catches the thread of all sorrows
and you see the size of the cloth.

Then it is only kindness that makes sense anymore,
only kindness that ties your shoes
and sends you out into the day to mail letters and purchase bread,
only kindness that raises its head
from the crowd of the world to say
It is I you have been looking for,
and then goes with you everywhere
like a shadow or a friend.

NAOMI SHIHAB NYE

7

Daily Round

Poetry connects us to what is deepest in ourselves. It gives us
access to our own feelings, which are often shadowy, and
engages us in the art of making meaning. It widens the space
of our inner lives. It is a magical, mysterious, inexplicable
(though not incomprehensible) event in language.

EDWARD HIRSCH

DAILY ROUND brings together poems charting modern urban life, the tribula-
tions of work and the city. The poems at the end of the section relate to earlier
daily rounds, to the rhythms of the seasons, work on the land and other kinds
of hardships.

Contemporary poems about city living often concentrate on the negative
side, not just in relation to people's lives but also the physical environment.
Many poets are drawn to writing about destruction and demolition, degradation
and urban squalor, alienation and loss of community. But there are also many
poets who celebrate particular cities in their work: Roy Fisher's Birmingham
(in *City* and *Birmingham River*, neither of which lend themselves to extracts),
Brendan Kennelly's Dublin (321) and Ciaran Carson's Belfast (323), as well as
Larkin's Hull (but his locations aren't specific). Other poems in this section are
set in London (Ken Smith), Manchester (David Constantine), Toronto (Roo
Borson), San Francisco (Thom Gunn) and Jersey City (August Kleinzahler).
Philip Levine and Jack Gilbert revisit the heavy industrial cities where they
grew up (Detroit and Pittsburgh) in many poems in their collections.

Cities have been compared in literature (as well as film) to Hell, especially
the big industrial cities, and many poems about the London Underground and
subway systems elsewhere use Dante's Hell as a central metaphor. In Helen
Dunmore's poem 'To Virgil' she calls for assistance from Dante's guide, and
the Tube features in other poems here by Maura Dooley (316) and Jo Shapcott
(316). Dante's Hell is also invoked in 'Grief' (314) by American poet William
Matthews, which opens with line spoken by one of the damned in his *Inferno*
('*E detto l'ho perche doler ti debbia*') which reappears as the clinching final line
translated into English: '*And I have told you this to make you grieve.*'

Orkney's George Mackay Brown remakes the seasonal myth of John Barley-
corn in his ballad (347), a tale echoed in Grace Nichols' Caribbean story of
'Sugar Cane' (349), where violence done to the crop invites identification with
the harsh treatment of the peasant workers, who were originally slaves.

The Way

There is the world, we say, and mean a kind
of mechanism, big machine that stands
there mornings when we come on. We check the gauge
and pull a lever we learned to pull, and wait,
and stuff comes out. We put stuff in. And wait.
Nights, we go home and rest. After a while of this,
we stop; and, mornings, someone else comes on.

This is a way we made to look at things.
The way is always there, you can bank on that,
though the flow of the slot is fuller here or there
or it dwindles away. We scheme then, over moves
to make more stuff come out, or a trick technique
to overlay whole sections like a new
machine, devise a way: it works somehow.

These changes are written down: what ones were made
and who served where and when – how many days.
It makes it seem more real except that real
is what it doesn't seem at all: the skips
at night, the end a blank. What went wrong?
It isn't the way things are, but only a way
we made to look at things, among various ways.

It has rewards: the pellets of food we get
are the soothing boon of problems and problems solved
because they were solvable. We grasp at that.
We wish it might be so who sleep and die
– do what we call those names, not knowing what
we do, yet wanting a life outside the one
that sleeping drifts towards, death illuminates.

WILLIAM BRONK

The Nerve

Somewhere at the side of the rough shape
your life makes in your town,
    you cross a line,
    perhaps

in a dusty shop you pause in, or a bar
you never tried, and a smell
    will do as well;
    then you're

suddenly very far from what you know.
You found it as a child,
    when the next field
    to you

was the world's end, a breeze of being gone.
Now it begins to give,
    a single nerve,
    low down:

it sags, as if it felt the gravity
at long last. You are chilled
    to have been told
    that way —

but you ought to recognise it, it's the one
that may well fail one day,
    fail utterly,
    go wrong,

be Judas, while the others, without thought
of you, or of your pain,
    show no sign,
    are mute,

assume they're safe with you. Treasure the nerve
suggesting otherwise;
    treasure its dis-
    belief:

it's straining to see the outline of somewhere
inhospitable,
    with other rules,
    unfair

and arbitrary, something to endure,
which nonetheless you spot,
    contemplate,
    start for;

where you will face the choices that the nerve
has suffered: to be plucked
    and, for that act
    of love,

to have brought the soldiers running; to lie low,
and, for that act of fear,
    have perished years
    ago.

GLYN MAXWELL

Killing Time #2

Time in the brain cells swearing like a nail bomb,
trouble with the heartbeat spitting like a Sten gun,
    cut to the chase,
    pick up the pace;
no such thing as a walkabout fun-run,
    shoot yourself a glance in the chrome in the day-room.
don't hang about, you're running out of space, son.

Red light, stop sign, belly full of road rage,
ticket from the fuzz if you dawdle in the slow lane,
    pull up your socks,
    get out of the blocks;
twelve-hour day-shift grafting at the coal face,
    turning up the gas brings blood to the boat race,
strike with the iron or you're sleeping in the stone age.

Don't dilly dally or the trail goes cold, sir,
don't hold back till you're mouldy old dough, sir,
    sprint for the line,
    turn on a dime;
sit tight, hang fire, I'm putting you on hold, sir,
    too late, snail pace, already sold, sir,
blame it on the kids but it's you getting old, sir.

Short cut, fast track, trolley dash at Kwik Save,
four minute warning, boil yourself an egg, babe,
    crack the whip,
    shoot from the hip;
close shave, tear arse, riding on a knife blade,
    twenny-four-seven in the brain-drain rat race,
finger on the pulse but you'd better watch your heart rate.

Cheap thrills, speed kills, pop yourself a pill, mate,
thumb a free ride on amphetamine sulphate,
    run with the pack,
    don't look back;
pedal to the floor when you're burning up the home straight,
    her indoors doesn't want you getting home late,
love's in the freezer and your dinner's in the dog-grate.

Ten to the dozen to the grave from the carry-cot,
bolt like a thoroughbred, talk like a chatterbox,
    oil the wheels,
    pick up your heels;
ginseng tea turns out to be tommyrot,
    reach for the future with a hand full of liver-spots,
fuse-wire burns in the barrel of a body-clock.

Cut yourself in half doing life at the sharp end,
meet your own self coming back around the U-bend,
    get with the beat,
    turn up the heat;
sink like a stone by going off the deep end,
    fifty quid an hour for a top-flight shrink, said
start killing time, it's later than you think, friend.

SIMON ARMITAGE

Bagpipe music

It's no go the merrygoround, it's no go the rickshaw,
All we want is a limousine and a ticket for the peepshow.
Their knickers are made of crêpe-de-chine, their shoes are made of
    python,
Their halls are lined with tiger rugs and their walls with heads of
    bison.

John MacDonald found a corpse, put it under the sofa,
Waited till it came to life and hit it with a poker,
Sold its eyes for souvenirs, sold its blood for whisky,
Kept its bones for dumb-bells to use when he was fifty.

It's no go the Yogi-Man, it's no go Blavatsky,
All we want is a bank balance and a bit of skirt in a taxi.

Annie MacDougall went to milk, caught her foot in the heather,
Woke to hear a dance record playing of Old Vienna.
It's no go your maidenheads, it's no go your culture,
All we want is a Dunlop tyre and the devil mend the puncture.

The Laird o' Phelps spent Hogmanay declaring he was sober,
Counted his feet to prove the fact and found he had one foot over.
Mrs Carmichael had her fifth, looked at the job with repulsion,
Said to the midwife 'Take it away; I'm through with over-production'.

It's no go the gossip column, it's no go the Ceilidh,
All we want is a mother's help and a sugar-stick for the baby.

Willie Murray cut his thumb, couldn't count the damage,
Took the hide of an Ayrshire cow and used it for a bandage.
His brother caught three hundred cran when the seas were lavish,
Threw the bleeders back in the sea and went upon the parish.

It's no go the Herring Board, it's no go the Bible,
All we want is a packet of fags when our hands are idle.

It's no go the picture palace, it's no go the stadium,
It's no go the country cot with a pot of pink geraniums,
It's no go the Government grants, it's no go the elections,
Sit on your arse for fifty years and hang your hat on a pension.

It's no go my honey love, it's no go my poppet;
Work your hands from day to day, the winds will blow the profit.
The glass is falling hour by hour, the glass will fall for ever,
But if you break the bloody glass you won't hold up the weather.

LOUIS MacNEICE

Life

Life gives
        us something
to live for:
        we will do
whatever it takes
        to make it last.
Kill in just wars
        for its survival.
Wolf fast-food
        during half-time breaks.
Wash down
        chemical cocktails,
as prescribed.
        Soak up
hospital radiation.
        Prey on kidneys
at roadside pile-ups.
        Take heart
from anything
        that might
conceivably grant it
        a new lease.
We would give
        a right hand
to prolong it.
        Cannot imagine
living without it.

DENNIS O'DRISCOLL

City Lights

To board the train for Toronto and glance over at the other
tracks as that train starts rolling and the woman there,
opposite, dozing, opens her eyes.
To look into eyes and know there are many directions.
To have it all at once: cinnamon buns
from the Harbord Bakery and the late poems of Wang Wei.
To step out, bringing traffic to a halt.
To bemoan with total strangers the state of the lettuce,
to be queried concerning the uses of star fruit,
and expostulate thereon.
To guide an unsteady gentleman across the street
and refuse payment in eternity.
To happen on the long light down certain streets as the sun is
          setting,
to pass by all that tempts others without a thought.
For cigar smoke and Sony Walkmans and random belligerence,
the overall sense of delighted industry
which is composed of idle hatred, inane self-interest,
compassion, and helplessness, when looked at closely.
To wait in queues, anonymous as the price code in a supermarket.
To board a bus where everyone is talking at once,
and count eight distinct languages and not know any.
For the Chinese proprietress of the Bagel Paradise Restaurant,
who is known to her customers as the joyful
otter is known to the clear salt water of Monterey Bay.
To know that everyone who isn't reading, daydreaming,
or on a first date is either full of plans or
playing Sherlock Holmes on the subway.
For eerie cloudlit nights, and skyscrapers,
and raccoons, jolly as bees.
For the joy of walking out the front door and becoming
instantly, and resolutely, lost.
To fall, when one is falling,
into a safety net, and find one's friends.
To be one among many.
To be many.

ROO BORSON

Snow in North Jersey

Snow is falling along the Boulevard
and its little cemeteries hugged by transmission shops
and on the stone bear in the park
and the WWI monument, making a crust
on the soldier with his chin strap and bayonet
It's blowing in from the west
over the low hills and meadowlands
swirling past the giant cracking stills
that flare all night along the Turnpike
It is with a terrible deliberateness
that Mr Ruiz reaches into his back pocket
and counts out $18 and change for his LOTTO picks
while in the upstairs of a thousand duplexes
with the TV on, cancers tick   tick   tick
and the snow continues to fall and blanket
these crowded rows of frame and brick
with their heartbreaking porches and castellations
and the red '68 Impala on blocks
and Joe he's drinking again and Myra's boy Tommy
in the old days it would have been a disgrace
and Father Keenan's not been having a good winter
and it was nice enough this morning
till noon anyhow with the sun sitting up there like a crown
over a great big dome of mackerel sky
But it's coming down now, all right
falling on the Dixon-Crucible Pencil factory
and on the spur to Bayonne
along the length of the Pulaski Skyway
and on St Bridget's and the Alibi Saloon
closed now, 'ho dear, I can't remember how long
and lordjesussaveus they're still making babies
and what did you expect from this life
and they're calling for snow tonight and through tomorrow
an inch an hour over 9 Ridge Road and the old courthouse
and along the sluggish, gray Passaic
as it empties itself into Newark Bay
and on Grandpa's store that sells curries now
and St Peter's almost made it to the semis this year

It's snowing on the canal and railyards, the bus barns and trucks
and on all the swells in their big houses along the river bluff
It's snowing on us all
and on a three-story *fix-up* off of Van Vorst Park
a young lawyer couple from Manhattan bought
where for no special reason in back of a closet
a thick, dusty volume from the '30s sits open
with a broken spine and smelling of mildew
to a chapter titled *Social Realism*

AUGUST KLEINZAHLER

Grief

> *E detto l'ho perche doler ti debbia*
> DANTE
> Inferno, XXIV, 151

Snow coming in parallel to the street,
a cab spinning its tires (a rising whine
like a domestic argument, and then
the words get said that never get forgot),

slush and backed-up runoff waters at each
corner, clogged buses smelling of wet wool...
The acrid anger of the homeless swells
like wet rice. *This slop is where I live, bitch*,

a sogged panhandler shrieks to whom it may
concern. But none of us slows down for scorn;
there's someone's misery in all we earn.
But like a bur in a dog's coat his rage

has borrowed legs. We bring it home. It lives
like kin among the angers of the house,
and leaves the same sharp zinc taste in the mouth:
And I have told you this to make you grieve.

WILLIAM MATTHEWS

314

To Virgil

Lead me with your cold, sure hand,
make me press the correct buttons
on the automatic ticket machine,
make me not present my ticket upside down
to the slit mouth at the barriers,

then make the lift not jam
in the hot dark of the deepest lines.
May I hear the voice on the loudspeaker
and understand each syllable
of the doggerel of stations.

If it is rush-hour, let me be close to the doors,
I do not ask for space,
let no one crush me into a corner
or accidentally squeeze hard on my breasts
or hit me with bags or chew gum in my face.

If there are incidents, let them be over,
let there be no red-and-white tape
marking the place, make it not happen
when the tunnel has wrapped its arms around my train
and the lights have failed.

Float me up the narrow escalator
not looking backward, losing my balance
or letting go of your cold, sure hand.
Let there not be a fire
in the gaps, hold me secure.
Let me come home to the air.

HELEN DUNMORE

315

Mind the Gap

We have settled on either side of a bridge, under arches,
medieval, Dickensian or twentieth-century. Over the bridge
a flutter of commuters, under the bridge the Thames,
beside the bridge a nest of survivors in cardboard.
Heading North, at night, with a suitcase and new coat
you hear rats in the Underground scratching over what's left,
a recorded voice   calling   Mind the Gap   Mind the Gap.

That swift, sad jump is replayed second by second
in the corner of your eye. But why today when sunlight
made the river almost lovely? Perhaps because it put him
beyond stomach pump or reason and when the sun
came out he was blinded by sorrow, hung up like sheets
for the wind to fill, billowing out over London, gathering dirt.
O take him down, bring him in, bundle him up in time,

before the clouds gather, before the rain comes.

MAURA DOOLEY

My Life Asleep

Everything is loud: the rasp of bed-sheets,
clamour of hair-tangles, clink of teeth.
Small sweat takes up residence in each crease
of the body, but breathing's even, herself warm,
room safe as a London room can be.
The tube rumbles only metres underneath
and planes for Heathrow circle on the roof.
You'll find the body and all the air it exhales
smellier than by day; she's kinder, more supple.
Bend close to catch the delicacies of sleep,
to hear skin tick, to taste the mandragora
of night sweat. Lean forward and put a finger
on the spot you think the dream is.

JO SHAPCOTT

New Year Behind the Asylum

There was the noise like when the men in droves
Are hurrying to the match only this noise was
Everybody hurrying to see the New Year in
In town under the clock but we, that once,

He said would I come our usual Saturday walk
And see it in out there in the open fields
Behind the asylum. Even on sunny days
How it troubled me more and more the nearer we got

And he went quiet and as if he was ashamed
For what he must always do, which was
Go and grip the bars of the iron gates and stand
Staring into the garden until they saw him.

They were like the animals, so glad and shy
Like overgrown children dressed in things
Handed down too big or small and they came in a crowd
And said hello with funny chunnering noises

And through the bars, looking so serious,
He put his empty hand out. But that night
We crept past quickly and only stopped
In the middle of the empty fields and there

While the clock in the square where the normal people stood
And all the clocks in England were striking twelve
We heard the rejoicings for the New Year
From works and churches and the big ships in the docks

So faint I wished we were hearing nothing at all
We were so far away in our black fields
I felt we might not ever get back again
Where the people were and it was warm, and then

Came up their sort of rejoicing out of the asylum,
Singing or sobbing I don't know what it was
Like nothing on earth, their sort of welcoming in
Another New Year and it was only then

When the bells and the cheerful hooters couldn't be heard
But only the inmates, only the poor mad people
Singing or sobbing their hearts out for the New Year
That he gripped me fast and kissed my hair

And held me in against him and clung on tight to me
Under a terrible number of bare stars
So far from town and the lights and house and home
And shut my ears against the big children crying

But listened himself, listened and listened
That one time. And I've thought since and now
He's dead I'm sure that what he meant was this:
That I should know how much love would be needed.

DAVID CONSTANTINE

Great Things Have Happened

We were talking about the great things
that have happened in our lifetimes;
and I said, 'Oh, I suppose the moon landing
was the greatest thing that has happened
in my time.' But, of course, we were all lying.
The truth is the moon landing didn't mean
one-tenth as much to me as one night in 1963
when we lived in a three-room flat in what once had been
the mansion of some Victorian merchant prince
(our kitchen had been a clothes closet, I'm sure),
on a street where by now nobody lived
who could afford to live anywhere else.
That night, the three of us, Claudine, Johnnie and me,
woke up at half-past four in the morning
and ate cinnamon toast together.

'Is that all?' I hear somebody ask.

Oh, but we were silly with sleepiness
and, under our windows, the street-cleaners
were working their machines and conversing in Italian, and

everything was strange without being threatening,
even the tea-kettle whistled differently
than in the daytime: it was like the feeling
you get sometimes in a country you've never visited
before, when the bread doesn't taste quite the same,
the butter is a small adventure, and they put
paprika on the table instead of pepper,
except that there was nobody in this country
except the three of us, half-tipsy with the wonder
of being alive, and wholly enveloped in love.

ALDEN NOWLAN

Night Taxi
(for Rod Taylor, wherever he is)

Open city
uncluttered as a map.
I drive through empty streets
scoured by the winds
of midnight. My shift
is only beginning and I am fresh
and excitable, master of the taxi.
I relish my alert reflexes
where all else
is in hiding. I have
by default it seems
conquered me a city.

My first address: I
press the doorbell, I lean back
against the hood, my headlights
scalding a garage door, my engine
drumming in the driveway,
the only sound on the block.
There the fare finds me
like a date, jaunty,
shoes shined, I am
proud of myself, on my toes,
obliging but not subservient.

I take short cuts, picking up
speed, from time to time
I switch on the dispatcher's
litany of addresses,
China Basin to Twin Peaks,
Harrison Street to the Ocean.

I am thinking tonight
my fares are like affairs
– no, more like tricks to turn:
quick, lively, ending up
with a cash payment.
I do not anticipate a holdup.
I can make friendly small talk.
I do not go on about Niggers,
women drivers or the Chinese.
It's all on my terms but
I let them think it's on theirs.

Do I pass through the city
or does it pass through me?
I know I have to be loose,
like my light embrace of the wheel,
loose but in control
– though hour by hour I tighten
minutely in the routine,
smoking my palate to ash,
till the last hour of all
will be drudgery, nothing else.

I zip down Masonic Avenue,
the taxi sings beneath the streetlights
a song to the bare city, it is
my instrument, I woo with it,
bridegroom and conqueror.

I jump out to open the door,
fixing the cap on my head
to, you know, firm up my role,
and on my knuckle
feel a sprinkle of wet.

Glancing upward I see
high above the lamppost
but touched by its farthest light
a curtain of rain already blowing
against black eucalyptus tops.

THOM GUNN

Message on the machine

Your protagonist is not at home just now.
He's out, a one-way window in his head
with everything coming in fast across the city
and always an alarm bell ringing in the buildings,

a jammed horn streets away, the town winds
lifting documents along the Broadway,
along Commercial Road a signboard
banging in the night reads *Smack*

Disposal Systems, he fears skinheads
in the drains and angels in the elevator
and the number 5 bus will never come now.
After the tone leave a brief message.

KEN SMITH

Clearing a Space

A man should clear a space for himself
Like Dublin city on a Sunday morning
About six o'clock.
Dublin and myself are rid of our traffic then
And I'm walking.

Houses are solitary and dignified
Streets are adventures
Twisting in and out and up and down my mind.
The river is talking to itself
And doesn't care if I eavesdrop.

No longer cluttered with purpose
The city turns to the mountains
And takes time to listen to the sea.
I witness all three communing in silence
Under a relaxed sky.

Bridges look aloof and protective.
The gates of the parks are closed
Green places must have their privacy too.
Office-blocks are empty, important and a bit
Pathetic, if they admitted it!

The small hills in this city are truly surprising
When they emerge in that early morning light.
Nobody has ever walked on them,
They are waiting for the first explorers
To straggle in from the needy north

And squat down here this minute
In weary legions
Between the cathedral and the river.
At the gates of conquest, they might enjoy a deep
Uninterrupted sleep.

To have been used so much, and without mercy,
And still to be capable of rediscovering
In itself the old nakedness
Is what makes a friend of the city
When sleep has failed.

I make through that nakedness to stumble on my own,
Surprised to find a city is so like a man.
Statues and monuments check me out as I pass
Clearing a space for myself the best I can,
One Sunday morning, in the original sun, in Dublin.

BRENDAN KENNELLY

Clearance

The Royal Avenue Hotel collapses under the breaker's pendulum:
Zigzag stairwells, chimney-flues, and a 'thirties mural
Of an elegantly-dressed couple doing what seems to be the Tango,
    in Wedgewood
Blue and white – happy days! Suddenly more sky
Than there used to be. A breeze springs up from nowhere –

There, through a gap in the rubble, a greengrocer's shop
I'd never noticed until now. Or had I passed it yesterday? Everything –
Yellow, green and purple – is fresh as paint. Rain glistens on the
    aubergines
And peppers; even from this distance, the potatoes smell of earth.

CIARAN CARSON

Turn Again

There is a map of the city which shows the bridge that was never
    built.
A map which shows the bridge that collapsed; the streets that never
    existed.
Ireland's Entry, Elbow Lane, Weigh-House Lane, Back Lane,
    Stone-Cutter's Entry –
Today's plan is already yesterday's – the streets that were there are
    gone.
And the shape of the jails cannot be shown for security reasons.

The linen backing is falling apart – the Falls Road hangs by a
    thread.
When someone asks me where I live, I remember where I used to
    live.
Someone asks me for directions, and I think again. I turn into
A side-street to try to throw off my shadow, and history is changed.

CIARAN CARSON

In Spite of Everything, the Stars

Like a stunned piano, like a bucket
of fresh milk flung into the air
or a dozen fists of confetti
thrown hard at a bride
stepping down from the altar,
the stars surprise the sky.
Think of dazed stones
floating overhead, or an ocean
of starfish hung up to dry. Yes,
like a conductor's expectant arm
about to lift toward the chorus,
or a juggler's plates defying gravity,
or a hundred fastballs fired at once
and freezing in midair, the stars
startle the sky over the city.

And that's why drunks leaning up
against abandoned buildings, women
hurrying home on deserted side streets,
policemen turning blind corners, and
even thieves stepping from alleys
all stare up at once. Why else do
sleepwalkers move toward the windows,
or old men drag flimsy lawn chairs
onto fire escapes, or hardened criminals
press sad foreheads to steel bars?
Because the night is alive with lamps!
That's why in dark houses all over the city
dreams stir in the pillows, a million
plumes of breath rise into the sky.

At midnight the soul dreams of a small fire
of stars flaming on the other side of the sky,
but the body stares into an empty night sheen,
a hollow-eyed darkness. Poor luckless angels,
feverish old loves: don't separate yet.
Let what rises live with what descends.

EDWARD HIRSCH

Searching for Pittsburgh

The fox pushes softly, blindly through me at night,
between the liver and the stomach. Comes to the heart
and hesitates. Considers and then goes around it.
Trying to escape the mildness of our violent world.
Goes deeper, searching for what remains of Pittsburgh
in me. The rusting mills sprawled gigantically
along three rivers. The authority of them.
The gritty alleys where we played every evening were
stained pink by the inferno always surging in the sky,
as though Christ and the Father were still fashioning
the Earth. Locomotives driving through the cold rain,
lordly and bestial in their strength. Massive water
flowing morning and night throughout a city
girded with ninety bridges. Sumptuous-shouldered,
sleek thighed, obstinate and majestic, unquenchable.
All grip and flood, mighty sucking and deep-rooted grace.
A city of brick and tired wood. Ox and sovereign spirit.
Primitive Pittsburgh. Winter month after month telling
of death. The beauty forcing us as much as harshness.
Our spirits forged in that wilderness, our minds forged
by the heart. Making together a consequence of America,
The fox watched me build my Pittsburgh again and again.
In Paris afternoons on Buttes-Chaumont. On Greek islands
with their fields of stone. In beds with women, sometimes,
amid their gentleness. Now the fox will live in our ruined
house. My tomatoes grow ripe among weeds and the sound
of water. In this happy place my serious heart has made.

JACK GILBERT

Zombies

1980, I was returned to the city exposed
in black and white as the lights went on and on.
A back-alley neon sign, the first I'd seen,
drew us sweetly down and in to brightness:

a doll's parasol, a spike of green cherries,
the physic of apricot brandy, actual limes
and morning-to-night shades of rum.
Newly old enough and government-moneyed,
we knocked them back, melting the ice
between us and the unaccustomed looseness
of being legitimate and free. What possessed us?
Was it the kick of spirits or the invisible syrup
in which they swam that worked in our veins,
charming us into a car and forty miles east

to the fields of our years of boredom...
Did we not remember the curse of this place?
How Sundays drank our blood as we watched
dry paint or the dust on the television screen.
How people died bursting out of a quiet life,
or from being written into a small world's stories.
Who can see such things and live to tell?
How we hunted all night for noise and love,
striking out once across ploughed and frozen earth,
lurching from rut to rut until at the edge
we smashed our way out through a hedge, to fall
eight feet to the road. Of course, we felt nothing.
Was it not ourselves who frightened us most?
As if brightness or sweetness could save us.

LAVINIA GREENLAW

Home

when all is said and done
what counts is having someone
you can phone at five to ask

for the immersion heater
to be switched to 'bath'
and the pizza taken from the deepfreeze

DENNIS O'DRISCOLL

What Work Is

We stand in the rain in a long line
waiting at Ford Highland Park. For work.
You know what work is – if you're
old enough to read this you know what
work is, although you may not do it.
Forget you. This is about waiting,
shifting from one foot to another.
Feeling the light rain falling like mist
into your hair, blurring your vision
until you think you see your own brother
ahead of you, maybe ten places.
You rub your glasses with your fingers,
and of course it's someone else's brother,
narrower across the shoulders than
yours but with the same sad slouch, the grin
that does not hide the stubbornness,
the sad refusal to give in to
rain, to the hours wasted waiting,
to the knowledge that somewhere ahead
a man is waiting who will say, 'No,
we're not hiring today,' for any
reason he wants. You love your brother
now suddenly you can hardly stand
the love flooding you for your brother,
who's not beside you or behind or
ahead because he's home trying to
sleep off a miserable night shift
at Cadillac so he can get up
before noon to study his German.
Works eight hours a night so he can sing
Wagner, the opera you hate most,
the worst music ever invented.
How long has it been since you told him
you loved him, held his wide shoulders,
opened your eyes wide and said those words,
and maybe kissed his cheek? You've never
done something so simple, so obvious,
not because you're too young or too dumb,
not because you're jealous or even mean

or incapable of crying in
the presence of another man, no,
just because you don't know what work is.

PHILIP LEVINE

Alive or Not

It's like a story
because it takes so long to happen:

a block away on an Ottawa street
I see this woman about to fall
and she collapses slowly
in sections the way you read about
and there just might be time
for me to reach her
running as fast as I can
before her head hits the sidewalk
Of course it's my wife
I am running toward her now
and there is a certain amount of horror
a time lag in which other things happen
I can almost see flowers break into blossom
while I am running toward the woman
my wife it seems
orchids in the Brazilian jungle
exist like improvable ideas
until a man in a pith helmet
steps on one and yells Eureka or something
– and while I am thinking about this
her body splashes on the street
her glasses fall broken beside her
with a musical sound under the traffic
and she is probably dead too
Of course I cradle her in my arms
a doll perhaps without life
while someone I do not know

signals a taxi
as the bystanders stare
What this means years later
as I grow older and older
is that I am still running toward her:
the woman falls very slowly
she is giving me more and more time
to reach her and make the grab
and each time each fall she may die
or not die and this will go on forever
this will go on forever and ever
As I grow older and older
my speed afoot increases
each time I am running and reach
the place before she falls every time
I am running too fast to stop
I run past her farther and farther
it's almost like a story
as an orchid dies in the Brazilian jungle
and there is a certain amount of horror

AL PURDY

At the Florist's

A man enters a florist's
and chooses some flowers
the florist wraps up the flowers
the man puts his hand in his pocket
to find the money
the money to pay for the flowers
but at the same time he puts
all of a sudden
his hand on his heart
and he falls

At the same time that he falls
the money rolls on the floor
and then the flowers fall

at the same time as the man
at the same time as the money
and the florist stands there
with the money rolling
with the flowers spoiling
with the man dying
obviously all this is very sad
and she's got to do something
the florist
but she doesn't know quite where to start
she doesn't know
at which end to begin

There's so many things to do
with this man dying
with these flowers spoiling
and this money
this money that rolls
that doesn't stop rolling.

JACQUES PRÉVERT
translated from the French by Lawrence Ferlinghetti

Her Retirement

Just a little party, nothing swank,
I told the founder, but you know Mr B.
There are so many of you here to thank.

I leave you the later tube trains, dank
At the hand-rails from a human sea,
Dreaming down to Morden via Bank.

I've homed quietly to port while others sank,
By keeping at my stenography.
There are so many of you here to thank.

I scan the backs of houses, rank on rank:
The comfy lamps, the oblique misery
Streaming down to Morden via Bank.

Our gardens keep us from the abyss, I think.
With the cheque I'll buy a trellis, or a tree.
There are so many of you here to thank.

And unaccustomed as I am to drink,
I toast you all who follow me
– There are so many of you here to thank –
In dreaming down to Morden, via Bank.

ANNE ROUSE

Toads

Why should I let the toad *work*
    Squat on my life?
Can't I use my wit as a pitchfork
    And drive the brute off?

Six days of the week it soils
    With its sickening poison –
Just for paying a few bills!
    That's out of proportion.

Lots of folk live on their wits:
    Lecturers, lispers,
Losels, loblolly-men, louts –
    They don't end as paupers;

Lots of folk live up lanes
    With fires in a bucket,
Eat windfalls and tinned sardines –
    They seem to like it.

Their nippers have got bare feet,
    Their unspeakable wives
Are skinny as whippets – and yet
    No one actually *starves*.

Ah, were I courageous enough
   To shout *Stuff your pension!*
But I know, all too well, that's the stuff
   That dreams are made on:

For something sufficiently toad-like
   Squats in me, too;
Its hunkers are heavy as hard luck,
   And cold as snow,

And will never allow me to blarney
   My way to getting
The fame and the girl and the money
   All at one sitting.

I don't say, one bodies the other
   One's spiritual truth;
But I do say it's hard to lose either,
   When you have both.

PHILIP LARKIN

The Panic Bird

just flew inside my chest. Some
days it lights inside my brain,
but today it's in my bonehouse,
rattling ribs like a birdcage.

If I saw it coming, I'd fend it
off with machete or baseball bat.
Or grab its scrawny hackled neck,
wring it like a wet dishrag.

But it approaches from behind.
Too late I sense it at my back –
carrion, garbage, excrement.
Once inside me it preens, roosts,

vulture on a public utility pole.
Next it flaps, it cries, it glares,
it rages, it struts, it thrusts
its clacking beak into my liver,

my guts, my heart, rips off strips.
I fill with black blood, black bile.
This may last minutes or days.
Then it lifts sickle-shaped wings,

rises, is gone, leaving a residue –
foul breath, droppings, molted midnight
feathers. And life continues.
And then I'm prey to panic again.

ROBERT PHILLIPS

Managing the Common Herd:
two approaches for senior management

THEORY X: People are naturally lazy.
They come late, leave early, feign illness.
When they sit at their desks
it's ten to one they're yakking to colleagues
on the subject of who qualifies as a gorgeous hunk.
They're coating their lips and nails with slop,
a magazine open to 'What your nails say about you'
or 'Ten exercises to keep your bottom in top form'
under this year's annual report.
These people need punishment;
they require stern warnings
and threats – don't be a coward,
don't be intimidated by a batting eyelash.
Stand firm: a few tears, a Mars Bar,
several glasses of cider with her pals tonight
and you'll be just the same old
rat-bag, mealy-mouthed, small-minded tyrant
you were before you docked her
fifteen minutes pay for insubordination.

Never let these con-artists get the better of you.

THEORY Z: Staff need encouragement.
Give them a little responsibility
and watch their eager faces lighting up.
Let them know their input is important.
Be democratic – allow all of them
their two cents worth of gripes.
(Don't forget this is the Dr Spock generation.)
If eight out of twelve of them
prefer green garbage cans to black ones
under their desks, be generous –
the dividends in productivity
will be reaped with compound interest.
Offer incentives, show them
it's to their *own* advantage to meet targets.
Don't talk down to your employees.
Make staff believe that they
have valid and innovative ideas
and that not only are you interested,
but that you will act upon them.

Remember, they're human too.

JULIE O'CALLAGHAN

Fight Song

Sometimes you have to say it:
Fuck them all.

Yes fuck them all –
the artsy posers,
the office blowhards
and brown-nosers;

Fuck the type who gets the job done
and the type who stands on principle
the down-to-earth and understated;
the overhyped and underrated;

Project director?
Get a bullshit detector.

Client's mum?
Up your bum.

You can't be nice to everyone.

When your back is to the wall
When they don't return your call
When you're sick of saving face
When you're screwed in any case

Fuck culture scanners, contest winners,
subtle thinkers and the hacks who offend them;
people who give catered dinners
and (saddest of sinners) the sheep who attend them –

which is to say fuck yourself
and the person you were: polite and mature,
a trooper for good. The beauty is
they'll soon forget you

and if they don't
they probably should.

DEBORAH GARRISON

A Malediction

Spawn of a profligate hog.
May the hand of your self-abuse
be afflicted by a palsy.
May an Order in Council
deprive you of a testicle.
May your teeth be rubbed with turds
by a faceless thing from Grimsby.

May your past begin to remind you
of an ancient butter paper
found lying behind a fridge.
May the evil odour of an elderly male camel
fed since birth on buckets of egg mayonnaise
enter your garden and shrivel up all your plants.
May all reflective surfaces
henceforth teach you to shudder.
And may you thus be deprived
of the pleasures of walking by water.
And may you grow even fatter.
And may you, moreover, develop athlete's foot.
May your friends cease to excuse you,
your wife augment the thicket of horns on your brow,
and even your enemies weary of malediction.
May your girth already gross
embark on a final exponential increase.
And at the last may your body, in bursting,
make your name live for ever,
an unparalleled warning to children.

PETER DIDSBURY

Some People
(for Eoin)

Some people know what it's like,

to be called a cunt in front of their children
to be short for the rent
to be short for the light
to be short for school books
to wait in Community Welfare waiting-rooms full of smoke
to wait two years to have a tooth looked at
to wait another two years to have a tooth out (the same tooth)
to be half strangled by your varicose veins, but you're
198th on the list
to talk into a banana on a jobsearch scheme
to talk into a banana in a jobsearch dream

to be out of work
to be out of money
to be out of fashion
to be out of friends
to be in for the Vincent de Paul man
to be in space for the milk man
(sorry, mammy isn't in today she's gone to Mars for the weekend)
to be in Puerto Rico this week for the blanket man
to be in Puerto Rico next week for the blanket man
to be dead for the coal man
(sorry, mammy passed away in her sleep, overdose of coal
in the teapot)
to be in hospital unconscious for the rent man
(St Judes ward 4th floor)
to be second-hand
to be second-class
to be no class
to be looked down on
to be walked on
to be pissed on
to be shat on

and other people don't.

RITA ANN HIGGINS

TV

All the preachers claimed it was Satan.
Now the first sets seem more venerable
Than Abraham or Williamsburg
Or the avant-garde. Back then nothing,

Not even the bomb, had ever looked so new,
It seemed almost heretical watching it
When we visited relatives in the city,
Secretly delighting, but saying later,

After church, probably it would not last,
It would destroy things: standards
And the sacredness of words in books.
It was well into the age of color,

Korea and Little Rock long past,
Before anyone got one. Suddenly some
Of them in the next valley had one.
You would know them by their lights

Burning late at night, and the recentness
And distance of events entering their talk,
But not one in our valley; for a long time
No one had one, so when the first one

Arrived in the van from the furniture store
And the men had set the box on the lawn,
At first we stood back from it, circling it
As they raised its antenna and staked in

The guy-wires before taking it in the door,
And I seem to recall a kind of blue light
Flickering from inside and then a woman
Calling out that they had got it tuned in –

A little fuzzy, a ghost picture, but something
That would stay with us, the way we hurried
Down the dirt road, the stars, the silence,
Then everyone disappearing into the houses.

RODNEY JONES

The Way We Live

In rooms whose lights
On winter evenings
Make peepshows of our lives –

Behind each window
A stage so cluttered up
With props and furniture

It's not surprising
We make a mess of what began
So simply with *I love you.*

Look at us: some
Slumped in chairs
And hardly ever speaking

And others mouthing
The same tired lines to ears
That long ago stopped listening.

Once we must have dreamed
Or something better.
But even those who swapped

One partner for another
Have ended up
Just like the rest of us:

Behind doors, moving outside
Only to go to work
Or spend weekends with mother.

VICKI FEAVER

Every Blessed Day

First with a glass of water
tasting of iron and then
with more and colder water
over his head he gasps himself
awake. He hears the *cheep*
of winter birds searching
the snow for crumbs of garbage
and knows exactly how much light
and how much darkness is there
before the dawn, gray and weak,
slips between the buildings.

Closing the door behind him,
he thinks of places he
has never seen but heard
about, of the great desert
his father said was like
no sea he had ever crossed
and how at dusk or dawn
it held all the shades of red
and blue in its merging shadows,
and though his life was then
a prison he had come to live
for these suspended moments.
Waiting at the corner he feels
the cold at his back and stamps
himself awake again. Seven miles
from the frozen, narrow river.
Even before he looks he knows
the faces on the bus, some
going to work and some coming back,
but each sealed in its hunger
for a different life, a lost life.
Where he's going or who he is
he doesn't ask himself, he
doesn't know and doesn't know
it matters. He gets off
at the familiar corner, crosses
the emptying parking lots
toward Chevy Gear & Axle #3.
In a few minutes he will hold
his time card above a clock,
and he can drop it in
and hear the moment crunching
down, or he can not, for
either way the day will last
forever. So he lets it fall.
If he feels the elusive calm
his father spoke of and searched
for all his short life, there's
no way of telling, for now he's
laughing among them, older men
and kids. He's saying, 'Damn,
we've got it made.' He's

lighting up or chewing with
the others, thousands of miles
from their forgotten homes, each
and every one his father's son.

PHILIP LEVINE

Pity the Bastards

for Billy and Tadhg

who lived in the eternal bastard present all their lives,
knew bulldozed boundaries and ancient names
for fields and had no names themselves apart
from Christian names, who cycled miles to Mass
in market towns the livestock saw more often
than themselves, and swayed up boreens, pristine
in their Sunday best and pissed when the God of Churches
refused to let them do the hard work they were born to do.

Pity the bastards who clamped buck rabbits' heads
between their legs and funnelled *poitín* into them
until they bucked, the wide sky shrivelling in their
pissed eyes, who swore blind that spirits sweetened
the meat, bled them through their scraped-out holes
for eyes and tugged the fur off over skulls like tugging
crew-necked knitted jumpers over children's heads.

Pity the bastards who hunted free-range eggs in sheds
and bore them back in their flat caps like promises
or secrets, who worked for fags and died of lung complaints,
cows withholding milk for days because they missed
the rough, familiar touch, the singing in their flanks;
who tested suspect hay in sheds with bare arms slipped
between the haunches of the bales to feel, like a vet

buried to the armpit in a heifer, who grabbed at sops
like the wet heels of a runt calf and pulled and felt the crop
contract against the strain, clench against them,
scald them and relax; who did not need to be told twice

341

if a scum had built that the crop would light if it wasn't
dumped and torched that night, the way you dumped
the runt to save the heifer, who satisfied themselves

with saving sheds some summers instead of hay.
Pity the bastards who loved to leave their yard boots
on the loft stairs and stand to their ankles in the deep grain,
taking to turning it and falling into the rhythm
of the chore, the wheat trench dug and borne
across the boards to break against one gable end
and double back, *ad infinitum*, the glint and dust and brunt

of indoor work, when called for tea was to be called
back from the brink, the trance of being knee-deep
in it and rowing for their lives, of wheat waves
breaking on the upstairs walls, who turned
an ancient jumper inside out to break the trance
and went down for their tea, who put on boots
and felt like they had slipped off wings. *Pity the bastards*

who loved to stand out in a fine mist, to touch the damp
warmth stored on the undersides of stones; masters
or the punchline and the soundbite – 'What would you do
with the jawbone of an ass?', the answer roared
to scandalise the woman of the house, 'Kill thousands!';
who kept the billhook shone to keep the wound
it made from going septic, who hot-wired Zetors,

tampered with the diaphragms of chainsaws
and gave so long on all fours thinning mangolds
it often slipped their minds that they were men;
who owned no clothes except the clothes they wore,
were known for not being able to harm a fly and meant
no harm when they grabbed the hand of a married
brother's girl and rammed it down inside the waist-

band of a working pants where nature hardened
like a pickaxe handle. *Pity the bastards* and the
youngster sprinting from an outhouse in the dark,
her hand aloft like a torch to light the way,
whose nipples pinched by an uncle stung for days
under a blue school blouse, who knew to say
nothing. *Pity the bastards* landlocked all their

342

lives, who took a row boat out on a calm lake
once and felt brute power flow into the oars,
whose lungs ignited with a cold lake air, who,
once or twice, caught the drift of it and got it right,
whose bulk became all cut and thrust and heave,
on whom the dip and drip of blades conferred
a sense of having slipped into the stream of things,

who strained and stroked and rowed till
they were flat out, limbered up and numbed,
who came around and scrambled for the bank
and learned the farther inland they could see
the farther out from land they went, who abandoned
oars at the boathouse door, stowed the craft
on her stanchions and felt it as a kind of grace

when the hoisted shell assumed its given mass.
Pity the bastards who perfected the dead-butt
from the back wall, predicted the foul hop
kept a clear eye on the dropping ball, a cool head
in defence, who swore by pesticides, believed in land,
supported Man United all their lives and suffered
Munich as a personal disaster, who took off

Elvis in the local after closing and cried like
children when he died, whose shit-caked boots
were as close as they ever came to blue suede shoes.
Pity the bastards who voted for Europe in the local
national schools where masters hammered
'seventeen different colours of shit' out of them
on a regular basis and, and, in the process, educated them,

who never got to grips with 'quotas'
because they loved churns, who understood
instinctively that milk likes peace and curdles
if disturbed, to leave it in the draught between
two doors, who dipped fingers in it to the wrist
to coax an ailing weanling into drinking.
Pity the bastards whose winters made them

good at lighting fires, who kicked Moroccan
orange crates to bits for tinder, whose mothers
were their sisters and their fathers rogues,
who lived in dread of County Homes and dreamed

of dying in their own beds, who loved the epic
feat of memory and recollected all the Presidents
of the United States in order of incumbency,

the dates of the battles of Clontarf and Hastings,
who treated cows at milking time to every line
of 'A bunch of the boys were whooping it up
at the Malamute saloon', emasculated cattle
with a steel Burdizzo and took malicious pleasure
in fingering the testicles expertly, like devotees
fingering shrivelled leather purses for their beads,

who remembered the headland of the field
they were working in precisely when Kennedy
got that high velocity bullet in the head
and fantasised about what they'd do to Oswald.
Pity the bastards who knew the knack with
landing a good punch was to time it right,
who karate-chopped rabbits to put them out

of their misery, who smeared Swarfega into
injured skins and loved the stink of it, who were
anti-Christ butchers when it came to roses
but thought a law protecting gentians sound.
Pity the bastards who were stuck to the ground
by a hard frost once like Gulliver, who spent
their lifetimes travelling sixteen acres extensively,

who spoke no language only English and thought
it lovely when the young ones picked up German.
Pity the bastards who cut crops from the centre
out to give the corncrakes time to make a break,
who dandled concertinas on their knees like babies
and loved the only note the wind could play
on the top of a gate because it had no fingers,

who loved to sing 'Put another nickel in
the nickelodeon', and didn't know what
the words they were singing meant, and cared
less. *Pity the bastards* who slept in extra rooms
they helped build, in beds that smelled of fields
and sheds, who vividly recalled the automatic
Telecom exchange when it was Carey's forge,

who sacrificed one lung to TB or the God
of nicotine, who coughed until they coughed
blood, who thought themselves lucky. *Pity*
the bastards who bore the full weight of a bull
on their chests once and wore the gouged-out
hollows of its legs like negative breasts
and never claimed they'd got the better

of the beast but missed him when the sergeant
stopped out with a captive bolt in a cardboard box
to drop the old stud at his manger on the spot,
who prayed for the creature that had wanted them
dead because it knew no better, and only said
they'd smelled the breath of death that reeked,
they said, of meadowsweet, wild flowers, ramsey,

half-digested grass. *Pity the bastards* whose Requiem
Masses were long, convoluted, concelebrated affairs
attended by kin who went into the Church
and wound up on the Missions in Brazil.
And pity them, because they left behind them
nothing, and took their names, and if they played
could imitate a hurt plover or a baby wailing

by pressing a rusty latch key against the strings,
who heard the waves at evening breaking in the key
of E, who went into the lakes, the earth, the sea,
holding stones inside their clothes like infants
to their chests, whistling into sheds with homemade ropes,
who took more jigs and reels and slow airs with them
than a human could play in a lifetime, to their graves.

TOM FRENCH

Photographs of Pioneer Women

You can see from their faces
Life was not funny,
The streets, when there were streets,
Tugging at axles,
The settlement ramshackle as a stack of cards.

And where there were no streets, and no houses,
Save their own roof of calico or thatch,
The cows coming morning and afternoon
From the end-of-world swamp,
Udders cemented with mud.

There is nothing to equal pioneering labour
For wrenching a woman out of shape,
Like an old willow, uprooted, thickening.
See their strong arms, their shoulders broadened
By the rhythmical swing of the axe, or humped
Under loads they donkeyed on their backs.
Some of them found time to be photographed,
With bearded husband, and twelve or thirteen children,
Looking shocked, but relentless,
After first starching the frills in their caps.

RUTH DALLAS

Names of Horses

All winter your brute shoulders strained against collars, padding
and steerhide over the ash hames, to haul
sledges of cordwood for drying through spring and summer,
for the Glenwood stove next winter, and for the simmering range.

In April you pulled cartloads of manure to spread on the fields,
dark manure of Holsteins, and knobs of your own clustered with oats.
All summer you mowed the grass in meadow and hayfield, the
        mowing machine
clacketing beside you, while the sun walked high in the morning;

and after noon's heat, you pulled a clawed rake through the same acres,
gathering stacks, and dragged the wagon from stack to stack,
and the built hayrack back, uphill to the chaffy barn,
three loads of hay a day from standing grass in the morning.

Sundays you trotted the two miles to church with the light load
of a leather quartertop buggy, and grazed in the sound of hymns.
Generation on generation, your neck rubbed the windowsill
of the stall, smoothing the wood as the sea smooths glass.

When you were old and lame, when your shoulders hurt bending
    to graze,
one October the man, who fed you and kept you, and harnessed you
    every morning,
led you through corn stubble to sandy ground above Eagle Pond,
and dug a hole beside you where you stood shuddering in your skin,

and lay the shotgun's muzzle in the boneless hollow behind your ear,
and fired the slug into your brain, and felled you into your grave,
shoveling sand to cover you, setting goldenrod upright above you,
where by the next summer a dent in the ground made your monument.

For a hundred and fifty years, in the pasture of dead horses,
roots of pine trees pushed through the pale curves of your ribs,
yellow blossoms flourished above you in autumn, and in winter
frost heaved your bones in the ground – old toilers, soil makers:

O Roger, Mackerel, Riley, Ned, Nellie, Chester, Lady Ghost.

DONALD HALL

The Ballad of John Barleycorn,
The Ploughman, and the Furrow

As I was ploughing in my field
The hungriest furrow ever torn
Followed my plough and she did cry
'Have you seen my mate John Barleycorn?'

Says I, 'Has he got a yellow beard?
Is he always whispering night and morn?
Does he up and dance when the wind is high?'
Says she, 'That's my John Barleycorn.

One day they took a cruel knife
(O, I am weary and forlorn!)
They struck him at his golden prayer.
They killed my priest, John Barleycorn.

347

They laid him on a wooden cart,
Of all his summer glory shorn,
And threshers broke with stick and stave
The shining bones of Barleycorn.

The miller's stone went round and round,
They rolled him underneath with scorn,
The miller filled a hundred sacks
With the crushed pride of Barleycorn.

A baker came by and bought his dust.
That was a madman, I'll be sworn.
He burned my hero in a rage
Of twisting flames, John Barleycorn.

A brewer came by and stole his heart.
Alas, that ever I was born!
He thrust it in a brimming vat
And drowned my dear John Barleycorn.

And now I travel narrow roads,
My hungry feet are dark and worn,
But no one in this winter world
Has seen my dancer Barleycorn.'

I took a bannock from my bag.
Lord, how her empty mouth did yawn!
Says I, 'Your starving days are done,
For here's your lost John Barleycorn.'

I took a bottle from my pouch,
I poured out whisky in a horn.
Says I, 'Put by your grief, for here
Is the merry blood of Barleycorn.'

She ate, she drank, she laughed, she danced.
And home with me she did return.
By candle-light in my ingle-nook
She wept no more for Barleycorn.

GEORGE MACKAY BROWN

Sugar Cane

1

There is something
about sugar cane

he isn't what
he seem –

indifferent hard
and sheathed in blades

his waving arms
is a sign for help

his skin thick
only to protect
the juice inside
himself

2

His colour
is the aura
of jaundice
when he ripe

he shiver
like ague
when it rain

he suffer
from bellywork
burning fever
and delirium

just before
the hurricane
strike
smashing him to pieces

3

Growing up
is an art

he don't have
any control of

it is us
who groom and
weed him

who stick him
in the earth
in the first place

and when he
growing tall

with the help
of the sun
and rain

we feel the
need to strangle
the life

out of him

But either way he can't survive

4

Slowly
pain-
fully
sugar
cane
pushes
his
knotted
joints
upwards
from
the
earth
slowly
pain-
fully
he
comes
to learn
the
truth
about
himself
the
crimes
committed
in
his
name

5

He cast his shadow
to the earth

the wind is
his only mistress

I hear them
moving
in rustling tones

she shakes
his hard reserve

smoothing
stroking
caressing
all his length
shamelessly

I crouch
below them
quietly

GRACE NICHOLS

Fish Tea Rice

It is on the Earth that all things transpire,
and only on the Earth. On it, up out of it,
down into it. Wading and stepping, pulling
and lifting. The heft in the seasons.

Knowledge in the bare ankle under water
amid the rows of rice seedlings. The dialogue
of the silent back and forth, the people moving
together in flat fields of water with the patina
of the sky upon it, the green shoots rising up
from the mud, sticking up seamlessly above the water.
The water buffalo stepping through as they work,
carrying the weight of their bodies along the rows.
The wrists of the people wet under the water,
planting or pulling up. It is this Earth that all
meaning is. If love unfolds, it unfolds here.
Here where Heaven shows its face. Christ's agony
flowers into grace, spikes through the hands
holding the body in place, arms reaching wide.
It breaks our heart on Earth. Ignorance mixed
with longing, intelligence mixed with hunger.
The genius of night and sleep, being awake
and at work. The sacred in the planting, the wading
in mud. Eating what is here. Fish, bread, tea, rice.

LINDA GREGG

Everything Is Going To Be All Right

How should I not be glad to contemplate
the clouds clearing beyond the dormer window
and a high tide reflected on the ceiling?
There will be dying, there will be dying,
but there is no need to go into that.
The lines flow from the hand unbidden
and the hidden source is the watchful heart.
The sun rises in spite of everything
and the far cities are beautiful and bright.
I lie here in a riot of sunlight
watching the day break and the clouds flying.
Everything is going to be all right

DEREK MAHON

The Round

Light splashed this morning
on the shell-pink anemones
swaying on their tall stems;
down blue-spiked veronica
light flowed in rivulets
over the humps of the honeybees;
this morning I saw light kiss
the silk of the roses
in their second flowering,
my late bloomers
flushed with their brandy.
A curious gladness shook me.

So I have shut the doors of my house,
so I have trudged downstairs to my cell,
so I am sitting in semi-dark
hunched over my desk
with nothing for a view
to tempt me
but a bloated compost heap,
steamy old stinkpile,
under my window;
and I pick my notebook up
and I start to read aloud
the still-wet words I scribbled
on the blotted page:
'Light splashed...'

I can scarcely wait till tomorrow
when a new life begins for me,
as it does each day,
as it does each day.

STANLEY KUNITZ

8

Lives

Sometimes a poem can change people's lives, strengthen
and focus people's beliefs. And if people can change,
that can change the world.

ADRIAN MITCHELL

LIVING HISTORY is one of the themes explored in this section, which begins
with myth and story-telling, ancestry and cultural inheritance, before going
on to trace the lives of migrants, exiles and refugees. Maya Angelou's defiant
'Still I Rise' (363) has been a clarion call for many African Americans, while
Gwendolyn Brooks' simple ballad 'Sadie and Maud' (365) manages to com-
press two whole lives into five verses. Many New Zealanders have identified
with Denis Glover's poem 'The Magpies' (366), while Paul Muldoon uses a
similarly effective nonsensical refrain in 'The Loaf' (367), which summons
the ghosts of the poor Irish migrant workers in America, many of whom left
Ireland because of famine and religious or political oppression. Vona Groarke
gets inside the lives of those caught up in the 1916 Easter Rising in 'Imperial
Measure' (368) by spicing up the role of food in that historical episode.

Imtiaz Dharker's 'Honour Killing' (376) recalls a recent incident in Lahore
when a woman was shot by her family in her lawyer's office. Her "crime" was
asking for a divorce, but the Pakistan Senate refused to condemn this 'honour
killing'. Poems by Tom Paulin (372) and Derek Mahon (373) present vividly
realised responses to religious intolerance in Northern Ireland, while Andrew
Waterhouse (374) and Peter Reading (375) use satire to attack fundamentalist
extremism. Reading's weapon in the extract from his book-length poem *Going
On* is Alcmanic verse, a metre used in Greek drama consisting of catalectic
dactylic tetrameters (see *Staying Alive* glossary, 464) whose incantatory rhythms
are deliberately and jauntily at odds with his subject-matter.

After W.H. Auden's 'Refugee Blues' (written in 1939), other poems retrace
journeys made by writers and fellow exiles, including George Szirtes' escape
from Hungary at the age of 8 after the 1956 Uprising and Choman Hardi's
flight from Kurdistan aged 14. These are followed by poems relating the loss
of language to loss of identity, and then poems showing how people's lives
are affected by conflict, change and exile by writers from different ethnic and
cultural backgrounds, including Arab poets Saadi Youssef (Iraq) and Mahmoud
Darwish (Palestine), Israel's Yehuda Amichai and Muslim Kashmiri-American
poet Agha Shahid Ali.

Lives

(for Seamus Heaney)

First time out
I was a torc of gold
And wept tears of the sun.

That was fun
But they buried me
In the earth two thousand years

Till a labourer
Turned me up with a pick
In eighteen fifty-four

And sold me
For tea and sugar
In Newmarket-on-Fergus.

Once I was an oar
But stuck in the shore
To mark the place of a grave

When the lost ship
Sailed away. I thought
Of Ithaca, but soon decayed.

The time that I liked
Best was when
I was a bump of clay

In a Navaho rug,
Put there to mitigate
The too god-like

Perfection of that
Merely human artifact.
I served my maker well –

He lived long
To be struck down in
Denver by an electric shock

354

The night the lights
Went out in Europe
Never to shine again.

So many lives,
So many things to remember!
I was a stone in Tibet,

A tongue of bark
At the heart of Africa
Growing darker and darker...

It all seems
A little unreal now,
Now that I am

An anthropologist
With my own
Credit card, dictaphone,

Army-surplus boots
And a whole boatload
Of photographic equipment.

I know too much
To be anything any more;
And if in the distant

Future someone
Thinks he has once been me
As I am today,

Let him revise
His insolent ontology
Or teach himself to pray.

DEREK MAHON

The Story

The story was not born with Robbie Cox
Nor with his father
Nor his father's father
But farther back than any could remember.

Cox told the story
Over twelve nights of Christmas.
It was the story
Made Christmas real.
When it was done
The new year was in,
Made authentic by the story.
The old year was dead,
Buried by the story.
The man endured,
Deepened by the story.

When Cox died
The story died.
Nobody had time
To learn the story.
Christmas shrivelled,
The old year was dust,
The new year nothing special,
So much time to be endured.

The people withered.
This withering hardly troubled them.
The story was a dead crow in a wet field,
An abandoned house, a rag on a bush,
A sick whisper in a dying room,
The shaking gash of an old man's mouth
Breaking like burnt paper
Into black ashes the wind scatters,
People fleeing from famine.
Nobody has ever heard of them.
Nobody will ever speak for them.

I know the emptiness
Spread by the story's death.

This emptiness is in the roads
And in the fields,
In men's eyes and children's voices,
In summer nights when stars
Play like rabbits behind Cox's house,
House of the story
That once lived on lips
Like starlings startled from a tree,
Exploding in a sky of revelation,
Deliberate and free.

BRENDAN KENNELLY

Transmutation
(FROM *Might a Shape of Words*)

Every evening a mother makes up another episode of the same story for her son. The next morning, he retells it to his grandmother who in turn can't resist relaying his account to her daughter, and also his detailed speculation as to what might happen: how the princess might escape from the castle, who she might meet in the forest.

The boy begins to realise the role of his grandmother but says nothing, scarcely able to contain himself with delight, certainly not able to decide which is the more wonderful: the continued uncertainty as to how it may develop or the recognition of his own fantasies given substance by the voice of another.

GAEL TURNBULL

Acting

I most remember the class where we lie
on our backs, on the cold floor, eyes closed, listening
to a story set in tall grasses, a land of flash floods.

Ten babies slept in a wagon as a stream risen from nothing
trampled like white horses toward them.
We heard the horses, pulling their terrible silence.
Then he asked us to open our eyes. Our teacher
took from his pocket an orange square, dropped it:
this had wrapped one of the babies.
This was found after the water receded.

I remember the woman with red hair
kneeling before the scarf, afraid to touch it,
our teacher telling her she could stop
by saying, *OK, Good.*
I remember the boy named Michael, who
once told me he loved me. Michael
approached with tiny steps, heel to toe,
as if he were measuring land,
and, all at once, he fell
on the scarf. It could have been funny,
loud, clumsy. Another context, another moment,
it would have been ridiculous.
Head down, he held the scarf to his eyes.

My turn, I didn't move. I stared
at the orange scarf, but not as long
as I'd have liked to, for this was a class
and there were others in line for their grief.
I touched it, lightly, with one hand,
folded it into a square, a smaller square, smaller.

What is lived in a life?
Our teacher making up that story
as he watched us lie on the dusty floor,
our rising, one by one,
to play with loss, to practice,
what is *lived, to live*? What was that desire
to move through ourselves to the orange
cotton, agreed upon, passed
from one to another?

SUZANNE CLEARY

The sea question

The sea asks 'How is your life now?'
It does so obliquely, changing colour.
It is never the same on any two visits.

It is never the same in any particular
Only in generalities: tide and such matters
Wave height and suction, pebbles that rattle.

It doesn't presume to wear a white coat
But it questions you like a psychologist
As you walk beside it on its long couch.

ELIZABETH SMITHER

The Sea

One night the tide went out
and never came back in
its shoals of moonlight lost
beyond our horizon.

We woke to a desert
a salt-crusted silence.
For weeks the churches were full.
Then they were empty.

The sea became a myth
our thin children don't believe in.
They mock our obsolete knowledge
of trade winds and currents.

They turn their backs on the docks
where the boats are all sinking,
white masts leaning at angles
like a forest of dying birches.

We grow long-sighted
watching for sails
in the shimmering heat.
We fall asleep

listening to shells.

ESTHER MORGAN

No Problem, But Not Easy

This is the Green Man
He lives at the corner of Hello Street and Goodbye.
He lives in a house, Alchemy House.

When you stand close to him
He is surely a man, you can see that
Sometimes, even, he has a beard.

And there are times when you see him
From afar, say, from across the room
He is also a woman.

Now, she is the Green Woman.
This is the way it is.

Sometimes he is friendly
Always in a hurry to be singing.
Sometimes she is not unfriendly
She is full of lightness, and music.

And there are times when he is quite terrible
Full of fire, you had better watch out.
And sometimes she is quite bossy
Even wicked, be careful.

Which is the way it is.

And you know, sometimes even they go to war.
There is destruction all over the place.

And of course there are times
When they lie down in each other's arms
And they touch each other again and again

And this is the way it is:
No problem, but not easy.

MICHAEL HARLOW

Seder Night with My Ancestors

On this night,
my ancestors arrive,
uninvited but expected,
to have their usual word.

They sit around the table
but refuse my offer of food.

I switch the television off
and wait,
the air thickening
with disapproval.

At last I ask them:
What do you want from me?
What have you got to do with me?
Why do you come here, every year
on this night?

And what do they say?

They say:
For this God brought us forth from Egypt?
For this we starved in the desert?
For this we fled the inquisition?
For this we fled the pogroms?

Did we die
refusing unclean meat
for you to fill your fridge with filth?

Did we disguise
our Hebrew prayers
with Christian melodies
so that you could forget them?

For you we did these things?
Do you think the Lord
would have thought you worth saving?

I say that all I want
is to live my life.

Without us you would have no life.

JOANNE LIMBURG

The Dacca Gauzes

> *...for a whole year he sought to accumulate*
> *the most exquisite Dacca gauzes*
> OSCAR WILDE,
> The Picture of Dorian Gray

Those transparent Dacca Gauzes
known as woven air, running
water, evening dew:

a dead art now, dead over
a hundred years. 'No one
now knows,' my grandmother says,

'what it was to wear
or touch that cloth.' She wore
it once, an heirloom sari from

her mother's dowry, proved
genuine when it was pulled, all
six yards, through a ring.

362

Years later when it tore,
many handkerchiefs embroidered
with gold-thread paisleys

were distributed among
the nieces and daughters-in-law.
Those too now lost.

In history we learned: the hands
of weavers were amputated,
the looms of Bengal silenced,
and the cotton shipped raw
by the British to England.
History of little use to her,

my grandmother just says
how the muslins of today
seem so coarse and that only

in autumn, should one wake up
at dawn to pray, can one feel that same texture again.

One morning, she says, the air
was dew-starched: she pulled
it absently through her ring.

AGHA SHAHID ALI

Still I Rise

You may write me down in history
With your bitter, twisted lies,
You may trod me in the very dirt
But still, like dust, I'll rise.

Does my sassiness upset you?
Why are you beset with gloom?
'Cause I walk like I've got oil wells
Pumping in my living room.

Just like moons and like suns,
With the certainty of tides,
Just like hopes springing high,
Still I'll rise.

Did you want to see me broken?
Bowed head and lowered eyes?
Shoulders falling down like teardrops,
Weakened by my soulful cries?

Does my haughtiness offend you?
Don't you take it awful hard
'Cause I laugh like I've got gold mines
Diggin' in my own backyard.

You may shoot me with your words,
You may cut me with your eyes,
You may kill me with your hatefulness,
But still, like air, I'll rise.

Does my sexiness upset you?
Does it come as a surprise
That I dance like I've got diamonds
At the meeting of my thighs?

Out of the huts of history's shame
I rise
Up from a past that's rooted in pain
I rise
I'm a black ocean, leaping and wide,
Welling and swelling I bear in the tide.

Leaving behind nights of terror and fear
I rise
Into a daybreak that's wondrously clear
I rise
Bringing the gifts that my ancestors gave,
I am the dream and the hope of the slave.
I rise
I rise
I rise.

MAYA ANGELOU

Sadie and Maud

Maud went to college.
Sadie stayed at home.
Sadie scraped life
With a fine-tooth comb.

She didn't leave a tangle in.
Her comb found every strand.
Sadie was one of the livingest chits
In all the land.

Sadie bore two babies
Under her maiden name.
Maud and Ma and Papa
Nearly died of shame.

When Sadie said her last so-long
Her girls struck out from home.
(Sadie had left as heritage
Her fine-tooth comb.)

Maud, who went to college,
Is a thin brown mouse.
She is living all alone
In this old house.

GWENDOLYN BROOKS

Glasgow Schoolboys, Running Backwards

High wind...They turn their backs to it, and push.
Their crazy strides are chopped in little steps.
And all their lives, like that, they'll have to rush
Forwards in reverse, always holding their caps.

DOUGLAS DUNN

The Magpies

When Tom and Elizabeth took the farm
The bracken made their bed,
And *Quardle oodle ardle wardle doodle*
The magpies said.

Tom's hand was strong to the plough
Elizabeth's lips were red,
And *Quardle oodle ardle wardle doodle*
The magpies said.

Year in year out they worked
While the pines grew overhead,
And *Quardle oodle ardle wardle doodle*
The magpies said.

But all the beautiful crops soon went
To the mortgage-man instead,
And *Quardle oodle ardle wardle doodle*
The magpies said.

Elizabeth is dead now (it's years ago);
Old Tom went light in the head;
And *Quardle oodle ardle wardle doodle*
The magpies said.

The farm's still there. Mortgage corporations
Couldn't give it away.
And *Quardle oodle ardle wardle doodle*
The magpies say.

DENIS GLOVER

The Loaf

When I put my finger to the hole they've cut for a dimmer switch
in a wall of plaster stiffened with horsehair
it seems I've scratched a two-hundred-year-old itch

with a pink and a pink and a pinkie-pick.

When I put my ear to the hole I'm suddenly aware
of spades and shovels turning up the gain
all the way from Raritan to the Delaware

with a clink and a clink and a clinky-click.

When I put my nose to the hole I smell the flood-plain
of the canal after a hurricane
and the spots of green grass where thousands of Irish have lain

with a stink and a stink and a stinky-stick.

When I put my eye to the hole I see one holding horse dung to
      the rain
in the hope, indeed, indeed,
of washing out a few whole ears of grain

with a wink and a wink and a winkie-wick.

And when I do at last succeed
in putting my mouth to the horsehair-fringed niche
I can taste the small loaf of bread he baked from that whole seed

with a link and a link and a linky-lick.

PAUL MULDOON

Imperial Measure

*We have plenty of the best food, all the meals being as good as if
served in a hotel. The dining-room here is very comfortable.*

P.H. PEARSE, the GPO, Easter 1916, in a letter to his mother

The kitchens of the Metropole and Imperial hotels yielded
    up to the Irish Republic
their armoury of fillet, brisket, flank. Though destined for
    more palatable tongues,
it was pressed to service in an Irish stew and served on fine
    bone china
with bread that turned to powder in their mouths. Brioche,
    artichokes, tomatoes
tasted for the first time: staunch and sweet on Monday, but
    by Thursday,
they had overstretched to spill their livid plenitude on the
    fires of Sackville Street.

A cow and her two calves were commandeered. One calf was
    killed,
its harnessed blood clotting the morning like news that
    wasn't welcome
when, eventually, it came. The women managed the blood
    into black puddings
washed down with milk from the cow in the yard who smelt
    smoke on the wind
and fire on the skin of her calf. Whose fear they took for loss
    and fretted with her
until daylight crept between crossfire and the sights of
    Marrowbone Lane.

Brownies, Simnel cake, biscuits slumped under royal icing.
    Éclairs with their cream
already turned. Crackers, tonnes of them: the floor of
    Jacobs' studded with crumbs,
so every footfall was a recoil from a gunshot across town, and the
    flakes
a constant needling in mouths already seared by the one drink
    – a gross
or two of cooking chocolate, stewed and taken without
    sweetener or milk.
Its skin was riven every time the ladle dipped but, just as
    quickly, it seized up again.

Nellie Gifford magicked oatmeal and a half-crowned loaf to
    make porridge
in a grate in the College of Surgeons where drawings of field
    surgery
had spilled from Ypres to drench in wounds the whitewashed
    walls
of the lecture hall. When the porridge gave out, there was
    rice:
a biscuit-tin of it for fourteen men, a ladleful each that
    scarcely knocked
the corners off their undiminished appetites; their vast,
    undaunted thirst.

The sacks of flour ballasting the garrison gave up their
    downy protest under fire.
It might have been a fall of Easter snow sent to muffle the
    rifles or to deaden the aim.
Every blow was a flurry that thickened the air of Boland's
    Mill, so breath
was ghosted by its own white consequence. The men's
    clothes were talced with it,
as though they were newborns, palmed and swathed, their
    foreheads kissed,
their grip unclenched, their fists and arms first blessed and,
    then, made much of.

The cellars of the Four Courts were intact at the surrender,
    but the hock
had been agitated, the Riesling set astir. For years, the wines
    were sullied
with a leaden aftertaste, although the champagne had as full a
    throat as ever,
and the spirits kept their heady confidence, for all the stock-
    piled bottles
had chimed with every hit, and the calculating scales above it
    all
had had the measure of nothing, or nothing if not smoke, and
    then wildfire.

VONA GROARKE

Nostalgia

Remember the 1340s? We were doing a dance called the Catapult.
You always wore brown, the color craze of the decade,
and I was draped in one of those capes that were popular,
the ones with unicorns and pomegranates in needlework.
Everyone would pause for beer and onions in the afternoon,
and at night we would play a game called 'Find the Cow'.
Everything was hand-lettered then, not like today.

Where has the summer of 1572 gone? Brocade and sonnet
marathons were the rage. We used to dress up in the flags
of rival baronies and conquer one another in cold rooms of stone.
Out on the dance floor we were all doing the Struggle
while your sister practiced the Daphne all alone in her room.
We borrowed the jargon of farriers for our slang.
These days language seems transparent a badly broken code.

The 1790s will never come again. Childhood was big.
People would take walks to the very tops of hills
and write down what they saw in their journals without speaking.
Our collars were high and our hats were extremely soft.
We would surprise each other with alphabets made of twigs.
It was a wonderful time to be alive, or even dead.

I am very fond of the period between 1815 and 1821.
Europe trembled while we sat still for our portraits.
And I would love to return to 1901 if only for a moment,
time enough to wind up a music box and do a few dance steps,
or shoot me back to 1922 or 1941, or at least let me
recapture the serenity of last month when we picked
berries and glided through afternoons in a canoe.

Even this morning would be an improvement over the present.
I was in the garden then, surrounded by the hum of bees
and the Latin names of flowers, watching the early light
flash off the slanted windows of the greenhouse
and silver the limbs on the rows of dark hemlocks.

As usual, I was thinking about the moments of the past,
letting my memory rush over them like water
rushing over the stones on the bottom of a stream.

I was even thinking a little about the future, that place
where people are doing a dance we cannot imagine,
a dance whose name we can only guess.

BILLY COLLINS

Plague Victims Catapulted
over Walls into Besieged City

Early germ
warfare. The dead
hurled this way turn like wheels
in the sky. Look: there goes
Larry the Shoemaker, barefoot, over the wall,
and Mary Sausage Stuffer, see how she flies,
and the Hatter twins, both at once, soar
over the parapet, little Tommy's elbow bent
as if in a salute,
and his sister, Mathilde, she follows him,
arms outstretched, through the air,
just as she did on earth.

THOMAS LUX

Part of the crowd that day

They watched the pilgrims leave for Santiago
gawping by the roadside. In the harbour
watching the boats gather they knew something
was afoot, so many horses and these armed men.
Mostly it was all too difficult to believe.
They watched the stones rise in the cathedral.
They watched the stars. They watched winter
follow summer and the birds fly south again.
They watched the thieves carted up the road
to Tyburn and the beggars whipped through town.

371

They were townsfolk, craftsmen, shopkeepers,
the labouring poor who came in from the fields.
They watched the witches burn, the heretics.
They watched the ships leave for the Americas.
They were on the bridge at Sarajevo the first time.
They saw. They wondered. They shouted
burn her, hang him, slaughter the Albigensians.
They were the onlookers, the crowd a gasp runs
mouth to mouth down the grumbling street
as Marie Antoinette goes by, and this time
they are shouting for her head. There goes
the Iron Duke, there the beaten Corsican,
and this the little father of all the Russians,
this the firing squad. They were on the hills
looking down on burning Rome, and still around
when Il Duce came to town, and how they cheered.
They gawp at the hungry, they gawp at the dead.
In the end they are not spared. In their turn
everything happens to them. Of any half dozen
one has a secret vice, one an incurable disease,
one a deep faith in God and the rest don't care
one way or the other. But they see it all happen.

KEN SMITH

Desertmartin

At noon, in the dead centre of a faith,
Between Draperstown and Magherafelt,
This bitter village shows the flag
In a baked absolute September light.
Here the Word has withered to a few
Parched certainties, and the charred stubble
Tightens like a black belt, a crop of Bibles.

Because this is the territory of the Law
I drive across it with a powerless knowledge –
The owl of Minerva in a hired car.

A Jock squaddy glances down the street
And grins, happy and expendable,
Like a brass cartridge. He is a useful thing,
Almost at home, and yet not quite, not quite.

It's a limed nest, this place. I see a plain
Presbyterian grace sour, then harden,
As a free strenuous spirit changes
To a servile defiance that whines and shrieks
For the bondage of the letter: it shouts
For the Big Man to lead his wee people
To a clean white prison, their scorched tomorrow.

Masculine Islam, the rule of the Just,
Egyptian sand dunes and geometry,
A theology of rifle-butts and executions:
These are the places where the spirit dies.
And now, in Desertmartin's sandy light,
I see a culture of twigs and bird-shit
Waving a gaudy flag it loves and curses.

TOM PAULIN

Ecclesiastes

God, you could grow to love it, God-fearing, God-
    chosen purist little puritan that,
for all your wiles and smiles, you are (the
    dank churches, the empty streets,
the shipyard silence, the tied-up swings) and
    shelter your cold heart from the heat
of the world, from woman-inquisition, from the
    bright eyes of children. Yes, you could
wear black, drink water, nourish a fierce zeal
    with locusts and wild honey, and not
feel called upon to understand and forgive
    but only to speak with a bleak
afflatus, and love the January rains when they
    darken the dark doors and sink hard

into the Antrim hills, the bog meadows, the heaped
    graves of your fathers. Bury that red
bandana and stick, that banjo; this is your
    country, close one eye and be king.
Your people await you, their heavy washing
    flaps for you in the housing estates –
a credulous people. God, you could do it, God
    help you, stand on a corner stiff
with rhetoric, promising nothing under the sun.

DEREK MAHON

Now the City Has Fallen

The radio station is filled with goats,
all telephone lines recoiled to their source,
the city gates closed and locked for the last time

Women are shackled and painted red,
the men given false beards and new names;
I am *He Who Looks Nervously Behind*,
my friend is *He Who Looks Nervously Above*.
They want us all to be very nervous.

The first born of a first born has to give
an organ to God. The rich buy poor men's livers
from secret markets. There is never a shortage.

All trees are being felled as they keep heaven
from earth. The invaders eat only human flesh.
Our children are taken from us and reared
in darkness. It is unclean to wash the body,
only the soul can be touched and scoured bright.
It must be left out on the roof tops
for the sun and moon. This is the law.

ANDREW WATERHOUSE

from Going On

This is unclean: to eat turbots on Tuesdays,
tying the turban unclockwise at cockcrow,
cutting the beard in a south-facing mirror,
wearing the mitre whilst sipping the Bovril,
chawing the pig and the hen and the ox-tail,
kissing of crosses with peckers erected,
pinching of bottoms (except in a yashmak),
flapping of cocks at the star-spangled-banner,
snatching the claret-pot off of the vicar,
munching the wafer without genuflexion,
facing the East with the arse pointing backwards,
thinking of something a little bit risqué,
raising the cassock to show off the Y-fronts,
holding a Homburg without proper licence,
chewing the cud with another man's cattle,
groping the ladies – or gentry – o'Sundays,
leaving the tip on the old-plum-tree-shaker,
speaking in physics instead of the Claptrap,
failing to pay due obeisance to monkeys,
loving the platypus more than the True Duck,
death without Afterlife, smirking in Mecca,
laughing at funny hats, holding the tenet
how that the Word be but fucking baloney,
failing to laud the Accipiter which Our Lord saith is Wisdom.

Started by *Australopithecus*, these are
time-honoured Creeds (and all unHoly doubters
shall be enlightened by Pious Devices:
mayhems of tinytots, low-flying hardwares,
kneecappings, letterbombs, deaths of the firstborns,
total extinctions of infidel unclean wrong-godded others).

PETER READING

375

Honour killing

At last I'm taking off this coat,
   this black coat of a country
   that I swore for years was mine,
   that I wore more out of habit
   than design.
   Born wearing it,
   I believed I had no choice.

I'm taking off this veil,
   this black veil of a faith
   that made me faithless
   to myself,
   that tied my mouth,
   gave my god a devil's face,
   and muffled my own voice.

I'm taking off these silks,
   these lacy things
   that feed dictator dreams,
   the mangalsutra and the rings
   rattling in a tin cup of needs
   that beggared me.

I'm taking off this skin,
   and then the face, the flesh,
   the womb.

Let's see
   what I am in here
   when I squeeze past
   the easy cage of bone.

Let's see
   what I am out here,
   making, crafting,
   plotting
   at my new geography.

IMTIAZ DHARKER

Geography Lesson

Here we have the sea of children; here
A tiny piece of Europe with dark hair.
She's crying. I am sitting next to her.

Thirty yellow suns blobbed on cheap paper,
Thirty skies blue as a Smith's Salt-wrapper
Are fading in the darkness of this weeper.

She's Czechoslovakia. And all the desks
Are shaking now. The classroom window cracks
And melts. I've caught her sobs like chicken-pox.

Czechoslovakia, though I've never seen
Your cities, I have somehow touched your skin.
You're all the hurt geography I own.

CAROL RUMENS

Refugee Blues

Say this city has ten million souls,
Some are living in mansions, some are living in holes:
Yet there's no place for us, my dear, yet there's no place for us.

Once we had a country and we thought it fair,
Look in the atlas and you'll find it there:
We cannot go there now, my dear, we cannot go there now.

In the village churchyard there grows an old yew,
Every spring it blossoms anew:
Old passports can't do that, my dear, old passports can't do that.

The consul banged the table and said,
'If you've got no passport you're officially dead':
But we are still alive, my dear, but we are still alive.

Went to a committee; they offered me a chair;
Asked me politely to return next year:
But where shall we go today, my dear, but where shall we go today?

Came to a public meeting; the speaker got up and said:
'If we let them in, they will steal our daily bread';
He was talking of you and me, my dear, he was talking of you and me.

Thought I heard the thunder rumbling in the sky;
It was Hitler over Europe, saying, 'They must die';
We were in his mind, my dear, we were in his mind.

Saw a poodle in a jacket fastened with a pin,
Saw a door opened and a cat let in:
But they weren't German Jews, my dear, but they weren't German Jews.

Went down the harbour and stood upon the quay,
Saw the fish swimming as if they were free:
Only ten feet away, my dear, only ten feet away.

Walked through a wood, saw the birds in the trees;
They had no politicians and sang at their ease:
They weren't the human race, my dear, they weren't the human race.

Dreamed I saw a building with a thousand floors,
A thousand windows and a thousand doors;
Not one of them was ours, my dear, not one of them was ours.

Stood on a great plain in the falling snow;
Ten thousand soldiers marched to and fro:
Looking for you and me, my dear, looking for you and me.

W.H. AUDEN

My father carries me across a field

My father carries me across a field.
It's night and there are trenches filled with snow.
Thick mud. We're careful to remain concealed

From something frightening I don't yet know.
And then I walk and there is space between
The four of us. We go where we have to go.

Did I dream it all, this ghostly scene,
The hundred-acre wood where the owl blinked
And the ass spoke? Where I am cosy and clean

In bed, but we are floating, our arms linked
Over the landscape? My father moves ahead
Of me, like some strange, almost extinct

Species, and I follow him in dread
Across the field towards my own extinction.
Spirits everywhere are drifting over blasted

Terrain. The winter cold makes no distinction
Between them and us. My father looks round
And smiles then turns away. We have no function

In this place but keep moving, without sound,
Lost figures who leave only a blank page
Behind them, and the dark and frozen ground

They pass across as they might cross a stage.

GEORGE SZIRTES

Escape Journey, 1988

They force you to crawl, these mountains,
even if you are only fourteen.
Who made the first journey over them?
Whose feet created this track?

The exhausted mules carry us
along with the smuggled goods.
Sitting on their backs, climbing mountains
feels much safer than going down.

The steepness makes me lean backwards,
my back nearly touching the mule's,
then holding on becomes impossible
and I dismount.
It is easier, safer to walk sideways.

And from high up, I can see the white valley.
'A valley of plaster,' I tell my sister.
The mule owner says: 'It is snow.'
But I cannot imagine being rescued from this rough mountain
only to walk over the snow, covering the river.
I cannot imagine listening to the rushing water
passing by holes where the river exposes itself.

'You are too young to complain,'
the mule owner says,
and I look at my father, his little body,
and listen to his difficult breathing.
But then again, he's been here before.

CHOMAN HARDI

Someone else's life

It was a day of slow fever
and roses in the doorway, wrapped
in yesterday's news of death.

Snow fell like angels' feathers
from a dark new sky, softly announcing
that some things would never be the same.

I listened carefully to doubts and revisions
of someone else's life, safe in my room of tomorrow,
a passing witness to sorrow and wonder.

Then night came and I was quickly
drifting inside that life. I was leaving mine.
Snowflakes continued to fall.

The street was deserted and dim.
Shrapnel wounds blossomed in stone walls.
There was no proof of the current decade,

and I could not recall
the names of faces that I knew
the smell of places where I'd lived

and why I lay alone now
so close to a vast, empty floor, so far
from the sun, so far.

KAPKA KASSABOVA

Migration

First, there was the waking,
each day, to a lightness
they couldn't place. The air
stretched tight as a sheet;
the sun on their whitewashed

walls was flexible, or at any rate
warm and rounded to the touch.
It clung about them; they moved
shadowless, footsteps dropping like
stones to the light-resounding bay.

Daily their home gathered weed,
names, string. Sea-changed,
their eyes lost transparency;
they saw the house as it was:
a wholly new thing.

When the dreams came:
tarred and feathered bundles
of prehistory, their webbed feet
clay. They came overnight,
silently, as homing birds

to their owners, whose waking
each day was to a clogged grey
dawn, whose night-time shadows
had wings, scything steeply
above their narrow beds.

JANE GRIFFITHS

Limited

I am riding on a limited express, one of the crack trains of the nation.
Hurtling across the prairie into blue haze and dark air go fifteen
       all-steel coaches holding a thousand people.
(All the coaches shall be scrap and rust and all the men and women
       laughing in the diners and sleepers shall pass to ashes.)
I ask a man in the smoker where he is going and he answers: 'Omaha.'

CARL SANDBURG

Arrival 1946

The boat docked in at Liverpool.
From the train Tariq stared
at an unbroken line of washing
from the North West to Euston.

These are strange people, he thought –
an Empire, and all this washing,
the underwear, the Englishman's garden.
It was Monday, and very sharp.

MONIZA ALVI

The City

You said: 'I'll go to another country, go to another shore,
find another city better than this one.
Whatever I try to do is fated to turn out wrong
and my heart – like something dead – lies buried.
How long can I let my mind moulder in this place?
Wherever I turn, wherever I look,
I see the black ruins of my life, here,
where I've spent so many years, wasted them, destroyed them totally.'

You won't find a new country, won't find another shore.
This city will always pursue you.
You'll walk the same streets, grow old
in the same neighbourhoods, turn grey in these same houses.
You'll always end up in this city. Don't hope for things elsewhere:
there's no ship for you, there's no road.
Now that you've wasted your life here, in this small corner,
you've destroyed it everywhere in the world.

C.P. CAVAFY
translated from the Greek by Edmund Keeley & Philip Sherrard

Malenki robot
(for János, Nagyszelmenc, Slovakia)

'Over there in the other country
my sister had daughters I've seen once
in forty years, nor visited my dead.
It's too late now, they're poor there,
and here I'm just an old working man,
and the only thing left for me to do is die.

'These are my blunt carpenter's hands,
and this on their backs the frost
that gnawed them at Szolyva, three winters,
two years I was a prisoner there.
Monday I build doors, Tuesday put on roofs.
Roofs. Doors. My life. Vodka.

It was the priest told me to go,
three days he said, a little light work,
malenki robot, two years building roofs,
and that because I had a trade.
I survived wearing the clothes of those who died,
after a while I survived because I had survived,
and then came home and here the border.'

The wire runs through the heart, dammit,
therefore we will drink cheap Russian vodka
in János' kitchen, and later take a walk
down to the border and look back
into the other world, the village in the mirror
that is the other half of us, here,
where the street stops at the wire
and goes on again on the other side,
and maybe the Gypsies will come to serenade us.

KEN SMITH

The Mouse

Here you are alone again
as though you had never traveled
through everyone's earth.
Here you are alone like a bird
tossed by the north winds to Kuwait.
Is this what you wished?
        To be alone
turning your eyes, waiting for the mail
as if the pages of the letters were waves
that would carry
your tired heart away.
And slowly in the darkness of the sea
        you will see her hands
waving among flowers,
light filling her eyes.
Return!
Return to yourself, you tramp,
you who roam without a house.

Return to yourself; damn the poets. You are in Kuwait
like a mouse looking for a job,
looking for white cheese to eat.
Leave that girl alone.
And when you fill your stomach tomorrow,
send her a thousand songs.

SAADI YOUSSEF
translated from the Arabic by Khaled Mattawa

The Emigrée

There was once a country... I left it as a child
but my memory of it is sunlight-clear
for it seems I never saw it in that November
which, I am told, comes to the mildest city.
The worst news I receive of it cannot break
my original view, the bright, filled paperweight.
It may be at war, it may be sick with tyrants,
but I am branded by an impression of sunlight.

The white streets of that city, the graceful slopes
glow even clearer as time rolls its tanks
and the frontiers rise between us, close like waves.
That child's vocabulary I carried here
like a hollow doll, opens and spills a grammar.
Soon I shall have every coloured molecule of it.
It may by now be a lie, banned by the state
but I can't get it off my tongue. It tastes of sunlight.

I have no passport, there's no way back at all
but my city comes to me in its own white plane.
It lies down in front of me, docile as paper;
I comb its hair and love its shining eyes.
My city takes me dancing through the city
of walls. They accuse me of absence, they circle me.
They accuse me of being dark in their free city.
My city hides behind me. They mutter death,
and my shadow falls as evidence of sunlight.

CAROL RUMENS

The Ideal

This is where I came from.
I passed this way.
This should not be shameful
Or hard to say.

A self is a self.
It is not a screen.
A person should respect
What he has been.

This is my past
Which I shall not discard.
This is the ideal.
This is hard.

JAMES FENTON

A Poet's Confession

'I did it. I killed my mother tongue.
I shouldn't have left her
there on her own.
All I wanted was a bit of fun
with another body
but now that she's gone –
it's a terrible silence.

She was highly strung,
quite possibly jealous.
After all, I'm young
and she, the beauty,
had become a crone
despite all the surgery.

Could I have saved her?
made her feel at home?

Without her reproaches.
I feel so numb,
not free, as I'd thought...

Tell my lawyer to come.
Until he's with me,
I'm keeping mum.'

GWYNETH LEWIS

Tongue

Inadvertently I passed the border of her teeth and swallowed her agile tongue. It lives inside me now, like a Japanese fish. It brushes against my heart and my diaphragm as if against the walls of an aquarium. It stirs silt from the bottom.

She whom I deprived of a voice stares at me with big eyes and waits for a word.

Yet I do not know which tongue to use when speaking to her – the stolen one or the one which melts in my mouth from an excess of heavy goodness.

ZBIGNIEW HERBERT
translated from the Polish by Czeslaw Milosz

Conversation

'I've got a talking chair.'

'I haven't heard a chair talk in years.'

'Come and have a chat with her. Her chair is very clear.'

'I'm not really fluent in chair – I can understand it OK but I can't speak chair as well as I do table.'

'I haven't got any talking tables.'

'The cupboard next door has learnt table as a second language.'

'Chair and cupboard are very similar.'

'Door is much the same too.'

'But door's a dead language.'

'It's a classical language like window – there's only a few left who
   speak it.'

'But the mirror language is spreading throughout the room.'

'These mirrors have got no roots.'

'Before long there'll be mirrors everywhere. On the floor, on the
   ceiling, even on the chairs.
You won't hear a word of chair after that.'

MIHANGEL MORGAN
translated from the Welsh by Martin Davis

Losing a Language

A breath leaves the sentences and does not come back
yet the old still remember something that they could say

but they know now that such things are no longer believed
and the young have fewer words

many of the things the words were about
no longer exist

the noun for standing in mist by a haunted tree
the verb for I

the children will not repeat
the phrases their parents speak

somebody has persuaded them
that it is better to say everything differently

so that they can be admired somewhere
farther and farther away

where nothing that is here is known
we have little to say to each other

we are wrong and dark
in the eyes of the new owners

the radio is incomprehensible
the day is glass

when there is a voice at the door it is foreign
everywhere instead of a name there is a lie

nobody has seen it happening
nobody remembers

this is what the words were made
to prophesy

here are the extinct feathers
here is the rain we saw

W.S. MERWIN

From the Technology of Tears

In our present state of knowledge only false tears are suitable for
treatment and regular production. Genuine tears are hot, for which
reason it is very difficult to remove them from the face. After their
reduction to a solid state, they have proved to be extremely fragile.
The problem of commercially exploiting genuine tears is a real head-
ache for technologists.

False tears before being quick-frozen are submitted to a process
of distillation, since they are by nature impure, and they are reduced
to a state in which, with respect to purity, they are hardly inferior
to genuine tears. They are very hard, very durable and thus are
suitable not only for ornamentation but also for cutting glass.

ZBIGNIEW HERBERT
translated from the Polish by Peter Dale Scott

from The Country Without a Post Office

...letters sent
To dearest him that lives alas! away
GERARD MANLEY HOPKINS

I read them, letters of lovers, the mad ones,
and mine to him from whom no answers came.
I light lamps, send my answers, Calls to Prayer
to deaf worlds across continents. And my lament
is cries countless, cries like dead letters sent
to this world whose end was near, always near.
My words go out in huge packages of rain,
go there, to addresses, across the oceans.

It's raining as I write this. I have no prayer.
It's just a shout, held in, It's Us! It's Us!
whose letters are cries that break like bodies
in prisons. Now each night in the minaret
I guide myself up the steps. Mad silhouette,
I throw paisleys to clouds. The lost are like this:
They bribe the air for dawn, this their dark purpose.
But there's no sun here. There is no sun here.

Then be pitiless you whom I could not save –
Send your cries to me, if only in this way:
I've found a prisoner's letters to a lover –
One begins: 'These words may never reach you.'
Another ends: 'The skin disssolves in dew
without your touch.' And I want to answer:
I want to live forever. What else can I say?
It rains as I write this. Mad heart, be brave.

AGHA SHAHID ALI

'The Rustle of History's Wings,'
as They Used to Say Then

Not far from the railroad tracks, near the fickle post office,
I saw a ceramic plaque on an old house with the name of
the son of a man whose girlfriend I took away
years ago: she left him for me

and his son was born to another woman and didn't know
about any of this.

Those were days of great love and great destiny:
the British imposed a curfew on the city and locked us up
for a sweet togetherness in our room,
guarded by well-armed soldiers.

For five shillings I changed the Jewish name of my ancestors
to a proud Hebrew name that matched hers.

That whore ran away to America, married
some spice broker – cinnamon, pepper, cardamom –
and left me alone with my new name and with the war.

'The rustle of history's wings,' as they used to say then,
which almost finished me off in battle,
blew gently over her face in her safe address.

And with the wisdom of war, they told me to carry
my first-aid bandage over my heart,
the foolish heart that still loved her
and the wise heart that would forget.

YEHUDA AMICHAI
translated from the Hebrew by Chana Bloch & Stephen Mitchell

Jerusalem

On a roof in the Old City
laundry hanging in the late afternoon sunlight:
the white sheet of a woman who is my enemy,
the towel of a man who is my enemy,
to wipe off the sweat of his brow.

In the sky of the Old City
a kite.
At the other end of the string,
a child
I can't see
because of the wall.

We have put up many flags,
they have put up many flags.
To make us think that they're happy.
To make them think that we're happy.

YEHUDA AMICHAI
translated from the Hebrew by Chana Bloch & Stephen Mitchell

Jerusalem

I

Stone cries to stone,
Heart to heart, heart to stone,
And the interrogation will not die
For there is no eternal city
And there is no pity
And there is nothing underneath the sky
No rainbow and no guarantee –
There is no covenant between your God and me.

II

It is superb in the air.
Suffering is everywhere
And each man wears his suffering like a skin.
My history is proud.

Mine is not allowed.
This is the cistern where all wars begin,
The laughter from the armoured car.
This is the man who won't believe you're what you are.

III

This is your fault.
This is a crusader vault.
The Brook of Kidron flows from Mea She'arim.
I will pray for you.
I will tell you what to do.
I'll stone you. I shall break your every limb.
Oh I am not afraid of you
But maybe I should fear the things you make me do.

IV

This is not Golgotha.
This is the Holy Sepulchre,
The Emperor Hadrian's temple to a love
Which he did not much share.
Golgotha could be anywhere.
Jerusalem itself is on the move.
It leaps and leaps from hill to hill
And as it makes its way it also makes its will.

V

The city was sacked.
Jordan was driven back.
The pious Christians burned the Jews alive.
This is a minaret.
I'm not finished yet.
We're waiting for reinforcements to arrive.
What was your mother's real name?
Would it be safe today to go to Bethlehem?

VI

This is the Garden Tomb.
No, *this* is the Garden Tomb.
I'm an Armenian. I am a Copt.
This is Utopia.
I came here from Ethiopia.
This hole is where the flying carpet dropped
The Prophet off to pray one night
And from here one hour later he resumed his flight.

VII

Who packed your bag?
I packed my bag.
Where was your uncle's mother's sister born?
Have you ever met an Arab?
Yes I am a scarab.
I am a worm. I am a thing of scorn.
I cry Impure from street to street
And see my degradation in the eyes I meet.

VIII

I am your enemy.
This is Gethsemane.
The broken graves look to the Temple Mount.
Tell me now, tell me when
When shall we all rise again?
Shall I be first in that great body count?
When shall the tribes be gathered in?
When, tell me, when shall the Last Things begin?

IX

You are in error.
This is terror.
This is your banishment. This land is mine.
This is what you earn.
This is the Law of No Return.
This is the sour dough, this the sweet wine.
This is my history, this my race
And this unhappy man threw acid in my face.

X

Stone cries to stone,
Heart to heart, heart to stone.
These are the warrior archaeologists.
This is us and that is them.
This is Jerusalem.
These are the dying men with tattooed wrists.
Do this and I'll destroy your home.
I have destroyed your home. You have destroyed my home.

JAMES FENTON

In This Land

What makes life worth living is here in this land:
    the hesitations of April
    the smell of freshly-baked bread at dawn
    women's perceptions of men
    the writings of Aeschylus
    the first flush of love
    herbs that spring from bare stone
    mothers entranced by the sound of a flute
    – and the invaders' dread of memories.
What makes life worth living is here in this land:
    the very last days of September
    a woman nearing forty still in full bloom
    that brief hour of sunlight in prison
    a mackerel sky
    the people's applause for those who face death with a smile
    – and the tyrant's terror of songs.
What makes life worth living is here in this land:
    this land, my motherland,
    the mother of the beginning, the mother of the end –
    that once was called Palestine, that later becomes Palestine.
    My mother, I deserve to live.
    Because you are my mother, I do deserve to live.

MAHMOUD DARWISH
translated from the Arabic by Sarah Maguire & Sabry Hafez

The Sari

Inside my mother
I peered through a glass porthole.
The world beyond was hot and brown.

They were all looking in on me –
Father, Grandmother,
the cook's boy, the sweeper-girl,
the bullock with the sharp
shoulderblades,
the local politicians.

395

My English grandmother
took a telescope
and gazed across continents.

All the people unravelled a sari.
It stretched from Lahore to Hyderabad,
wavered across the Arabian Sea,
shot through with stars,
fluttering with sparrows and quails.
They threaded it with roads,
undulations of land.

Eventually
they wrapped and wrapped me in it
whispering *Your body is your country.*

MONIZA ALVI

Wind

This is the wind, the wind in a field of corn.
Great crowds are fleeing from a major disaster
Down the long valleys, the green swaying wadis,
Down through the beautiful catastrophe of wind.

Families, tribes, nations and their livestock
Have heard something, seen something. An expectation
Or a gigantic misunderstanding has swept over the hilltop
Bending the ear of the hedgerow with stories of fire and sword.

I saw a thousand years pass in two seconds.
Land was lost, languages rose and divided.
This lord went east and found safety.
His brother sought Africa and a dish of aloes.

Centuries, minutes later, one might ask
How the hilt of a sword wandered so far from the smithy.
And somewhere they will sing: 'Like chaff we were borne
In the wind.' This is the wind in a field of corn.

JAMES FENTON

9

Mad World

Of course poetry is irrelevant to the "real" world of power
and politics, but so is philosophy, painting, music and any
other human activity where something genuine can be found.

CHARLES SIMIC

FOUR OF THE opening poems from this section were recommended by the poet
W.S. Merwin to personnel at U.S. Navy bases in Puget Sound in 2000. Asked
by a bookseller who serviced these bases to nominate poems which might make
the individuals responsible for triggering a nuclear attack think twice before
pressing the button, Merwin suggested Gerald Stern's 'The Dog' (398), Emily
Dickinson's 'I reason, Earth is short' (399), William Stafford's 'Earth Dweller'
(400) and Hans Magnus Enzensberger's 'The End of the Owls' (400), along with
Stanley Kunitz's 'Touch Me', in section 4 (206). Whether they were eventually
displayed on Navy noticeboards isn't clear, but it seemed appropriate to give
all these poems a place in *Being Alive*; although Emily Dickinson's poem was
written a century before most of the work in this book – around 1862 – her own
text of 'I reason, Earth is short' was not published until 1955.

Adam Zagajewski's 'Try to Praise the Mutilated World' (436) and Vijay
Seshadri's 'The Disappearances' (403) appeared in *The New Yorker* after 11 Sept-
ember 2001; both were recent poems but gained new resonance in the aftermath
of the Al-Qaeda attacks. John Burnside's 'History' (430) was his immediate,
personal response, while C.K. Williams's 'The Hearth' (432) was written in
February 2003 just before the Iraq War. An earlier chronicler inspires the
psychic metaphors in Sinéad Morrissey's 'The Wound Man' (429), Spanish
poet Federico García Lorca, who witnessed the Wall Street Crash of 1929.

Primo Levi survived Auschwitz (but committed suicide over 40 years later).
His 'Shemà' (409) and poems by Poland's Tadeusz Rozewicz (408, 410) and
Austrian Jewish exile Erich Fried (411, 418) – and the one attributed to Pastor
Martin Niemöller (411) – bear witness to the Holocaust and its legacy. Czeslaw
Milosz's 'Dedication' (424) was written at the end of the war, in 1945, in 'the
broken city' of Warsaw. 'Revenge' by Luis Enrique Mejía Godoy (423) is a song
based on words by Tómas Borge addressed to his jailers and torturers; after the
Nicaraguan Rev-olution in 1979, Borge became Minister for the Interior and
had his revenge by forgiving them. Michael Longley's 'Ceasefire' (see *Staying
Alive*, 350, 344n) is another powerful contemporary poem on forgiveness.

Other poems here hold out hope: through resistance, through not submit-
ting, not forgetting, not doing nothing.

ABC

Any body can die, evidently. Few
Go happily, irradiating joy,

Knowledge, love. Many
Need oblivion, painkillers,
Quickest respite.

Sweet time unafflicted,
Various world:

X=your zenith.

ROBERT PINSKY

The Dog

What I was doing with my white teeth exposed
like that on the side of the road I don't know,
and I don't know why I lay beside the sewer
so that the lover of dead things could come back
with his pencil sharpened and his piece of white paper.
I was there for a good two hours whistling
dirges, shrieking a little, terrifying
hearts with my whimpering cries before I died
by pulling the one leg up and stiffening.
There is a look we have with the hair of the chin
curled in mid-air, there is a look with the belly
stopped in the midst of its greed. The lover of dead things
stoops to feel me, his hand is shaking. I know
his mouth is open and his glasses are slipping.
I think his pencil must be jerking and the terror
of smell – and sight – is overtaking him;
I know he has that terrified faraway look
that death brings – he is contemplating. I want him
to touch my forehead once again and rub my muzzle
before he lifts me up and throws me into

that little valley. I hope he doesn't use
his shoe for fear of touching me; I know,
or used to know, the grasses down there; I think
I knew a hundred smells. I hope the dog's way
doesn't overtake him, one quick push,
barely that, and the mind freed, something else,
some other thing to take its place. Great heart,
great human heart, keep loving me as you lift me,
give me your tears, great loving stranger, remember,
the death of dogs, forgive the yapping, forgive
the shitting, let there be pity, give me your pity.
How could there be enough? I have given
my life for this, emotion has ruined me, oh lover,
I have exchanged my wildness – little tricks
with the mouth and feet, with the tail, my tongue is a parrot's,
I am a rampant horse, I am a lion,
I wait for the cookie, I snap my teeth –
as you have taught me, oh distant and brilliant and lonely.

GERALD STERN

'I reason, Earth is short...'

I reason, Earth is short –
And Anguish – absolute –
And many hurt,
But, what of that?

I reason, we could die –
The best Vitality
Cannot excel Decay,
But, what of that?

I reason, that in Heaven –
Somehow, it will be even –
Some new Equation, given –
But, what of that?

EMILY DICKINSON

Earth Dweller

It was all the clods at once become
precious; it was the barn, and the shed,
and the windmill, my hands, the crack
Arlie made in the ax handle: oh, let me stay
here humbly, forgotten, to rejoice in it all;
let the sun casually rise and set.
If I have not found the right place,
teach me; for somewhere inside, the clods are
vaulted mansions, lines through the barn sing
for the saints forever, the shed and windmill
rear so glorious the sun shudders like a gong.

Now I know why people worship, carry around
magic emblems, wake up talking dreams
they teach to their children: the world speaks.
The world speaks everything to us.
It is our only friend.

WILLIAM STAFFORD

The End of the Owls

I speak for none of your kind,
I speak for the end of the owls.
I speak for the flounder and whale
in their unlighted house,
for the seven cornered sea,
for the glaciers
they will have calved too soon,
raven and dove, feathery witnesses,
for all those that dwell in the sky
and the woods, and the lichen in gravel,
for those without paths, for the colourless bog
and the desolate mountains.

Glaring on radar screens,
interpreted one final time
around the briefing table, fingered
to death by antennas, Florida's swamps
and the Siberian ice, beast
and bush and basalt strangled
by early bird, ringed
by the latest manoeuvres, helpless
under the hovering fireballs,
in the ticking of crises.

We're as good as forgotten.
Don't fuss with the orphans,
just empty your mind
of its longing for nest eggs,
glory or psalms that won't rust.
I speak for none of you now,
all you plotters of perfect crimes,
not for me, not for anyone.

I speak for those who can't speak,
for the deaf and dumb witnesses.
for otters and seals,
for the ancient owls of the earth.

HANS MAGNUS ENZENSBERGER
translated from the German by Jerome Rothenberg

The end of the world

The bird had come to the very end of its song
and the tree was dissolving under its claws.

And in the sky the clouds were twisting
and darkness flowed through all the cracks
into the sinking vessel of the landscape.

Only in the telegraph wires
a message still
crackled:

C·—·—·o———m——e· h···o———m——e·
y—·—o———u··— h···a·—v···—e·
a·— s···o———n—.

MIROSLAV HOLUB
translated from the Czech by Ewald Osers

The Horses

Barely a twelvemonth after
The seven days war that put the world to sleep,
Late in the evening the strange horses came.
By then we had made our covenant with silence,
But in the first few days it was so still
We listened to our breathing and were afraid.
On the second day
The radios failed; we turned the knobs; no answer.
On the third day a warship passed us, heading north,
Dead bodies piled on the deck. On the sixth day
A plane plunged over us into the sea. Thereafter
Nothing. The radios dumb;
And still they stand in corners of our kitchens,
And stand, perhaps, turned on, in a million rooms
All over the world. But now if they should speak,
If on a sudden they should speak again,
If on the stroke of noon a voice should speak,
We would not listen, we would not let it bring
That old bad world that swallowed its children quick
At one great gulp. We would not have it again.
Sometimes we think of the nations lying asleep,
Curled blindly in impenetrable sorrow,
And then the thought confounds us with its strangeness.
The tractors lie about our fields; at evening
They look like dank sea-monsters couched and waiting.
We leave them where they are and let them rust:
'They'll moulder away and be like other loam.'
We make our oxen drag our rusty ploughs,
Long laid aside. We have gone back
Far past our fathers' land.

And then, that evening

Late in the summer the strange horses came.
We heard a distant tapping on the road,
A deepening drumming; it stopped, went on again
And at the corner changed to hollow thunder.
We saw the heads
Like a wild wave charging and were afraid.
We had sold our horses in our fathers' time
To buy new tractors. Now they were strange to us
As fabulous steeds set on an ancient shield
Or illustrations in a book of knights.
We did not dare go near them. Yet they waited,
Stubborn and shy, as if they had been sent
By an old command to find our whereabouts
And that long-lost archaic companionship.
In the first moment we had never a thought
That they were creatures to be owned and used.
Among them were some half-a-dozen colts
Dropped in some wilderness of the broken world,
Yet new as if they had come from their own Eden.
Since then they have pulled our ploughs and borne our loads,
But that free servitude still can pierce our hearts.
Our life is changed; their coming our beginning.

EDWIN MUIR

The Disappearances

'Where was it one first heard of the truth?'

On a day like any other day,
like 'yesterday or centuries before',
in a town with the one remembered street,
shaded by the buckeye and the sycamore –
the street long and true as a theorem,
the day like yesterday or the day before,
the street you walked down centuries before –
the story the same as the others flooding in
from the cardinal points is
turning to take a good look at you.

Every creature, intelligent or not, has disappeared –
the humans, phosphorescent,
the duplicating pets, the guppies and spaniels,
the Woolworth's turtle that cost forty-nine cents
(with the soiled price tag half-peeled on its shell) –
but from the look of things, it only just happened.
The wheels of the upside-down tricycle are spinning.
The swings are empty but swinging.
And the shadow is still there, and there
is the object that made it,
riding the proximate atmosphere,
oblong and illustrious above
the dispeopled bedroom community,
venting the memories of those it took,
their corrosive human element.
This is what you have to walk through to escape,
transparent but alive as coal dust.
This is what you have to hack through,
bamboo-tough and thickly clustered.
The myths are somewhere else, but here are the meanings,
and you have to breathe them in
until they burn your throat
and peck at your brain with their intoxicated teeth.
This is you as seen by them, from the corner of an eye
(was that the way you were always seen?).
This is you when the President died
(the day is brilliant and cold).
This is you poking a ground-wasps' nest.
This is you at the doorway, unobserved,
while your aunts and uncles keen over the body.
This is your first river, your first planetarium, your first popsicle.
The cold and brilliant day in six-color prints –
but the people on the screen are black and white.
Your friend's mother is saying,
Hush, children! Don't you understand history is being made?
You do, and you still do. Made and made again.
This is you as seen by them, and them as seen by you,
and you as seen by you, in five dimensions,
in seven, in three again, then two,
then reduced to a dimensionless point
in a universe where the only constant is the speed of light.
This is you at the speed of light.

VIJAY SESHADRI

The Shield of Achilles

         She looked over his shoulder
            For vines and olive trees,
         Marble well-governed cities
            And ships upon untamed seas,
         But there on the shining metal
            His hands had put instead
         An artificial wilderness
            And a sky like lead.

A plain without a feature, bare and brown,
   No blade of grass, no sign of neighborhood,
Nothing to eat and nowhere to sit down,
   Yet, congregated on its blankness, stood
   An unintelligible multitude,
A million eyes, a million boots in line,
Without expression, waiting for a sign.

Out of the air a voice without a face
   Proved by statistics that some cause was just
In tones as dry and level as the place:
   No one was cheered and nothing was discussed;
   Column by column in a cloud of dust
They marched away enduring a belief
Whose logic brought them, somewhere else, to grief.

         She looked over his shoulder
            For ritual pieties,
         White flower-garlanded heifers,
            Libation and sacrifice,
         But there on the shining metal
            Where the altar should have been,
         She saw by his flickering forge-light
            Quite another scene.

Barbed wire enclosed an arbitrary spot
   Where bored officials lounged (one cracked a joke)
And sentries sweated for the day was hot:
   A crowd of ordinary decent folk
   Watched from without and neither moved nor spoke
As three pale figures were led forth and bound
To three posts driven upright in the ground.

The mass and majesty of this world, all
That carries weight and always weighs the same
Lay in the hands of others; they were small
And could not hope for help and no help came:
What their foes liked to do was done, their shame
Was all the worst could wish; they lost their pride
And died as men before their bodies died.

          She looked over his shoulder
             For athletes at their games,
          Men and women in a dance
             Moving their sweet limbs
          Quick, quick, to music,
             But there on the shining shield
          His hands had set no dancing-floor
             But a weed-choked field.

A ragged urchin, aimless and alone,
   Loitered about that vacancy; a bird
Flew up to safety from his well-aimed stone:
   That girls are raped, that two boys knife a third,
   Were axioms to him, who'd never heard
Of any world where promises were kept,
Or one could weep because another wept.

          The thin-lipped armorer,
             Hephaestos, hobbled away,
          Thetis of the shining breasts
             Cried out in dismay
          At what the god had wrought
             To please her son, the strong
          Iron-hearted man-slaying Achilles
             Who would not live long.

W.H. AUDEN

Five Ways to Kill a Man

There are many cumbersome ways to kill a man:
you can make him carry a plank of wood
to the top of a hill and nail him to it. To do this
properly you require a crowd of people
wearing sandals, a cock that crows, a cloak
to dissect, a sponge, some vinegar and one
man to hammer the nails home.

Or you can take a length of steel,
shaped and chased in a traditional way,
and attempt to pierce the metal cage he wears.
But for this you need white horses,
English trees, men with bows and arrows,
at least two flags, a prince and
a castle to hold your banquet in.

Dispensing with nobility, you may, if the wind
allows, blow gas at him. But then you need
a mile of mud sliced through with ditches,
not to mention black boots, bomb craters,
more mud, a plague of rats, a dozen songs
and some round hats made of steel.

In an age of aeroplanes, you may fly
miles above your victim and dispose of him by
pressing one small switch. All you then
require is an ocean to separate you, two
systems of government, a nation's scientists,
several factories, a psychopath and
land that no one needs for several years.

These are, as I began, cumbersome ways
to kill a man. Simpler, direct, and much more neat
is to see that he is living somewhere in the middle
of the twentieth century, and leave him there.

EDWIN BROCK

Pigtail

When all the women in the transport
had their heads shaved
four workmen with brooms made of birch twigs
swept up
and gathered up the hair

Behind clean glass
the stiff hair lies
of those suffocated in gas chambers
there are pins and side combs
in this hair

The hair is not shot through with light
is not parted by the breeze
is not touched by any hand
or rain or lips

In huge chests
clouds of dry hair
of those suffocated
and a faded plait
a pigtail with a ribbon
pulled at school
by naughty boys.

[*The Museum, Auschwitz, 1948*]

TADEUSZ RÓŻEWICZ
translated from the Polish by Adam Czerniawski

Shemà

You who live secure
In your warm houses,
Who return at evening to find
Hot food and friendly faces:

Consider whether this is a man.
Who labors in the mud
Who knows no peace
Who fights for a crust of bread
Who dies at a yes or a no.
Consider whether this is a woman,
Without hair or name
With no more strength to remember
Eyes empty and womb cold
As a frog in winter.

Consider that this has been:
I commend these words to you.
Engrave them on your hearts
When you are in your house, when you walk on your way,
When you go to bed, when you rise.
Repeat them to your children.
Or may your house crumble,
Disease render you powerless,
Your offspring avert their faces from you.

[10 January 1946]

PRIMO LEVI
translated from the Italian by Ruth Feldman & Brian Stone

The survivor

I am twenty-four
led to slaughter
I survived.

The following are empty synonyms:
man and beast
love and hate
friend and foe
darkness and light.

The way of killing men and beasts is the same
I've seen it:
truckfuls of chopped-up men
who will not be saved.

Ideas are mere words:
virtue and crime
truth and lies
beauty and ugliness
courage and cowardice.

Virtue and crime weigh the same
I've seen it:
in a man who was both
criminal and virtuous.

I seek a teacher and a master
may he restore my sight hearing and speech
may he again name objects and ideas
may he separate darkness from light.

I am twenty-four
led to slaughter
I survived.

TADEUSZ RÓŻEWICZ
translated from the Polish by Adam Czerniawski

'First they came for the Jews...'

First they came for the Jews.
and I did not speak out –
because I was not a Jew.

Then they came for the Communists
and I did not speak out –
because I was not a Communist.

Then they came for the Trade Unionists.
and I did not speak out –
because I was not a Trade Unionist.

Then they came for the Catholics.
and I did not speak out –
because I was a Protestant.

Then they came for me –
and there was no one left
to speak out for me.

attributed to **MARTIN NIEMÖLLER**
translated from the German

What Happens

It has happened
and it goes on happening
and will happen again
if nothing happens to stop it

The innocent know nothing
because they are too innocent
and the guilty know nothing
because they are too guilty

The poor do not notice
because they are too poor
and the rich do not notice
because they are too rich

The stupid shrug their shoulders
because they are too stupid
and the clever shrug their shoulders
because they are too clever

The young do not care
because they are too young
and the old do not care
because they are too old

That is why nothing happens
to stop it
and that is why it has happened
and goes on happening and will happen again

ERICH FRIED
translated from the German by Stuart Hood

To Whom It May Concern
(*Tell Me Lies about Vietnam*)

I was run over by the truth one day.
Ever since the accident I've walked this way
    So stick my legs in plaster
    Tell me lies about Vietnam.

Heard the alarm clock screaming with pain,
Couldn't find myself so I went back to sleep again
    So fill my ears with silver
    Stick my legs in plaster
    Tell me lies about Vietnam.

Every time I shut my eyes all I see is flames.
Made a marble phone book and I carved all the names
    So coat my eyes with butter
    Fill my ears with silver
    Stick my legs in plaster
    Tell me lies about Vietnam.

I smell something burning, hope it's just my brains.
They're only dropping peppermints and daisy-chains
    So stuff my nose with garlic
    Coat my eyes with butter
    Fill my ears with silver
    Stick my legs in plaster
    Tell me lies about Vietnam.

Where were you at the time of the crime?
Down by the Cenotaph drinking slime
    So chain my tongue with whisky
    Stuff my nose with garlic
    Coat my eyes with butter
    Fill my ears with silver
    Stick my legs in plaster
    Tell me lies about Vietnam.

You put your bombers in, you put your conscience out,
You take the human being and you twist it all about
    So scrub my skin with women
    Chain my tongue with whisky
    Stuff my nose with garlic
    Coat my eyes with butter
    Fill my ears with silver
    Stick my legs in plaster
    Tell me lies about Vietnam.

ADRIAN MITCHELL

'When Statesmen gravely say'

When Statesmen gravely say 'We must be realistic',
The chances are they're weak and, therefore, pacifistic,
But when they speak of Principles, look out: perhaps
Their generals are already poring over maps.

W.H. AUDEN

Explaining the Declaration

It starts in the pub, in the back room
where seven drunks are gathered together,
war; it smoulders
in the crèche; the Academy
of Sciences hatches it;
no, in a delivery room in Gori
or Braunau it flourishes, on the net,
in the mosque; it sweats
from the small brain of the patriotic poet;
because someone is offended, because someone
has tasted blood, in God's name,
war rages, on grounds of colour,
in the bunker, for a joke, or by mistake;
because there have to be sacrifices
to save mankind, and these
especially at night, because of the oilfields;
for this, that even self-mutilation
has its attractions and because there's money
war starts, in a delirium
because of a football match;
for no such thing, for heaven's sake; yes, then;
though nobody wanted it; aha;
just like that, for pleasure, heroically
and because we can't think of anything better to do.

HANS MAGNUS ENZENSBERGER
translated from the German by David Constantine

414

Untitled

Time of fools is coming,
time of the fairground tent
and the one with a clown's face
   cursing God.

Time of the peacock quill,
the quill that glides from right to left
over the paper downside up.

Time when you won't lift your little finger
without dipping into something
they call indecent.

Time of fools is coming,
time of the know-nothing professor
and the book that can't be cracked open
   at either edge.

ALEKSANDAR RISTOVIĆ
translated from the Serbian by Charles Simic

War Has Been Given a Bad Name

I am told that the best people have begun saying
How, from a moral point of view, the Second World War
Fell below the standard of the First. The Wehrmacht
Allegedly deplores the methods by which the SS effected
The extermination of certain peoples. The Ruhr industrialists
Are said to regret the bloody manhunts
Which filled their mines and factories with slave workers. The
      intellectuals
So I heard, condemn industry's demand for slave workers
Likewise their unfair treatment. Even the bishops

Dissociate themselves from this way of waging war; in short the
     feeling
Prevails in every quarter that the Nazis did the Fatherland
A lamentably bad turn, and that war
While in itself natural and necessary, has, thanks to the
Unduly uninhibited and positively inhuman
Way in which it was conducted on this occasion, been
Discredited for some time to come.

BERTOLT BRECHT
translated from the German by John Willett

He Embraces His Murderer

He embraces his murderer to win him over.
Will you be furious if I survive?
My brother... my brother...
What can I possibly have done to make you destroy me?
Look, two birds are flying above our heads –
aim at them instead! aim this hell away from me!
Why don't we go to my mother's place where she'll cook beans for us –
What do you say? Why not?
You're fed up with my embrace and sick of my smell?
Aren't you worn out by the fear that's inside me?
So chuck that pistol in the river!
How about it? Yes?
An enemy on the riverbank has got us covered with a machinegun?
So shoot him instead!
Then we'll both escape his fire, and you'll be released from this crime.
What do you think?
You're going to kill me and let the enemy go home – to our home?
And then you'll return to the law of the jungle?
What did you do with my mother's coffee – with our mother's coffee?
What did I do to make you destroy me... my brother?
I won't let you out of my arms.
I will never release you.

MAHMOUD DARWISH
translated from the Arabic by Sarah Maguire & Sabry Hafez

from **A German War Primer**

General, your tank is a powerful machine.
It can flatten a forest and crush a hundred people.
But there's one thing wrong with it:
It needs a driver.

General, your bomber is powerful.
It can fly faster than the stormwind and carry more than an elephant.
But there's one thing wrong with it:
It needs a mechanic.

General, a human being is very useful.
He can fly and he can kill.
But there's one thing wrong with him:
He can think.

BERTOLT BRECHT
translated from the German by David Constantine

Song of the Juggler

General, dein Tank ist ein starker Wagen.
BRECHT

General, there's a battle
between your orders and my songs.
It goes on all the time:
night, day.
It knows neither tiredness nor sleep –
a battle that has gone on for many years,
so many that my eyes have never seen a sunrise
in which you, your orders, your arms, your trenches did not figure.

A rich battle
in which, aesthetically speaking, my rags
and your uniform face off.
A theatrical battle –
it only lacks dazzling stage sets

where comedians might come on from anywhere
raising a rumpus as they do in carnivals,
each one showing off his loyalty and valor.

General. I can't destroy your fleets or your tanks
and I don't know how long this war will last
but every night one of your orders dies without being followed,
and, undefeated, one of my songs survives.

HEBERTO PADILLA
translated from the Spanish by Alastair Reid & Andrew Hurley

Conversation with a Survivor

What did you do in those days
that you shouldn't have done?
'Nothing'

What did you not do
that you should have done?
'This and that:
a few things'

Why did you not do it?
'Because I was afraid'
Why were you afraid?
'Because I didn't want to die'

Did others die
because you didn't want to?
'I think
they did'

Have you got anything else to say
about what you didn't do?
'Yes: to ask you
what you would have done in my place?'

I do not know
and cannot sit in judgment on you.
Only one thing I know:
Tomorrow none of us
will stay alive
if today
we again do nothing

ERICH FRIED
translated from the German by Stuart Hood

Twelve Bar Bessie

See that day, Lord, did you hear what happened then?
A nine o'clock shadow always chases the sun.
And in the thick heavy air came the Ku Klux Klan
To the tent where the Queen was about to sing her song.

They were going to pull the Blues Tent down.
Going to move the Queen out of the town.
Take her twelve bar beat and squash it into the ground.
She tried to get her Prop Boys together, and they got scared.

She tried to get the Prop Boys together, and they got scared.
She said Boys, Boys, get those men out of here.
But they ran away and left the Empress on her own.
She went up to the men who had masks over their head

With her hand on her hips she cursed and she hollered,
'I'll get the whole damn lot of you out of here now
If I have to. You are as good as dead.
You just pick up the sheets and run. Go on.'

That's what she done. Her voice was cast-iron.
You should have seen them. You should have seen them.
Those masks made of sheets from somebody's bed.
Those masks flying over their heads. Flapping.

They was flapping like some strange bird migrating.
Some bird that smelt danger in the air, a blue song.
And flew. Fast. Out of the small mid western town.
To the sound of black hands clapping.

And the Empress saying, 'And as for you' to the ones who did
    nothing.

JACKIE KAY

from An Atlas of the Difficult World

Here is a map of our country:
here is the Sea of Indifference, glazed with salt
This is the haunted river flowing from brow to groin
we dare not taste its water
This is the desert where missiles are planted like corms
This is the breadbasket of foreclosed farms
This is the birthplace of the rockabilly boy
This is the cemetery of the poor
who died for democracy   This is a battlefield
from a nineteenth-century war   the shrine is famous
This is the sea-town of myth and story   when the fishing fleets
went bankrupt   here is where the jobs were   on the pier
processing frozen fishsticks   hourly wages and no shares
These are other battlefields   Centralia   Detroit
here are the forests primeval   the copper   the silver lodes
These are the suburbs of acquiescence   silence rising fumelike
        from the streets
This is the capital of money and dolor whose spires
flare up through air inversions whose bridges are crumbling
whose children are drifting blind alleys pent
between coiled rolls of razor wire
I promised to show you a map you say but this is a mural
then yes let it be   these are small distinctions
where do we see it from is the question

ADRIENNE RICH

At Last the Women Are Moving

Last, walking with stiff legs as if they carried bundles
Came mothers, housewives, old women who knew why they
    abhorred war.
Their clothes bunched about them, they hobbled with anxious steps
To keep with the stride of the marchers, erect, bearing wide banners.

Such women looked odd, marching on American asphalt.
Kitchens they knew, sinks, suds, stew-pots and pennies...
Dull hurry and worry, clatter, wet hands and backache.
Here they were out in the glare on the militant march.

How did these timid, the slaves of breakfast and supper
Get out in the line, drop for once dish-rag and broom?
Here they are as work-worn as stitchers and fitters.
Mama have you got some grub, now none of their business.

Oh, but these who know in their growing sons and their husbands
How the exhausted body needs sleep, how often needs food
These, whose business is keeping the body alive,
These are ready, if you talk their language, to strike.

Kitchen is small, the family story is sad.
Out of the musty flats the women come thinking:
*Not for me and mine only. For my class I have come
To walk city miles with many, my will in our work.*

GENEVIEVE TAGGARD

Ourstory

Let us now praise women
with feet glass slippers wouldn't fit;

not the patient, nor even the embittered
ones who kept their place,

but awkward women, tenacious with truth,
whose elbows disposed of the impossible;

who split seams, who wouldn't wait,
take no, take sedatives;

who sang their own numbers, went uninsured,
knew best what they were missing.

Our misfit foremothers are joining forces
underground, their dusts mingling

breast-bone with scapula, forehead
with forehead. Their steady mass

bursts locks; lends a springing foot
to our vaulting into enormous rooms.

CAROLE SATYAMURTI

The low road

What can they do
to you? Whatever they want.
They can set you up, they can
bust you, they can break
your fingers, they can
burn your brain with electricity,
blur you with drugs till you
can't walk, can't remember, they can
take your child, wall up
your lover. They can do anything
you can't stop them
from doing. How can you stop
them? Alone, you can fight,
you can refuse, you can
take what revenge you can
but they roll over you.

But two people fighting
back to back can cut through
a mob, a snake-dancing file
can break a cordon, an army
can meet an army.

Two people can keep each other
sane, can give support, conviction,
love, massage, hope, sex.
Three people are a delegation,
a committee, a wedge. With four
you can play bridge and start
an organisation. With six
you can rent a whole house,
eat pie for dinner with no
seconds, and hold a fund-raising party.
A dozen make a demonstration.
A hundred fill a hall.
A thousand have solidarity and your own newsletter;
ten thousand, power and your own paper;
a hundred thousand, your own media;
ten million, your own country.

It goes on one at a time,
it starts when you care
to act, it starts when you do
it again after they said no,
it starts when you say *We*
and know who you mean, and each
day you mean one more.

MARGE PIERCY

Revenge

My personal revenge will be your children's
right to schooling and to flowers.
My personal revenge will be this song
bursting for you with no more fears.

My personal revenge will be to make you see
the goodness in my people's eyes,
implacable in combat always
generous and firm in victory.

My personal revenge will be to greet you
'Good morning!' in streets with no beggars,
when instead of locking you inside
they say, 'Don't look so sad.'
When you, the torturer,
daren't lift your head.
My personal revenge will be to give you
these hands you once ill-treated
with all their tenderness intact.

LUIS ENRIQUE MEJÍA GODOY
translated from the Spanish by Dinah Livingstone

Dedication

You whom I could not save
Listen to me.
Try to understand this simple speech as I would be ashamed of another.
I swear, there is in me no wizardry of words.
I speak to you with silence like a cloud or a tree.

What strengthened me, for you was lethal.
You mixed up farewell to an epoch with the beginning of a new one,
Inspiration of hatred with lyrical beauty,
Blind force with accomplished shape.

Here is the valley of shallow Polish rivers. And an immense bridge
Going into white fog. Here is a broken city,
And the wind throws the screams of gulls on your grave
When I am talking with you.

What is poetry which does not save
Nations or people?
A connivance with official lies,
A song of drunkards whose throats will be cut in a moment,
Readings for sophomore girls.

That I wanted good poetry without knowing it,
That I discovered, late, its salutary aim,
In this and only this I find salvation.

They used to pour millet on graves or poppy seeds
To feed the dead who would come disguised as birds.
I put this book here for you, who once lived
So that you should visit us no more.

CZESLAW MILOSZ
translated from the Polish by the author

Ratatouille

I

Consider, please, this dish of ratatouille.
Neither will it invade Afghanistan
Or boycott the Olympic Games in a huff.
It likes the paintings of Raoul Dufy.
It feeds the playboy and the working-man.
Of wine and sun it cannot get enough.
It has no enemies, no, not even
Salade niçoise or phoney recipes,
Not Leonid Brezhnev, no, not Ronald Reagan.
It is the fruits of earth, this ratatouille,
And it has many friends, including me.
Come, lovers of ratatouille, and unite!

II

It is a sort of dream, which coincides
With the pacific relaxations called
Preferred Reality. Men who forget
Lovingly chopped-up cloves of *ail*, who scorn
The job of slicing two good peppers thinly,
Then two large onions and six aubergines –
Those long, impassioned and imperial purples –
Which, with six courgettes, you sift with salt
And cover with a plate for one round hour;
Or men who do not care to know about
The eight ripe *pommes d'amour* their wives have need of,
Preparing ratatouille, who give no thought to

The cup of olive oil that's heated in
Their heaviest pan, or onions, fried with garlic
For five observant minutes, before they add
Aubergines, courgettes, peppers, tomatoes;
Or men who give no thought to what their wives
Are thinking as they stand beside their stoves
When seasoning is sprinkled on, before
A *bouquet garni* is dropped in – these men
Invade Afghanistan, boycott the Games,
Call off their fixtures and prepare for war.

III

Cook for one hour, and then serve hot or cold.
Eat it, for preference, under the sun,
But, if you are Northern, you may eat
Your ratatouille imagining Provence.
Believe me, it goes well with everything,
As love does, as peace does, as summers do
Or any other season, as a lifetime does.
Acquire, then, for yourselves, ingredients;
Prepare this stew of love, and ask for more.
Quick, before it is too late. *Bon appétit!*

DOUGLAS DUNN

In Memory: The Miami Showband –
Massacred 31 July 1975

Beautiful are the feet of them that preach the gospel of peace,
Of them that bring glad tidings of good things

In a public house, darkly lit, a patriotic (sic)
Versifier whines into my face: 'You must take one side
Or the other, or you're but a fucking romantic.'
His eyes glitter hate and vanity, porter and whiskey,
And I realise that he is blind to the braille connection
Between a music and a music-maker.
'You must take one side or the other
Or you're but a fucking romantic':

The whine is icy
And his eyes hang loose like sheets from poles
On a bare wet hillside in winter
And his mouth gapes like a cave in ice;
It is a whine in the crotch of whose fear
Is fondled a dream gun blood-smeared;
It is in war – not poetry or music –
That men find their niche, their glory hole;
Like most of his fellows
He will abide no contradiction in the mind.
He whines: 'If there is birth, there cannot be death'
And – jabbing a hysterical forefinger into my nose and eyes –
'If there is death, there cannot be birth.'
Peace to the souls of those who unlike my fellow poet
Were true to their trade
Despite death-dealing blackmail by racists:
You made music, and that was all. You were realists
And beautiful were your feet.

PAUL DURCAN

Casual Wear

Your average tourist: Fifty. 2 3
Times married. Dressed, this year, in Ferdi Plinthbower
Originals. Odds 1 to 9
Against her strolling past the Embassy

Today at noon. Your average terrorist:
Twenty-five. Celibate. No use for trends,
At least in clothing. Mark, though, where it ends.
People have come forth made of colored mist

Unsmiling on one hundred million screens
To tell of his prompt phone call to the station,
'Claiming responsibility' – devastation
Signed with a flourish, like the dead wife's jeans.

JAMES MERRILL

427

The Diameter of the Bomb

The diameter of the bomb was thirty centimeters
and the diameter of its effective
range – about seven meters.
And in it four dead and eleven wounded.
And around them in a greater circle
of pain and time are scattered
two hospitals and one cemetery.
But the young woman who was
buried where she came from
over a hundred kilometers away
enlarges the circle greatly.
And the lone man who weeps over her death
in a far corner of a distant country
includes the whole world in the circle.
And I won't speak at all about the crying of orphans
that reaches to the seat of God
and from there onward, making
the circle without end and without God.

YEHUDA AMICHAI
translated from the Hebrew by Yehuda Amichai & Ted Hughes

The Red and the Black

We sat up late, talking –
thinking of the screams of the tortured
and the last silence of starving children,
seeing the faces of bigots and murderers.

Then sleep.

And there was the morning, smiling
in the dance of everything. The collared doves
guzzled the rowan berries and the sea
washed in, so gently, so tenderly.
Our neighbours greeted us
with humour and friendliness.

World, why do you do this to us,
giving us poison with one hand
and the bread of life with another?

And reason sits helpless at its desk,
adding accounts that never balance,
finding no excuse for anything.

NORMAN MacCAIG

The Wound Man
(for Federico García Lorca)

It would have been a kind of action replay,
only worse. The white handkerchiefs.
The unimaginable collapse. The day
the markets crashed and unleashed
unknowing through the New York streets

saw you transfixed, a witness in Times Square,
as the world went down in hysterical laughter
and diminishing shrieks. Then thudded over.
All hope in the gutter, blooded and lost. How you loathed
the reflections of clouds in the skyscrapers

and the glittering rings of the suicides.
It was all one in New York: the manacled roses, oil on the Hudson,
financial devastation. Had you survived,
Federico, say, Franco's henchmen,
or the war that was to open like a demon from his person,

or the later war, and all the intervening years
between that fall of faith and this, what would you think?
Would you know what has happened here,
the way we do not know what has happened? Where
would your fury go? We shiver on the brink

of an ending, and a war stretches in front of us,
we stand where you stood. As for me,
I see the Wound Man walking, tall and imperious,
through the streets of America, surly
and muscular, from the textbook of Paracelsus.

He's been badly hit. There are weapons through every part of him.
A knife in the cheek; an arrow in the thigh;
someone has severed his wrist bones, on a whim,
and thrust a sword into his eye.
They've flung razors at his flesh to pass the time.

And yet he rears. Sturdy and impossible. Strong.
Loose in the world. And out of proportion.

SINÉAD MORRISSEY

History
St Andrews: West Sands; September 2001

Today
    as we flew the kites
– the sand spinning off in ribbons along the beach
and that gasoline smell from Leuchars gusting across
the golf links;
        the tide far out
and quail-grey in the distance;
                people
jogging, or stopping to watch
as the war planes cambered and turned
in the morning light –

today
    – with the news in my mind, and the muffled dread
of what may come –

        I knelt down in the sand
with Lucas
    gathering shells
and pebbles
        finding evidence of life in all this
driftwork:
    snail shells; shreds of razorfish;
smudges of weed and flesh on tideworn stone.

430

At times I think what makes us who we are
is neither kinship nor our given states
but something lost between the world we own
and what we dream about behind the names

on days like this
                    our lines raised in the wind
our bodies fixed and anchored to the shore

and though we are confined by property
what tethers us to gravity and light
has most to do with distance and the shapes
we find in water
                    reading from the book
of silt and tides
                    the rose or petrol blue
of jellyfish and sea anemone
combining with a child's
first nakedness.

Sometimes I am dizzy with the fear
of losing everything – the sea, the sky,
all living creatures, forests, estuaries:
we trade so much to know the virtual
we scarcely register the drift and tug
of other bodies
                    scarcely apprehend
the moment as it happens: shifts of light
and weather
                    and the quiet, local forms
of history: the fish lodged in the tide
beyond the sands;
                    the long insomnia
of ornamental carp in public parks
captive and bright
                    and hung in their own
slow-burning
                    transitive gold;
                                    jamjars of spawn
and sticklebacks
                    or goldfish carried home
from fairgrounds
                    to the hum of radio

but this is the problem: how to be alive
in all this gazed-upon and cherished world
and do no harm

                    a toddler on a beach
sifting wood and dried weed from the sand
and puzzled by the pattern on a shell

his parents on the dune slacks with a kite
plugged into the sky
                    all nerve and line

patient; afraid; but still, through everything
attentive to the irredeemable.

JOHN BURNSIDE

The Hearth
(February 2003)

1

Alone after the news on a bitter
evening in the country, sleet slashing
the stubbled fields, the river ice;
I keep stirring up the recalcitrant fire,

but when I throw my plastic coffee cup
in with new kindling it perches intact
on a log for a strangely long time,
as though uncertain what to do,

until, in a somehow reluctant, almost
creaturely way, it dents, collapses
and decomposes to a dark slime
untwining itself on the stone hearth.

I once knew someone who was caught in a fire
and made it sound something like that.
He'd been loading a bomber and a napalm shell
had gone off; flung from the flames,

at first he felt nothing and thought
he'd been spared, but then came the pain,
then the hideous dark – he'd been blinded,
and so badly charred he spent years

in recovery: agonising debridements,
grafts, learning to speak through a mouth
without lips, to read Braille with fingers
lavaed with scar, to not want to die –

though that never happened. He swore,
even years later, with a family,
that if he were back there, this time allowed
to put himself out of his misery, he would.

2

There was dying here tonight, after
dusk, by the road: an owl,
eyes fixed and flared, breast
so winter-white he seemed to shine

a searchlight on himself, helicoptered
near a wire fence, then suddenly
banked, plunged and vanished
into the swallowing dark with his prey.

Such an uncomplicated departure;
no detonation, nothing to mourn;
if the creature being torn from its life
made a sound, I didn't hear it.

But in fact I wasn't listening, I was thinking,
as I often do these days, of war;
I was thinking of my children, and their children,
of the more than fear I feel for them,

and then of radar, rockets, shrapnel,
cities razed, soil poisoned
for a thousand generations; of suffering so vast
it nullifies everything else.

I stood in the wind in the raw cold
wondering how those with power over us
can effect such things, and by what
cynical reasoning pardon themselves.

The fire's ablaze now, its glow
on the windows makes the night even darker,
but it barely keeps the room warm.
I stoke it again, and crouch closer.

C.K. WILLIAMS

Musée des Beaux Arts

About suffering they were never wrong,
The Old Masters: how well they understood
Its human position; how it takes place
While someone else is eating or opening a window or just walking
      dully along;
How, when the aged are reverently, passionately waiting
For the miraculous birth, there always must be
Children who did not specially want it to happen, skating
On a pond at the edge of the wood:
They never forgot
That even the dreadful martyrdom must run its course
Anyhow in a corner, some untidy spot
Where the dogs go on with their doggy life and the torturer's horse
Scratches its innocent behind on a tree.

In Brueghel's *Icarus*, for instance: how everything turns away
Quite leisurely from the disaster; the ploughman may
Have heard the splash, the forsaken cry,
But for him it was not an important failure; the sun shone
As it had to on the white legs disappearing into the green
Water; and the expensive delicate ship that must have seen
Something amazing, a boy falling out of the sky,
Had somewhere to get to and sailed calmly on.

W.H. AUDEN

Reality Demands

Reality demands
that we also mention this:
Life goes on.
It continues at Cannae and Borodino,
at Kosovo Polje and Guernica.

There's a gas station
on a little square in Jericho,
and wet paint
on park benches in Bila Hora.
Letters fly back and forth
between Pearl Harbor and Hastings,
a moving van passes
beneath the eye of the lion at Cheronea,
and the blooming orchards near Verdun
cannot escape
the approaching atmospheric front.

There is so much Everything
that Nothing is hidden quite nicely.
Music pours
from the yachts moored at Actium
and couples dance on their sunlit decks.

So much is always going on,
that it must be going on all over.
Where not a stone still stands,
you see the Ice Cream Man
besieged by children.
Where Hiroshima had been
Hiroshima is again,
producing many products
for everyday use.

This terrifying world is not devoid of charms,
of the mornings
that make waking up worthwhile.
The grass is green
on Maciejowice's fields,

and it is studded with dew,
as is normal with grass.

Perhaps all fields are battlefields,
all grounds are battlegrounds,
those we remember
and those that are forgotten:
the birch, the cedar, and fir forests, the white snow,
the yellow sands, gray gravel, the iridescent swamps,
the canyons of black defeat,
where, in times of crisis,
you can cower under a bush.

What moral flows from this? Probably none.
Only the blood flows, drying quickly,
and, as always, a few rivers, a few clouds.

On tragic mountain passes
the wind rips hats from unwitting heads
and we can't help
laughing at that.

WISLAWA SZYMBORSKA
translated from the Polish by Stanislaw Baranczak & Clare Cavanagh

Try to Praise the Mutilated World

Try to praise the mutilated world.
Remember June's long days,
and wild strawberries, drops of wine, the dew.
The nettles that methodically overgrow
the abandoned homesteads of exiles.
You must praise the mutilated world.
You watched the stylish yachts and ships;
one of them had a long trip ahead of it,
while salty oblivion awaited others.
You've seen the refugees heading nowhere,
you've heard the executioners sing joyfully.

You should praise the mutilated world.
Remember the moments when we were together
in a white room and the curtain fluttered.
Return in thought to the concert where music flared.
You gathered acorns in the park in autumn
and leaves eddied over the earth's scars.
Praise the mutilated world
and the gray feather a thrush lost,
and the gentle light that strays and vanishes
and returns.

ADAM ZAGAJEWSKI
translated from the Polish by Clare Cavanagh

A Prison Evening

Each star a rung,
night comes down the spiral
staircase of the evening.
The breeze passes by so very close
as if someone just happened to speak of love.
In the courtyard,
the trees are absorbed refugees
embroidering maps of return on the sky.
On the roof,
the moon – lovingly, generously –
is turning the stars
into a dust of sheen.
From every corner, dark-green shadows,
in ripples, come towards me.
At any moment they may break over me,
like the waves of pain each time I remember
this separation from my lover.

This thought keeps consoling me:
though tyrants may command that lamps be smashed
in rooms where lovers are destined to meet,
they cannot snuff out the moon, so today,
nor tomorrow, no tyranny will succeed,

no poison of torture make me bitter,
if just one evening in prison
can be so strangely sweet,
if just one moment anywhere on this earth.

FAIZ AHMED FAIZ
translated from the Urdu by Agha Shahid Ali

To the Days

From you I want more than I've ever asked,
all of it – the newscasts' terrible stories
of life in my time, the knowing it's worse than that,
much worse – the knowing what it means to be lied to.

Fog in the mornings, hunger for clarity,
coffee and bread with sour plum jam.
Numbness of soul in placid neighborhoods.
Lives ticking on as if.

A typewriter's torrent, suddenly still.
Blue soaking through fog, two dragonflies wheeling.
Acceptable levels of cruelty, steadily rising.
Whatever you bring in your hands, I need to see it.

Suddenly I understand the verb without tenses.
To smell another woman's hair, to taste her skin.
To know the bodies drifting underwater.
To be human, said Rosa – I can't teach you that.

A cat drinks from a bowl of marigolds – his moment.
Surely the love of life is never-ending,
the failure of nerve, a charred fuse?
I want more from you than I ever knew to ask.

Wild pink lilies erupting, tasseled stalks of corn
in the Mexican gardens, corn and roses.
shortening days, strawberry fields in ferment
with tossed-aside, bruised fruit.

ADRIENNE RICH

Sometimes

Sometimes things don't go, after all,
from bad to worse. Some years, muscadel
faces down frost; green thrives; the crops don't fail,
sometimes a man aims high, and all goes well.

A people sometimes will step back from war;
elect an honest man; decide they care
enough, that they can't leave some stranger poor.
Some men become what they were born for.

Sometimes our best efforts do not go
amiss; sometimes we do as we meant to.
The sun will sometimes melt a field of sorrow
that seemed hard frozen: may it happen for you.

SHEENAGH PUGH

Spells

A curse on the lover with shyness as plausible cover for his black lies.
A curse on his leather furniture sticking to the skin.
A curse on his row after row of tasteful jazz
and the glass table's cutting edges.

A blessing on my cobalt blue vase
and a spray of lemon fuchsia, and forgetting.

A curse on 4 a.m., the light like soot or burnt milk in a pan.
A blessing on the dawn and dusk, when the sun and moon are large and
*   shimmering.*

A curse on the memories like storm clouds in my heart.
A blessing on the storm clouds outside my window.
A curse on the useless letters I never throw away.
A blessing on my right arm for its sharp delivery.
A curse on my sharp tongue for its sharp delivery.

439

A blessing on the Lyric muse when she is kind to me.
A curse on the Lyric muse, for she is on holiday in the Bahamas.
A blessing on the warm salt seas for their constancy and power.
A curse on the razor-clams slicing bare feet.

A blessing on foreign countries: their birds and trees, their people, their
clothing, their houses and songs.
A curse on their wars, our wars.
A blessing on their dawn, their dusk, their seas, even their deceitful men.
A blessing.

EVA SALZMAN

Glad of these times

Driving along the motorway
swerving the packed lanes
I am glad of these times.

Because I did not die in childbirth
because my children will survive me
I am glad of these times.

I am not hungry, I do not curtsey,
I lock my door with my own key
and I am glad of these times,

glad of central heating and cable TV
glad of email and keyhole surgery
glad of power showers and washing machines,

glad of polio inoculations
glad of three weeks' paid holiday
glad of smart cards and cash-back,

glad of twenty types of yoghurt
glad of cheap flights to Prague
glad that I work.

I do not breathe pure air or walk green lanes,
see darkness, hear silence,
make music, tell stories,

tend the dead in their dying
tend the newborn in their birthing,
tend the fire in its breathing,

but I am glad of my times,
these times, the age
we feel in our bones, our rage

of tyre music, speed
annulling the peasant graves
of all my ancestors,

glad of my hands on the wheel
and the cloud of grit as it rises
where JCBs move motherly
widening the packed motorway.

HELEN DUNMORE

Staple Island Swing

What I hate about love is its dog
EDWIN MORGAN,
'A View of Things'

What I love – the tall clock of thermals, blackbacks
turning on Sunday axles. A guillemot gaping
a mouth like a mussel shell. The grooved bright meat.

What I hate – cormorants –
when there's one chick too many, sprawled
on the rock like an over-loved fuzzy bear.

What I love – in two and threes,
the cormorants' greasy
green heraldries.

What I hate – eyes like sour sweeties.
Holiday cruelties: watching the veins in her calves,
the man watching the women walking.

What I hate – sickening for a poem,
counting birds into a poem.
What I love – a bird poem.

What I love – a bull seal kippering,
like those fish in red cellophane
we laid on palms to tell fortunes.

What I love – the fantailed terns
adorning your aura
like a devil and an angel.

What I love – the terns giving beak
baksheesh, darning our arms,
sticking our heads like hatpins.

What I love – outrage on the rocks,
a shifting bag of magma, hardening
to a bullseal in the slashed green water.

What I love, the guillemots with their shit tracers,
like me showing off in painty trousers,
playing at being a decorator.

What I love – beaks wagging like metronomes,
bakelite black of cormorants,
the guffy jazz of sea-cliffs.

JEN HADFIELD

10

Ends and Beginnings

Death poems are also celebration poems. We want
to celebrate...whoever has been taken away from us.

FLEUR ADCOCK

The imagination, the one reality in this imagined world.

WALLACE STEVENS

THIS SECTION includes several deeply felt laments for loved ones. Each loss is
particular, but the feelings evoked are universal. Carol Muske-Dukes's 'Love
Song' (463) is just one poem from her 2003 collection *Sparrow*, a whole book
of elegies for her late husband. Virginia Hamilton Adair's mention of 'a bul-
let in the head' in 'A Last Marriage' (460) is a painfully oblique reference to
her husband's suicide many years earlier. There are other poems relating to
suicide in the *Being and Loss* section (270-71) as well as the *Dead or Alive* sec-
tion (123-25) of *Staying Alive*; Andrew Waterhouse's 'Speaking About My
Cracked Sump' (270) is a powerful poem analysing his state of mind at times
of acute depression, written not long before he took his own life in 2001.

Celebration is the uplifting counterweight to grief. Others' lives were enriched
by the person mourned, as in the poems here by Elizabeth Smither (459), Meg
Bateman (460) and Lauris Edmond (462), while Bernard O'Donoghue (458) shows
how a death can bring people back together. Humour can also help, whether
the wit is acerbic (Edwin Brock, 456), gentle (Michael Longley, 457) or fondly
whimsical (Paul Durcan, 458). Critic Jahan Ramazani says we need these kinds
of disturbingly modern poems 'because our society often sugarcoats mourning
in dubious comfort, or retreats from it in embarrassed silence'.

Several poems here show human life following the natural cycles of the Earth;
when autumn comes, it is time to let go, for winter will be followed by rebirth
in spring. The writers believe in the possibility of resurrection at the same time
as they accept the inevitability of withdrawal, for death is not only inescapable
but a defining force in life itself. That sense of letting go also informs poems
which view death as a welcome release from painful illness or infirmity, as in
Jane Kenyon's 'In the Nursing Home' (450).

This section complements part 10 of *Staying Alive* ('Disappearing acts'). I've
also edited a separate anthology, *Do Not Go Gentle*, which offers a selection
of poems chosen specifically for reading at funerals and memorial services.

The Trees

The trees are coming into leaf
Like something almost being said;
The recent buds relax and spread,
Their greenness is a kind of grief.

Is it that they are born again
And we grow old? No, they die too.
Their yearly trick of looking new
Is written down in rings of grain.

Yet still the unresting castles thresh
In fullgrown thickness every May.
Last year is dead, they seem to say,
Begin afresh, afresh, afresh.

PHILIP LARKIN

Late Snow

An end. Or a beginning.
Snow had fallen again and covered
the old dredge and blackened mush
with a gleaming pelt; but high up there
in the sycamore top, Thaw
Thaw, the rooks cried,
sentinel by ruined nests.

Water was slacking into runnels
from drifts and pitted snowbacks,
dripping from the gutter and ragged
icicle fringes. Snow paused
in the shining embrace of bushes,
waiting in ledged curds and bluffs
to tumble into soft explosions.

And suddenly your absence
drove home its imperatives like frost,
and I ran to the high field
clumsily as a pregnant woman
to tread our names in blemished
brilliant drifts; because the time we have
is shrinking away like snow.

M.R. PEACOCKE

Candles

Days to come stand in front of us
like a row of burning candles –
golden, warm, and vivid candles.

Days past fall behind us,
a gloomy line of burnt-out candles;
the nearest are still smoking,
cold, melted, and bent.

I don't want to look at them: their shape saddens me,
and it saddens me to remember their original light.
I look ahead at my burning candles.

I don't want to turn, don't want to see, terrified
how quickly that dark line gets longer,
how quickly one more dead candle joins another.

C.P. CAVAFY
translated from the Greek by Edmund Keeley & Philip Sherrard

Night in Al-Hamra

A candle on the long road
A candle in the slumbering houses
A candle for the terrified stores
A candle for the bakeries
A candle for the journalist shuddering in an empty office
A candle for the fighter
A candle for the doctor at the sick bed
A candle for the wounded
A candle for honest talk
A candle for staircases
A candle for the hotel crowded with refugees
A candle for the singer
A candle for the broadcasters in a shelter
A candle for a bottle of water
A candle for the air
A candle for two lovers in a stripped apartment
A candle for the sky that has folded
A candle for the beginning
A candle for the end
A candle for the final decision
A candle for conscience
A candle in my hand

SAADI YOUSSEF
translated from the Arabic by Khaled Mattawa

Candle poem
(*after Saadi Youssef*)

A candle for the ship's breakfast
eaten while moving southward
through mild grey water
with the work all done,
a candle for the house seen from outside,
the voices and shadows
of the moment before coming home,

446

a candle for the noise of aeroplanes
going elsewhere, passing over,
for delayed departures, embarrassed silences
between people who love one another,
a candle for sandwiches in service stations
at four a.m., and the taste of coffee
from plastic cups, thickened with sugar
to keep us going,

a candle for the crowd around a coffin
and the terrible depth it has to fall
into the grave dug for everyone,
the deaths for decades to come,
our deaths; a candle for going home
and feeling hungry after saying
we would never be able to eat the ham,
the fruit cake, those carefully-buttered buns.

HELEN DUNMORE

A Piece of the Storm
(for Sharon Horvath)

From the shadow of domes in the city of domes,
A snowflake, a blizzard of one, weightless, entered your room
And made its way to the arm of the chair where you, looking up
From your book, saw it the moment it landed. That's all
There was to it. No more than a solemn waking
To brevity, to the lifting and falling away of attention, swiftly,
A time between times, a flowerless funeral. No more than that
Except for the feeling that this piece of the storm,
Which turned into nothing before your eyes, would come back,
That someone years hence, sitting as you are now, might say:
'It's time. The air is ready. The sky has an opening.'

MARK STRAND

Going Without Saying
(i.m. Joe Flynn)

It is a great pity we don't know
When the dead are going to die
So that, over a last companionable
Drink, we could tell them
How much we liked them.

Happy the man who, dying, can
Place his hand on his heart and say:
'At least I didn't neglect to tell
The thrush how beautifully she sings.'

BERNARD O'DONOGHUE

Wet Evening in April

The birds sang in the wet trees
And as I listened to them it was a hundred years from now
And I was dead and someone else was listening to them.
But I was glad I had recorded for him
    The melancholy.

PATRICK KAVANAGH

For the Anniversary of My Death

Every year without knowing it I have passed the day
When the last fires will wave to me
And the silence will set out
Tireless traveller
Like the beam of a lightless star

Then I will no longer
Find myself in life as in a strange garment
Surprised at the earth
And the love of one woman
And the shamelessness of men
As today writing after three days of rain
Hearing the wren sing and the falling cease
And bowing not knowing to what

W.S. MERWIN

Final Notations

it will not be simple, it will not be long
it will take little time, it will take all your thought
it will take all your heart, it will take all your breath
it will be short, it will not be simple

it will touch through your ribs, it will take all your heart
it will not be long, it will occupy your thought
as a city is occupied, as a bed is occupied
it will take all your flesh, it will not be simple

You are coming into us who cannot withstand you
you are coming into us who never wanted to withstand you
you are taking parts of us into places never planned
you are going far away with pieces of our lives

it will be short, it will take all your breath
it will not be simple, it will become your will

ADRIENNE RICH

Gravy

No other word will do. For that's what it was. Gravy.
Gravy, these past ten years.
Alive, sober, working, loving and
being loved by a good woman. Eleven years
ago he was told he had six months to live
at the rate he was going. And he was going
nowhere but down. So he changed his ways
somehow. He quit drinking! And the rest?
After that it was *all* gravy, every minute
of it, up to and including when he was told about,
well, some things that were breaking down and
building up inside his head. 'Don't weep for me,'
he said to his friends. 'I'm a lucky man.
I've had ten years longer than I or anyone
expected. Pure gravy. And don't forget it.'

RAYMOND CARVER

In the Nursing Home

She is like a horse grazing
a hill pasture that someone makes
smaller by coming every night
to pull the fences in and in.

She has stopped running wide loops,
stopped even the tight circles.
She drops her head to feed; grass
is dust, and the creekbed's dry.

Master, come with your light
halter. Come and bring her in.

JANE KENYON

Lovebirds

So she moved into the hospital the last nine days
to tend him with little strokes and murmurs
as he sank into the sheets. Nurse
set out a low bed for her, night-times, next to his.
He nuzzled up to her as she brushed
away the multiplying cells with a sigh,
was glad as she ignored the many
effluents and the tang of death. The second
last morning of his life he opened
his eyes, saying, 'I can't wake up'
but wouldn't close them for his nap
until he was sure she was there
Later he moved quietly to deeper sleep,
as Doctor said he would, still listening
to her twittering on and on until the last.

JO SHAPCOTT

Beyond Harm

A week after my father died
suddenly I understood
his fondness for me was safe – nothing
could touch it. In that last year,
his face would sometimes brighten when I would
enter the room, and his wife said
that once, when he was half asleep,
he smiled when she said my name. He respected
my spunk – when they tied me to the chair, that time
they were tying up someone he respected, and when
he did not speak, for weeks, I was one of the
beings to whom he was not speaking,
someone with a place in his life. The last
week he even said it, once,
by mistake. I walked into his room and said

'How are you,' and he said, 'I love you
too.' From then on, I had
that word to lose. Right up to the last
moment, I could make some mistake, offend him,
and with one of his old mouths of disgust he could
re-skew my life. I did not think of it much,
I was helping to take care of him,
wiping his face and watching him.
But then, a while after he died,
I suddenly thought, with amazement, he will always
love me now, and I laughed – he was dead, dead!

SHARON OLDS

The Entertainment of War

I saw the garden where my aunt had died
And her two children and a woman from next door;
It was like a burst pod filled with clay.

A mile away in the night I had heard the bombs
Sing and then burst themselves between cramped houses
With bright soft flashes and sounds like banging doors;

The last of them crushed the four bodies into the ground,
Scattered the shelter, and blasted my uncle's corpse
Over the housetop and into the street beyond.

Now the garden lay stripped and stale; the iron shelter
Spread out its separate petals around a smooth clay saucer,
Small, and so tidy it seemed nobody had ever been there.

When I saw it, the house was blown clean by blast and care:
Relations had already torn out the new fireplaces;
My cousin's pencils lasted me several years.

And in his office notepad that was given me
I found solemn drawings in crayon of blondes without dresses.
In his lifetime I had not known him well.

Those were the things I noticed at ten years of age:
Those, and the four hearses outside our house,
The chocolate cakes, and my classmates' half-shocked envy.

But my grandfather went home from the mortuary
And for five years tried to share the noises in his skull,
Then he walked out and lay under a furze-bush to die.

When my father came back from identifying the daughter
He asked us to remind him of her mouth.
We tried. He said 'I think it was the one'.

These were marginal people I had met only rarely
And the end of the whole household meant that no grief was seen;
Never have people seemed so absent from their own deaths.
This bloody episode of four whom I could understand better dead
Gave me something I needed to keep a long story moving;
I had no pain of it; can find no scar even now.

But had my belief in the fiction not been thus buoyed up
I might, in the sigh and strike of the next night's bombs
Have realised a little what they meant, and for the first time been
        afraid.

ROY FISHER

Mid-Term Break

I sat all morning in the college sick bay
Counting bells knelling classes to a close.
At two o'clock our neighbours drove me home.

In the porch I met my father crying –
He had always taken funerals in his stride –
And Big Jim Evans saying it was a hard blow.

The baby cooed and laughed and rocked the pram
When I came in, and I was embarrassed
By old men standing up to shake my hand

And tell me they were 'sorry for my trouble'.
Whispers informed strangers I was the eldest,
Away at school, as my mother held my hand

In hers and coughed out angry tearless sighs.
At ten o'clock the ambulance arrived
With the corpse, stanched and bandaged by the nurses.

Next morning I went up into the room. Snowdrops
And candles soothed the bedside; I saw him
For the first time in six weeks. Paler now,

Wearing a poppy bruise on his left temple,
He lay in the four-foot box as in his cot.
No gaudy scars, the bumper knocked him clear.

A four-foot box, a foot for every year.

SEAMUS HEANEY

Sounding the name

In this poem my mother is not dead.
The phone does not ring that October
morning of my fourteenth year.
The anonymous voice on the phone

does not say, Call Arthur to the phone.
Our hired man, a neighbor's son, quiet,
unpretentious, a man from the river hills
near our farm, does not turn from the phone,

he does not say, seeming to stress the time,
Your mother died at ten o'clock. My sister and I
do not look at each other, do not smile,
assuring each other (forever) that words are pretenders.

In this poem my mother is not dead,
she is in the kitchen, finishing the October
canning. I am helping in the kitchen.

I wash the cucumbers. My mother asks me
to go pick some dill. The ducks are migrating.
I forget to close the garden gate.

ROBERT KROETSCH

When a Friend

(for Ellis Settle, 1924-93)

When a friend dies, part
of oneself splits off
and spins into the outer dark.
No use calling it back.
No use saying I miss you.
Part of one's body has been riven.
One recollects gestures,
mostly trivial. The way
he pinched a cigarette,
the way he crouched on a chair.
Now he is less than a living flea.
Where has he gone, this person
whom I loved? He is vapor now;
he is nothing. I remember
talking to him about the world.
What a rich place it became
within our vocabulary. I did not
love it half so much until
he spoke of it, until it was sifted
through the adjectives of our discussion.
And now my friend is dead.
His warm hand has been reversed.
His movements across a room
have been erased. How I wish
he was someplace specific. He
is nowhere. He is absence.
When he spoke of the things
he loved – books, music, pictures,
the articulation of idea –
his body shook as if a wire
within him suddenly surged.

In passion, he filled the room.
Where has he gone, this friend
whom I loved? The way he shaved,
the way he cut his hair, even
the way he squinted when he talked,
when he embraced idea, held it –
all vanished. He has been reduced
to memory. The books he loved,
I see them on my shelves. The words
he spoke still group around me. But
this is chaff. This is the container
now that heart has been scraped out.
He is defunct now. His body is less
than cinders; less than a sentence
after being whispered. He is the zero
from which a man has vanished. He
was the smartest, most vibrant,
like a match suddenly struck, flaring;
now he is sweepings in a roadway.
Where is he gone? He is nowhere.
My friends, I knew a wonderful man,
these words approximate him,
as chips of stone approximate
a tower, as wind approximates a song.

STEPHEN DOBYNS

And another thing...

Why in Christ's name
can't somebody say something?
Nothing profound, just:
*It's OK under ground
the dirt doesn't get into your eyes!*
Or: *you'd be surprised
at the sounds that come down,
breezes, birdsong and heavy breathing!*
I mean, who needs
that Yorick sentimentality?
We want the bloody *skull* speaking!

And what about those friends
who've been through the fire?
Just a whisper as the smoke
flies higher to say: *it's OK
you never feel the blisters!*
An everyday postcard will do,
nothing as festive as Easter!
You see, it isn't our mortality
we fear, that's neither here
nor anywhere; it's the thought
of all that emptiness up there
that takes your breath away.

EDWIN BROCK

Detour

I want my funeral to include this detour
Down the single street of a small market town,
On either side of the procession such names
As Philbin, O'Malley, MacNamara, Keane.
A reverent pause to let a herd of milkers pass
Will bring me face to face with grubby parsnips,
Cauliflowers that glitter after a sunshower,
Then hay rakes, broom handles, gas cylinders.
Reflected in the slow sequence of shop windows
I shall be part of the action when his wife
Draining the potatoes into a steamy sink
Calls to the butcher to get ready for dinner
And the publican descends to change a barrel.
From behind the one locked door for miles around
I shall prolong a detailed conversation
With the man in the concrete telephone kiosk
About where my funeral might be going next.

MICHAEL LONGLEY

Tullynoe: Tête-à-Tête in the Parish Priest's Parlour

'Ah, he was a grand man.'
'He was: he fell out of the train going to Sligo.'
'He did: he thought he was going to the lavatory.'
'He did: in fact he stepped out the rear door of the train.'
'He did: God, he must have got an awful fright.'
'He did: he saw that it wasn't the lavatory at all.'
'He did: he saw that it was the railway tracks going away from him.'
'He did: I wonder if...but he was a grand man.'
'He was: he had the most expensive Toyota you can buy.'
'He had: well, it was only beautiful.'
'It was: he used to have an Audi.'
'He had: as a matter of fact he used to have two Audis.'
'He had: and then he had an Avenger.'
'He had: and then he had a Volvo.'
'He had: in the beginning he had a lot of Volkses.'
'He had: he was a great man for the Volkses.'
'He was: did he once have an Escort?'
'He had not: he had a son a doctor.'
'He had: and he had a Morris Minor too.'
'He had: he had a sister a hairdresser in Kilmallock.'
'He had: he had another sister a hairdresser in Ballybunion.'
'He had: he was put in a coffin which was put in his father's cart.'
'He was: his lady wife sat on top of the coffin driving the donkey.'
'She did: Ah, but he was a grand man.'
'He was: he was a grand man...'
'Good night, Father.'
'Good night, Mary.'

PAUL DURCAN

Concordiam in Populo

And Duncan's horses... 'Tis said they ate each other

After the heart attack, prodigious events
Took place: neighbours who hadn't talked
For twenty years, because of trees cut down,
Horses gone lame, or cattle straying,

Cooperated in organising lifts
To make arrangements for the funeral.

Husbands who'd not addressed a civil word
To wives for even longer referred to them
By christian name in everybody's hearing:
Lizzie or *Julanne* or *Nora May*.
The morning of the burial it rained and rained,
And we all huddled close by the graveside,

Trusting one another, small differences
Set aside, just as Kate had told us once
How she crept into bed when the thunder seemed
To throw giant wooden boxes at the house,
Beside the husband that she hadn't spoken to
Since the first month after their sorry wedding.

BERNARD O'DONOGHUE

A cortège of daughters

A quite ordinary funeral: the corpse
Unknown to the priest. The twenty-third psalm.
The readings by serious businessmen
One who nearly tripped on the unaccustomed pew.
The kneelers and the sitters like sheep and goats.

But by some prior determination a row
Of daughters and daughters-in-law rose
To act as pallbearers instead of men
All of even height and beautiful.
One wore in her hair a black and white striped bow.

And in the midst of their queenliness
One in dark flowered silk, the corpse
Had become a man before they reached the porch
So loved he had his own dark barge
Which their slow moving steps rowed
As a dark lake is sometimes surrounded by irises.

ELIZABETH SMITHER

After the Funeral

The widow stands at the door
and leans her head against the wall.
All is quiet.
The guests are fed
and mostly gone,
and the sea and the town are grey, grey,
with the fishing boats silently putting out.
She hears the talk of the women in the kitchen
and the old men with their drams
discussing a life well lived.
'It's kind of been a happy day,'
she says, looking at her boys,
each with his something
of his father in his face.

Suddenly the sun stabs out bars
of lemon-yellow light
over the fields of glowering corn,
dragons of mist are whisked up
and away across the bay,
and as she turns back to the house
you can still see in her face
the dead man's love for it all.

MEG BATEMAN
translated from the Gaelic by the author

A Last Marriage

The children gone, grown into other arms,
Man of her heart and bed gone underground,
Powder and chunks of ash in a shamefast urn,
Her mother long since buried in a blue gown,
Friends vanishing downward from the highway crash,
Slow hospital dooms, or a bullet in the head,
She came at last alone into her overgrown
Shapeless and forlorn garden. Death was there
Too, but tangible. She hacked and dragged away
Horrors of deadwood, webbed and sagging foliage,

460

Self-strangling roots, vines, suckers, arboreal
Deformities in viperish coils. Sweat, anger, pity
Poured from her. And her flesh was jabbed by thorns,
Hair jerked by twigs, eyes stung by mould and tears.

But day by day in the afterbath she recovered stillness.
Day by day the disreputable garden regained
Its green tenderness. They wooed one another. The living
Responses issued from clean beds of earth.
It was a new marriage, reclusive, active, wordless.
Early each morning even in rain she walked
The reviving ground where one day she would knock and enter.
She took its green tribute into her arms and rooms.
Through autumn the pruned wood gave her ceremonial
Fires, where she saw lost faces radiant with love.
Beyond the window, birds passed and the leaves with them.
Now was a season to sit still with time to know,
Drawing each breath like a fine crystal of snow.

VIRGINIA HAMILTON ADAIR

Musician's Widow

Plants she loved, all growing things.
Soil was nourishment richer than food for her,
richer than sex as she grew older. But she
hated death, hated his unjust death in particular.
The music of him tunnelled through her mind to pursue her.

For a time she remembered to return to him.
She left the upholstery of the new home, the ferns,
the fuchsias, the piano-furnished living-room,
and followed her spade into the cold warmth
his absence had hollowed out for her in earth.

Desire for him she burned with his body, though.
Detritus of nostalgia was a waste of good.
And she had to come back as woman to the world,
a green branched seedling of her purpose, need,
the life behind her gaping like a seed.

ANNE STEVENSON

Anniversary

The white rhododendron has come into flower
– one glistening cluster, ripe and virginal
at the same time; it's grown too, in the year
it's been marking the spot – yours, we said,
walking across to it under the apple trees carrying
our glasses of wine – 'yes, this is the place',
and I think we each did a bit with a trowel.

It wasn't the last word, though – you're here now
in the dusk, laughing somewhere behind me
at what you still had in store for us... but
it's so domestic! Look at me bending down
taking the spoon – a tablespoon (nothing paltry
about this measure) out of the box of... well,
look, it's you, isn't it, this white pile –

why do they call it ashes? My dear, you are grit,
all through; you rattle, you tinkle, as I take
one, two, good spoonfuls of you. It's hilarious
I can see, for the doubled-up ghost of you
over there under the trees, purged of this
heavy stuff, watching me, pointing out
how familiar it is, this kitcheny action –

after all, most of our time was in kitchens,
talking – or shouting – among cooking and kids,
running a complex show and keeping our spirits up,
eager, or cynical, or frivolous – dog-tired too,
of course. Under the leaves, that white sprinkle
gleams in the darkening garden. Remember the day...
oh to hell with it. I wish you were here.

LAURIS EDMOND

A Marriage

We met
    under a shower
of bird-notes.
    Fifty years passed,
love's moment
    in a world in
servitude to time.
    She was young;
I kissed with my eyes
    closed and opened
them on her wrinkles.
    'Come' said death,
choosing her as his
    partner for
the last dance. And she,
    who in life
had done everything
    with a bird's grace,
opened her bill now
    for the shedding
of one sigh no
    heavier than a feather.

R.S. THOMAS

Love Song

Love comes hungry to anyone's hand.
I found the newborn sparrow next to
the tumbled nest on the grass. Bravely

opening its beak. Cats circled, squirrels.
I tried to set the nest right but the wild
birds had fled. The knot of pinfeathers

sat in my hand and spoke. Just because
I've raised it by touch, doesn't mean it
follows. All day it pecks at the tin image of

463

a faceless bird. It refuses to fly,
though I've opened the door. What
sends us to each other? He and I

had a blue landscape, a village street,
some poems, bread on a plate. Love
was a camera in a doorway, love was

a script, a tin bird. Love was faceless,
even when we'd memorised each other's
lines. Love was hungry, love was faceless,

the sparrow sings, famished, in my hand.

CAROL MUSKE-DUKES

Poems

When you come back to me
it will be crow time
and flycatcher time,
with rising spirals of gnats
between the apple trees.
Every weed will be quadrupled,
coarse, welcoming
and spine-tipped.
The crows, their black flapping
bodies, their long calling
toward the mountain;
relatives, like mine,
ambivalent, eye-hooded;
hooting and tearing.
And you will take me in
to your fractal meaningless
babble; the quick of my mouth,
the madness of my tongue.

RUTH STONE

The Eyes

1

When his lover died
he made up his mind to grow old
in his closed house,
alone, with his memory and mirror
in which she gazed one bright day.
Like gold in the miser's coffer,
he chose not to keep
a whole yesterday in the clear mirror.
Time for him would not run.

2

After the first year,
'How were her eyes,' he wondered,
'brown or black? Pale green? Gray?
How were they? Good God! I can't remember.'

3

He went into the street one day
of spring and strolled silently
in double mourning, his heart locked.
From a window in the hollow shadow
he saw flashing eyes. He lowered his
and walked on. Like those!

ANTONIO MACHADO
translated from the Spanish by Willis Barnstone

Curtains

Putting up new curtains,
other windows intrude.
As though it is that first winter in Cambridge
when you and I had just moved in.
Now cold borscht alone in a bare kitchen.

What does it mean if I say this years later?

Listen, last night
I am on a crying jag
with my landlord, Mr Tempesta.
I sneaked in two cats.
He screams NO PETS! NO PETS!
I become my Aunt Virginia,
proud but weak in the head.
I remember Anna Magnani.
I throw a few books. I shout.
He wipes his eyes and opens his hands.
OK OK keep the dirty animals
but no nails in the walls.
We cry together.
I am so nervous, he says.

I want to dig you up and say, look,
it's like the time, remember,
when I ran into our living room naked
to get rid of that fire inspector.

See what you miss by being dead?

RUTH STONE

Not at Home

This room is dead; the occupant has gone.
Why are we frightened? Is it simply that
So much taut stillness, so much neatness stun
The rough intruder? Under that glass dome
A bird peers out. The furniture is flat
With knowledge of so many who've gone home.

Why do we come so eagerly who once
Shrank from her invitations? What is there
In this old, mothballed room, dead at a glance,
That holds us? Here there are no hauntings; we
Perhaps are held by the cold atmosphere,
The sudden stress on all we would not be.

We turn away and the whole room falls back
To junk-shop value; there is nothing more.
The things of worth would fit into a sack,
The rubbish keep a rag-and-bone man for
Longer than he'd believe. Yet, stripped and bare,
The room will hint of something still trapped there.

ELIZABETH JENNINGS

A Room

A room does not turn its back on grief.
Anger does not excite it.
Before desire, it neither responds
nor draws back in fear.

Without changing expression,
it takes
and gives back;
not a tuft in the mattress alters.

Windowsills evenly welcome
both heat and cold.
Radiators speak or fall silent as they must.

Doors are not equivocal,
floorboards do not hesitate or startle.
Impatience does not stir the curtains,
a bed is neither irritable nor rapacious.

Whatever disquiet we sense in a room
we have brought there.

And so I instruct my ribs each morning,
pointing to hinge and plaster and wood –

You are matter, as they are.
See how perfectly it can be done.
Hold, one day more, what is asked.

JANE HIRSHFIELD

We Are Living

What is this room
But the moments we have lived in it?
When all due has been paid
To gods of wood and stone
And recognition has been made
Of those who'll breathe here when we are gone
Does it not take its worth from us
Who made it because we were here?

Your words are the only furniture I can remember
Your body the book that told me most.
If this room has a ghost
It will be your laughter in the frank dark
Revealing the world as a room
Loved only for those moments when
We touched the purely human.

I could give water now to thirsty plants,
Dig up the floorboards, the foundation,
Study the worm's confidence,
Challenge his omnipotence
Because my blind eyes have seen through walls
That make safe prisons of the days.

We are living
In ceiling, floor and windows,
We are given to where we have been.
This white door will always open
On what our hands have touched,
Our eyes have seen.

BRENDAN KENNELLY

What the Living Do

Johnny, the kitchen sink has been clogged for days, some utensil
    probably fell down there.
And the Drano won't work but smells dangerous, and the crusty
    dishes have piled up

waiting for the plumber I still haven't called. This is the everyday
    we spoke of.
It's winter again: the sky's a deep, headstrong blue, and the sunlight
    pours through

the open living-room windows because the heat's on too high in here,
    and I can't turn it off.
For weeks now, driving, or dropping a bag of groceries in the street,
    the bag breaking,

I've been thinking: This is what the living do. And yesterday,
    hurrying along those
wobbly bricks in the Cambridge sidewalk, spilling my coffee down
    my wrist and sleeve,

I thought it again, and again later, when buying a hairbrush: This
    is it.
Parking. Slamming the car door shut in the cold. What you called
    that yearning.

What you finally gave up. We want the spring to come and the
    winter to pass. We want
whoever to call or not call, a letter, a kiss – we want more and more
    and then more of it.

But there are moments, walking, when I catch a glimpse of myself
    in the window glass,
say, the window of the corner video store, and I'm gripped by a
    cherishing so deep

for my own blowing hair, chapped face, and unbuttoned coat that
    I'm speechless:
I am living, I remember you.

MARIE HOWE

Sea to the West

When the sea's to the west
The evenings are one dazzle –
You can find no sign of water.
Sun upflows the horizon;
Waves of shine
Heave, crest, fracture,
Explode on the shore;
The wide day burns
In the incandescent mantle of the air.

Once, fifteen,
I would lean on handlebars,
Staring into the flare,
Blinded by looking,
Letting the gutterings and sykes of light
Flood into my skull.

Then, on the stroke of bedtime,
I'd turn to the town,
Cycle past purpling dykes
To a brown drizzle
Where black-scum shadows
Stagnated between backyard walls.
I pulled the warm dark over my head
Like an eiderdown.

Yet in that final stare when I
(Five times, perhaps, fifteen)
Creak protesting away –
The sea to the west,
The land darkening –
Let my eyes at the last be blinded
Not by the dark
But by dazzle.

NORMAN NICHOLSON

Girls

This top is the pitch of the world
and they've got there, two girls golden
as stamens of wheat, their bicycles burning
– all still now and tingling
receiving their fierce anointing of sun.

Past the high towns they came
Te Pohue Tarawera
tossed on the horn of the hill
past the rivers Rahunga Rangitikei Mohaka
past the sheep seen creeping like maggots
up tracks to the osier's body of shade –

now they stand shining
proclaiming Look! I'm alive!
I've got red hair that tilts
at the tips, I've got freckles
a melon-slice grin
– or I'm taller, more sallow
with boy's hips and a frizz...

we've arrived, we're located
we've found an address at the centre
of four horizons
a hawk hung in one corner
and a cattle truck dripping with dung
rolling by...

They are bright dust, two sparks
in a travelling galaxy
spun to this moment
for taking a sip of eternity
pause on the road to the hillsides of thunder
Turangakuma Titiokura – yes, yes
they know they're at last for the dark.
But look how they blaze in the light.

LAURIS EDMOND

471

A Mistake

I thought: all this is only preparation
For learning, at last, how to die.
Mornings and dusks, in the grass under a maple
Laura sleeping without pants, on a headrest of raspberries,
While Filon, happy, washes himself in the stream.
Mornings and years. Every glass of wine,
Laura, and the sea, land, and archipelago
Bring us nearer, I believed, to one aim
And should be used with a thought to that aim.

But a paraplegic in my street
Whom they move together with his chair
From shade into sunlight, sunlight into shade,
Looks at a cat, a leaf, the chrome steel on an auto,
And mumbles to himself, *'Beau temps, beau temps.'*

It is true. We have a beautiful time
As long as time is time at all.

CZESLAW MILOSZ
translated from the Polish by Renata Gorczynski & Robert Hass

Migration

This year Marie drives back and forth
from the hospital room of her dying friend
to the office of the adoption agency.

I bet sometimes she doesn't know
what threshold she is waiting at –

the hand of her sick friend, hot with fever;
the theoretical baby just a lot of paperwork so far.

But next year she might be standing by a grave,
wearing black with a splash of
                              banana vomit on it,

the little girl just starting to say *Sesame Street*
and *Cappuccino latte grande Mommy.*
The future ours for a while to hold, with its heaviness –

and hope moving from one location to another
like the holy ghost that it is.

TONY HOAGLAND

A Prayer for Sleep

Grant me good rest tonight, O Lord;
let no creatures prowl
the tangled pathways in my skull:
wipe out all wars,
throw guilt a bone;
let me dream, if I dream at all,
no child of Yours has come to harm.

    I know, of course, that death's the norm,
    that there are people who have yet to climb
    the Present's rungs, who lag behind
    (hyenas at the rim of civilisation's light),
    whose laughing hides a Stone Age howl,
    who wait till darkness comes to pounce
    and tear the guts of progress out.

Yet, grant me good rest tonight, my Lord,
blind my internal eyes;
guard my anxious baffled years
with Your protecting arm
and let me dream, if I dream at all,
no child of Yours has come to harm.

MICHAEL HARTNETT

The Task

Reverse the flight of Lucifer,
Hurl back to heaven the fallen star;
Recall Eve's fate, establish her
Again where the first glories are:
Again where Eden's rivers are.

Thrust back contention, merge in one
Warring dualities, make free
Night of the moon, day of the sun;
End the old war of land and sea,
Saying, There shall be no more sea.

With love of love now make an end;
Let male and female strive no more;
Let good and bad their quarrel mend
And with an equal voice adore;
The lion with the lamb adore.

Bow lofty saint, rise humble sin,
Fall from your throne, creep from your den:
The king, the kingdom is within,
That is for evermore, amen:
Was dead and is alive. Amen.

RUTH PITTER

from Autumn Testament

19

The bodies of the young are not the flower,
As some may imagine – it is the soul

Struggling in an iron net of terror
To become itself, to learn to love well,

To nourish the Other – when Mumma came from the bin
With scars from the wrist to the shoulder,

They combed her hair and put their arms around her
Till she began to blossom. The bread she baked for us

Was better kai than you'd get in a restaurant
Because her soul was in it. The bread we share in the churches

Contains a Christ nailed up in solitude,
And all our pain is to be crystal vases,

As if the mice were afraid of God the cat
Who'd plunge them into Hell for touching one another.

22

To pray for an easy heart is no prayer at all
Because the heart itself is the creaking bridge

On which we cross these Himalayan gorges
From bluff to bluff. To sweat out the soul's blood

Midnight after midnight is the ministry of Jacob,
And Jacob will be healed. This body that shivers

In the foggy cold, tasting the sour fat,
Was made to hang like a sack on its thief's cross,

Counting it better than bread to say the words of Christ,
'*Eli! Eli!*' The Church will be shaken like a

Blanket in the wind, and we are the fleas that fall
To the ground for the dirt to cover. Brother thief,

You who are lodged in my ribcage, do not rail at
The only gate we have to paradise.

JAMES K. BAXTER

Some Questions You Might Ask

Is the soul solid, like iron?
Or is it tender and breakable, like
the wings of a moth in the beak of the owl?
Who has it, and who doesn't?
I keep looking around me.
The face of the moose is as sad
as the face of Jesus.
The swan opens her white wings slowly.
In the fall, the black bear carries leaves into the darkness.
One question leads to another.
Does it have a shape? Like an iceberg?
Like the eye of a hummingbird?
Does it have one lung, like the snake and the scallop?
Why should I have it, and not the anteater
who loves her children?
Why should I have it, and not the camel?
Come to think of it, what about the maple trees?
What about the blue iris?
What about all the little stones, sitting alone in the moonlight?
What about roses, and lemons, and their shining leaves?
What about the grass?

MARY OLIVER

A Riddle: Of the Soul

I cannot give
    Unless I have
I cannot have
    Unless I save
Unless I have
    I cannot save
Unless I give
    I cannot have.

Unless I live
  I cannot be
Unless I am
  I cannot seem
I cannot be
  Unless I seem
I cannot live
  Unless I am.

I cannot be
  Unless I give
I cannot have
  Unless I die
Unless I grieve
  I cannot love
Unless I die
  I cannot live.

M.K. JOSEPH

'There will be a talking...'

There will be a talking of lovely things,
there will be cognisance of the seasons,
there will be men who know the flights of birds.
In new days there will be love for women:
we will walk the balance of artistry,
and things will have a middle and an end,
and be loved because they are beautiful.
Who in a walk will find a lasting vase
depicting dance and hold it in his hands
and sell it then? No man on the new earth
will barter with malice nor make of stone
a hollowed riddle; for art will be art,
the freak, the rare no longer commonplace.
There will be a going back to the laws.

MICHAEL HARTNETT

For the Children

The rising hills, the slopes,
of statistics
lie before us,
the steep climb
of everything, going up,
up, as we all
go down.

In the next century
or the one beyond that,
they say,
are valleys, pastures,
we can meet there in peace
if we make it.

To climb these coming crests
one word to you, to
you and your children:

stay together
learn the flowers
go light

GARY SNYDER

In the Next Galaxy

Things will be different.
No one will lose their sight,
their hearing, their gallbladder.
It will be all Catskills with brand-
new wraparound verandas.
The idea of Hitler will not
have vibrated yet.

While back here,
they are still cleaning out
pockets of wrinkled
Nazis hiding in Argentina.
But in the next galaxy,
certain planets will have true
blue skies and drinking water.

RUTH STONE

Let Evening Come

Let the light of late afternoon
shine through chinks in the barn, moving
up the bales as the sun moves down.

Let the cricket take up chafing
as a woman takes up her needles
and her yarn. Let evening come.

Let dew collect on the hoe abandoned
in long grass. Let the stars appear
and the moon disclose her silver horn.

Let the fox go back to its sandy den.
Let the wind die down. Let the shed
go black inside. Let evening come.

To the bottle in the ditch, to the scoop
in the oats, to air in the lung
let evening come.

Let it come, as it will, and don't
be afraid. God does not leave us
comfortless, so let evening come.

JANE KENYON

from Four Quartets

FROM East Coker

I [extract]

In my beginning is my end. In succession
Houses rise and fall, crumble, are extended,
Are removed, destroyed, restored, or in their place
Is an open field, or a factory, or a by-pass.
Old stone to new building, old timber to new fires,
Old fires to ashes, and ashes to the earth
Which is already flesh, fur and faeces,
Bone of man and beast, cornstalk and leaf.
Houses live and die: there is a time for building
And a time for living and for generation
And a time for the wind to break the loosened pane
And to shake the wainscot where the field-mouse trots
And to shake the tattered arras woven with a silent motto.

In my beginning is my end. Now the light falls
Across the open field, leaving the deep lane
Shuttered with branches, dark in the afternoon,
Where you lean against a bank while a van passes,
And the deep lane insists on the direction
Into the village, in the electric heat
Hypnotised. In a warm haze the sultry light
Is absorbed, not refracted, by grey stone.
The dahlias sleep in the empty silence.
Wait for the early owl.

V [extract]

Home is where one starts from. As we grow older
The world becomes stranger, the pattern more complicated
Of dead and living. Not the intense moment
Isolated, with no before and after,
But a lifetime burning in every moment
And not the lifetime of one man only
But of old stones that cannot be deciphered.
There is a time for the evening under starlight,
A time for the evening under lamplight
(The evening with the photograph album).

Love is most nearly itself
When here and now cease to matter.
Old men ought to be explorers
Here or there does not matter
We must be still and still moving
Into another intensity
For a further union, a deeper communion
Through the dark cold and the empty desolation,
The wave cry, the wind cry, the vast waters
Of the petrel and the porpoise. In my end is my beginning.

FROM Little Gidding

V

What we call the beginning is often the end
And to make an end is to make a beginning.
The end is where we start from. And every phrase
And sentence that is right (where every word is at home,
Taking its place to support the others,
The word neither diffident nor ostentatious,
An easy commerce of the old and the new,
The common word exact without vulgarity,
The formal word precise but not pedantic,
The complete consort dancing together)
Every phrase and every sentence is an end and a beginning,
Every poem an epitaph. And any action
Is a step to the block, to the fire, down the sea's throat
Or to an illegible stone: and that is where we start.
We die with the dying:
See, they depart, and we go with them.
We are born with the dead:
See, they return, and bring us with them.
The moment of the rose and the moment of the yew tree
Are of equal duration. A people without history
Is not redeemed from time, for history is a pattern
Of timeless moments. So, while the light fails
On a winter's afternoon, in a secluded chapel
History is now and England.

With the drawing of this Love and the voice of this Calling

We shall not cease from exploration
And the end of all our exploring
Will be to arrive where we started
And know the place for the first time.
Through the unknown, unremembered gate
When the last of earth left to discover
Is that which was the beginning;
At the source of the longest river
The voice of the hidden waterfall
And the children in the apple tree
Not known, because not looked for
But heard, half-heard, in the stillness
Between two waves of the sea.
Quick now, here, now, always –
A condition of complete simplicity
(Costing not less than everything)
And all shall be well and
All manner of thing shall be well
When the tongues of flame are in-folded
Into the crowned knot of fire
And the fire and the rose are one.

T.S. ELIOT

Appendices

FURTHER READING

INDIVIDUAL POETS

The acknowledgements pages give details of selected and collected editions by poets represented in this anthology as well as some key individual collections. As further starting-point for new readers, here are 20 books by poets I would strongly recommend: all are writers featured in *Staying Alive* or *Being Alive* with representative choices from their work.

Fleur Adcock: *Poems 1960-2000* (Bloodaxe, 2000)
Simon Armitage: *Selected Poems* (Faber, 2001)
Elizabeth Bishop: *Complete Poems* (Chatto, 1991)
Billy Collins: *Taking Off Emily Dickinson's Clothes: Selected Poems* (Picador, 2000)
Carol Ann Duffy: *Selected Poems* (Penguin, 1994)
Helen Dunmore: *Out of the Blue: Poems 1975-2001* (Bloodaxe, 2001)
Paul Durcan: *A Snail in My Prime: New & Selected Poems* (Harvill, 1993)
U.A. Fanthorpe: *Collected Poems* (Peterloo Poets, 2004)
Seamus Heaney: *Opened Ground: Poems 1966-1996* (Faber, 1998)
Michael Longley: *Selected Poems* (Cape, 1998)
Derek Mahon: *Collected Poems* (Gallery, 1999)
Czeslaw Milosz: *New and Collected Poems 1931-2001* (Penguin, 2001)
Paul Muldoon: *New Selected Poems 1968-1994* (Faber, 1996)
Pablo Neruda: *Full Woman, Fleshly Apple, Hot Moon* (HarperCollins, NY, 1997)
Alden Nowlan: *Between Tears and Laughter: Selected Poems* (Bloodaxe, 2004)
Sharon Olds: *The Wellspring* (Cape, 1996)
Mary Oliver: *Wild Geese: Selected Poems* (Bloodaxe, 2004)
Jo Shapcott: *Her Book: Poems 1988-1998* (Faber, 2000)
Ken Smith: *Shed: Poems 1980-2001* (Bloodaxe, 2002)
Wislawa Szymborska: *View with a Grain of Sand: Selected Poems* (Faber, 1998)

ANTHOLOGIES

Many poetry anthologies are useless to readers who aren't already familiar with the territory. Like poetry reviews in newspapers, they are produced by poets with other poets – not readers – in mind. But I recommend these books for their range or content or because their introductions or notes are helpful to new readers. The American anthologies can be ordered from www.amazon.com.

Neil Astley: *Staying Alive: real poems for unreal times* (Bloodaxe, 2002). *Being Alive* is the sequel to *Staying Alive*. The first anthology in this series has another 500 poems as well as an introductory essay on the relevance of contemporary poetry; 'The Sound of Poetry', an account of rhyme and rhythm, form and free verse (essential reading for anyone who believes that poetry *has* to rhyme or 'it's not poetry'); and a glossary of technical terms.

Neil Astley: *Being Human* (Bloodaxe, 2006). The forthcoming third volume in the series: a companion volume to both *Staying Alive* and *Being Alive*.

Edna Longley: *The Bloodaxe Book of 20th Century Poetry from Britain & Ireland* (Bloodaxe, 2000): The key 60 poets introduced with informative notes.

Seamus Heaney & Ted Hughes: *The Rattle Bag* (Faber, 1982): Classic and modern poems, including poetry in translation and from oral traditions.

Jo Shapcott & Matthew Sweeney: *Emergency Kit: Poems for Strange Times* (Faber, 1996). Lively selection of contemporary English-language poetry.

Mark Strand & Eavan Boland: *The Making of a Poem* (Norton, 2000). Traces the evolution of forms through the poems themselves, from early to modern.

Ruth Padel: *52 Ways of Looking at a Poem* (Chatto, 2002). Short essays from her newspaper column which strip poems down to their nuts and bolts.

Robert Hass: *Poet's Choice: poems for everyday life* (Ecco/HarperCollins, USA, 1998). The former U.S. Poet Laureate introduced readers of his syndicated column to a different poem every week, with thoughtful commentaries on mostly new work by American poets as well as some translations.

Robert Pinsky & Maggie Dietz: *Americans' Favorite Poems* (Norton, USA, 2000) AND *Poems to Read* (Norton, USA, 2002). Pinsky's task as Laureate was the National Favorite Poem Project: readers recorded their favourite poems, and their comments are included with the editors' notes in these two books.

Billy Collins: *Poetry 180: a turning back to poetry* (Random House, USA, 2003). Another inspired anthology by a U.S. Poet Laureate, this book draws on Billy Collins's Library of Congress website, whose focus was high school 'because all too often it is the place where poetry goes to die'.

Diane Boller, Don Selby & Chryss Yost: *Poetry Daily: 366 poems from the world's most popular poetry website* (Sourcebooks, USA, 2003). Selection from poems posted on the *Poetry Daily* website (www.poems.com) in its first six years.

Garrison Keillor: *Good Poems* (Viking, USA, 2002). Poems read by Keillor on his *Writer's Almanac* radio show, but as Rita Dove has noted, 'an anthology overwhelmingly populated by white poets is likely to send the message that only white folks deserve and/or are capable of writing "good poems".'

J.D. McClatchy: *The Vintage Book of Contemporary American Poetry* (Vintage, 1990): More comprehensive and recent than similarly titled anthologies from Faber and Penguin: selections from 65 poets with editorial notes on each.

J.D. McClatchy: *The Vintage Book of Contemporary World Poetry* (Vintage, 1996): Poets from four continents and two dozen languages, mostly in first-rate translations by distinguished poets, with short introductory notes.

E.A. Markham: *Hinterland: Caribbean Poetry from the West Indies & Britain* (Bloodaxe, 1989): 14 poets with photos, interviews and autobiographical essays.

Jeni Couzyn: *The Bloodaxe Book of Contemporary Women Poets* (Bloodaxe, 1985): Large selections – with essays on their work – by eleven leading poets.

Linda France: *Sixty Women Poets* (Bloodaxe, 1993): Selections by the main British and Irish women poets from the 1970s to the early 90s.

Maura Dooley: *Making for Planet Alice: New Women Poets* (Bloodaxe, 1997): Thirty poets who published their first collections during the 1990s.

Deryn Rees-Jones: *Modern Women Poets* (Bloodaxe, 2005): Companion anthology to her critical study *Consorting with Angels*. Over 100 poets from 1900 to the present, mostly British and Irish writers but including some influential figures from North America.

Michael Hulse, David Kennedy & David Morley: *The New Poetry* (Bloodaxe, 1993): The first anthology of the new British and Irish poets of the 1980s and 90s – multicultural, politicised, witty, often urban.

Sean O'Brien: *The Firebox: Poetry in Britain and Ireland after 1945* (Picador, 1999): Small selections of numerous poets, with helpful editorial headnotes.

Simon Armitage & Robert Crawford: *The Penguin Book of Poetry from Britain and Ireland since 1945* (Penguin, 1998). Similar selection to O'Brien's *Firebox*, with a fuller choice of Scottish and Welsh poets, but limited notes.

Patrick Crotty: *Modern Irish Poetry* (Blackstaff, 1995). Nearly 50 writers, each introduced with helpful notes, including some Irish language poets.

Selina Guinness: *The New Irish Poets* (Bloodaxe, 2004). In-depth selections of work by over 30 poets, with photos and editorial commentaries.

ESSAYS & HANDBOOKS

As with the anthologies, most critical guides to modern poetry are produced by writers who have little interest in helping new readers. Many books on modern poetry issued by academic publishers are written in a jargon-studded private language which even highly intelligent readers find baffling, so avoid any book of literary criticism published by a university press, and any book which refers to poems as *texts* or which uses the expressions *decode* or *foregrounding*. The following books are among the few exceptions:

W.N. Herbert & Matthew Hollis: *Strong Words: modern poets on modern poetry* (Bloodaxe, 2000): Absolutely indispensable: essential reading for poets as well as for readers, critics, teachers and students of creative writing. This judicious and comprehensive selection of manifestos starts with Yeats, Eliot, Pound, Auden, Stevens, Lowell, Plath and other key figures, then adds over 30 newly commissioned essays by contemporary poets.

Paul Hyland: *Getting into Poetry: A Readers' and Writers' Guide to the Poetry Scene*, 2nd edition (Bloodaxe, 1996): Hyland has written the book he wanted to read when he started getting into poetry, a handbook to help readers, writers and teachers to hack their way into the jungle of modern poetry.

Peter Sansom: *Writing Poems* (Bloodaxe, 1994). Practical guide with examples drawn from Sansom's long experience of running workshops and courses.

Matthew Sweeney & John Hartley Williams: *Writing Poetry* (Hodder, 1997): Entertaining guide for interested readers as well as would-be poets.

Seamus Heaney: *Finders Keepers: Selected Prose 1971-2001* (Faber, 2002). Essays on many essential poets, including work from *Preoccupations*, *The Government of the Tongue* and *The Redress of Poetry*. All Heaney's readings are informed by his insistence on the unity of poetry and life.

Dennis O'Driscoll: *Troubled Thoughts, Majestic Dreams: Selected Prose Writings* (Gallery Press, 2001). The most perceptive and knowledgeable critic of modern poetry, O'Driscoll is an excellent guide unhampered by critical baggage.

James Fenton: *An Introduction to English Poetry* (Viking, 2002). Lively guide to form in poetry by a poet-critic who practises what he preaches.

Randall Jarrell: *Poetry and the Age* (1955; Faber, 1973). America's most acute poet-critic, a savager of cant and a salvager of humanity. His essays on poetry and criticism are essential reading for anyone who cares about the art.

Sean O'Brien: *The Deregulated Muse: Essays on Contemporary British & Irish Poetry* (Bloodaxe, 1998). Densely written studies of 20 poets, with shorter comments on another dozen: not the best starting-point for new readers, but the least offputting, despite its male bias and overpoliticised readings.

Deryn Rees-Jones: *Consorting with Angels: Modern Women Poets* (Bloodaxe, 2005). Long awaited critical study of major women poets, published with a companion anthology, *Modern Women Poets* (same title as this book's subtitle).

Clare Brown & Don Paterson: *Don't Ask Me What I Mean: poets in their own words* (Picador, 2003). Short essays commissioned by the Poetry Book Society. The PBS offers readers a Choice and four Recommendations each quarter, all five titles discussed by the poets themselves in the *PBS Bulletin* (their short commentaries are far more illuminating than reviews of poetry). Joining the PBS is one of the easiest and most enjoyable ways of gaining a better knowledge of contemporary poetry. The PBS is at Book House, 45 East Hill, London SW18 2QZ. The PBS's new on-line book ordering service will supply any in-print book of contemporary poetry published in Britain (not just the PBS's own selections): see www.poetrybooks.co.uk.

ACKNOWLEDGEMENTS

The poems in this anthology are reprinted from the following books, all by permission of the publishers listed unless stated otherwise. Thanks are due to all the copyright holders cited below for their kind permission:

Virginia Hamilton Adair: *Ants on the Melon* (Random House, NY, 1996). Robert Adamson: *Reading the River: Selected Poems* (Bloodaxe Books, 2004). Kim Addonizio: *Tell Me* (BOA Editions, USA, 2000). Fleur Adcock: *Poems 1960-2000* (Bloodaxe Books, 2000). Kim Addonizio: *Tell Me* (BOA Editions, USA, 2000). John Agard: *Mangoes and Bullets* (Pluto Press, 1985; Serpent's Tail, 1990). Ai: *Vice: New & Selected Poems* (W.W. Norton & Company, 1999). Agha Shahid Ali: 'The Dacca Gauzes' and 'Stationery' from *The Half-Inch Himalayas* (Wesleyan University Press, 1987); extract from 'The Country Without a Post Office' from *The Country Without a Post Office* (W.W. Norton & Company, 1997), by permission of the publishers and Agha Shahid Ali Literary Trust. Moniza Alvi: *Carrying My Wife* (Bloodaxe Books, 2000). Yehuda Amichai: 'My Father', tr. Azila Talit Reisenberger, first published in *Poems to Read*, ed. Robert Pinsky (W W Norton & Company, 2000), by permission of the translator; 'The Diameter of the Bomb' from *Selected Poems*, ed. Ted Hughes & Daniel Weissbort (Faber & Faber, 2000); 'Jerusalem', 'To My Love, Combing Her Hair' and ' "The Rustle of History's Wings," as They Used to Say Then' from *The Selected Poetry of Yehuda Amichai*, tr. Chana Bloch & Stephen Mitchell (HarperCollins, 1986; rev. ed. University of California Press, 1996). Maya Angelou: *The Complete Collected Poems* (Virago Press, 1994). Simon Armitage: 'Kid' and 'Not the Furniture Game' from *Kid* (1992); 'Mother, any distance...' from *Book of Matches* (1993); 'Killing Time #2' from *Travelling Songs* (2002), all from Faber & Faber. Margaret Atwood: *Poems 1976-1986* (Virago Press, 1992). W.H. Auden: *Collected Poems*, ed. Edward Mendelson (Faber & Faber, 1991).

Meg Bateman: *Lightness and Other Poems* (Polygon, 1997), by permission of Birlinn Ltd. James K. Baxter: *Collected Poems*, ed. John Weir (Oxford University Press, NZ, 1980), by permission of Mrs Jacquie C. Baxter. Connie Bensley: *Choosing To Be a Swan* (Bloodaxe Books, 1994). Wendell Berry: *The Selected Poems of Wendell Berry* (Counterpoint, USA, 1998). John Berryman: *The Dream Songs* (Faber & Faber, 1993). Elizabeth Bishop: *The Complete Poems 1927-1979* (Chatto & Windus, 1983), by permission of Farrar, Straus & Giroux, Inc. Michael Blackburn: *The Ascending Boy* (Flambard Press, 1999). Robert Bly: 'The Third Body' from *Loving a Woman in Two Worlds* (1985), reprinted in *Eating the Honey of Words: New and Selected Poems* (HarperCollins, USA, 1999). Roo Borson: *Night Walk: Selected Poems* (Oxford University Press, Toronto, 1994), by permission of the author. Bertolt Brecht: 'War Has Been Given a Bad Name', tr. John Willett, from *Poems 1913-1956*, ed. John Willett & Ralph Manheim (Methuen, 2000), © 1976; 'General, Your Tank Is a Powerful Machine', tr. David Constantine, previously unpublished translation by permission of Suhrkamp Verlag. Edwin Brock: 'Five Ways to Kill a Man' from *Five Ways to Kill a Man: New and Selected Poems* (Enitharmon Press, 1990); 'And another thing...' from *And Another Thing* (Enitharmon Press, 1999), by permission of David Higham Associates. Gwendolyn Brooks: *Selected Poems* (HarperCollins, 1963/1999). William Bronk: *Life Support: New & Collected Poems* (North Point Press, USA, 1977). Eleanor Brown: *Maiden Speech* (Bloodaxe Books, 1996). George Mackay Brown: *Selected Poems* (The Hogarth Press, 1977), by permission of the Random House Group Ltd. David Budbill:

Moment to Moment: Poems of a Mountain Recluse (Copper Canyon Press, USA, 1999). **Charles Bukowski:** *Love is a Dog from Hell: Poems 1974-77* (Black Sparrow Press, USA, 1977), by permission of HarperCollins, Inc. **John Burnside:** *The Light Trap* (Jonathan Cape, 2002), by permission of the Random House Group Ltd. **Hayden Carruth:** *Collected Shorter Poems, 1946-1991* (Copper Canyon Press, USA, 1991). **Ciaran Carson:** *The Ballad of HMS Belfast: A compendium of Belfast poems* (Gallery Press, 1999). **Raymond Carver:** *All of Us: Collected Poems* (Harvill Press, 1996), by permission of International Creative Management, Inc., copyright © 1996 Tess Gallagher. **Charles Causley:** *Collected Poems 1951-2000* (Picador, 2000), by permission of David Higham Associates Ltd. **C.P. Cavafy:** *Collected Poems*, tr. Edmund Keeley & Philip Sherrard (Hogarth Press, 1990), by permission of the estate of C.P. Cavafy and Random House Group Ltd. **Kate Clanchy:** *Newborn* (Picador, 2004), by permission of Macmillan Publishers Ltd. **Polly Clark:** 'Elvis the Performing Octopus', previously unpublished poem by permission of the author. **Suzanne Cleary:** *Keeping Time* (Carnegie Mellon University Press, Pittsburgh, 2002). **Lucille Clifton:** 'the lost baby poem' from *Good Woman: Poems and a Memoir 1969-1980* (1987); 'poem to my uterus' and 'to my last period' from *Quilting: Poems 1987-1990* (1991), both from BOA Editions, USA. **Henri Cole:** *Middle Earth* (Farrar, Straus & Giroux, Inc, 2003). **Billy Collins:** 'Man in Space', 'Nostalgia', 'Putting Down the Cat' from *Taking Off Emily Dickinson's Clothes: Selected Poems* (Picador, 2000); 'Litany' from *Nine Horses* (Picador, 2003) by permission of Macmillan Publishers Ltd; 'Introduction to Poetry' from *The Apple that Astonished Paris* (University of Arkansas Press, Fayetteville, 1996). **Stewart Conn:** *Stolen Light: Selected Poems* (Bloodaxe Books, 1999). **David Constantine:** *Collected Poems* (Bloodaxe Books, 2004). **Wendy Cope:** *Serious Concerns* (Faber & Faber, 1992). **Julia Copus:** *In Defence of Adultery* (Bloodaxe Books, 2003). **Hart Crane:** *The Complete Poems*, ed. Marc Simon (Liveright Books, 2000), by permission of Liveright Publishing Corporation. **Robert Creeley:** *Collected Poems of Robert Creeley 1945-1975* (Uni-versity of California Press, 1982), copyright © The Regents of the University of California, by permission of author and publisher. **Lorna Crozier:** *Inventing the Hawk* (McClelland & Stewart, Toronto, 1992). **Jeni Couzyn:** *Life by Drowning: Selected Poems* (Bloodaxe Books, 1985), by permission of the author. **Ruth Dallas:** *Collected Poems* (University of Otago Press, Dunedin, NZ, 1987). **Julia Darling:** *Sudden Collapses in Public Places* (Arc, 2003). **Mahmoud Darwish:** 'He Embraces His Murderer' and 'In This Land', tr. Sarah Maguire & Sabry Hafez, by permission of the author and translators. **Peter Davison:** *The Great Ledge* (Alfred A. Knopf, Inc., NY, 1989). **Michael Davitt:** *Selected Poems/ Roghda Dánta 1968-1984* (Raven Arts Press, 1987). **C. Day Lewis:** *Selected Poems*, ed. Jill Balcon (Enitharmon Press, 2004). **Carl Dennis:** *Practical Gods* (Penguin USA, 2001). **Imtiaz Dharker:** 'Blessing' from *Postcards from god* (1997); 'This room' and 'Honour Killing' from *I Speak for the Devil* (2001); both from Bloodaxe Books and Penguin Books India. **Emily Dickinson:** *The Poems of Emily Dickinson*, ed. Ralph W. Franklin (Harvard University Press, 1998). **Peter Didsbury:** *Scenes from a Long Sleep: New & Collected Poems* (Bloodaxe Books, 2003). **Stephen Dobyns:** *Common Carnage* (Penguin Books, USA, 1996; Bloodaxe Books, 1997). **Michael Donaghy:** *Dances Learned Last Night: Poems 1975-1995* (Picador, 2000), by permission of Macmillan Publishers Ltd. **Maura Dooley:** *Sound Barrier: Poems 1982-2002* (Bloodaxe Books, 2002). **Mark Doty:** 'Brilliance' from *My Alexandria* (1995); 'Migratory' from *Atlantis* (1996); 'The Embrace' from *Sweet Machine* (1998), all from Jonathan Cape by permission of the Random House Group Ltd. **Rita Dove:** *Selected Poems* (Vintage Books, USA, 1993), by permission of the author. **Nick**

Drake: *The Man in the White Suit* (Bloodaxe Books, 1999). **Carlos Drummond de Andrade**: 'Infancy', tr. Elizabeth Bishop, from *An Anthology of 20th Century Brazilian Poetry*, ed. Elizabeth Bishop & Emanuel Brasil (Wesleyan University Press, USA, 1972). **Carol Ann Duffy**: 'Warming Her Pearls' from *Selling Manhattan* (1987), 'Valentine' from *Mean Time* (1993), both from Anvil Press Poetry; 'Mrs Midas' from *The World's Wife* (Picador, 1999), by permission of Macmillan Publishers Ltd. **Helen Dunmore**: all poems from *Out of the Blue: Poems 1975-2001* (Bloodaxe Books, 2001) except 'Glad of these times', previously unpublished poem by permission of the author. **Douglas Dunn**: 'Glasgow Schoolboys, Running Backwards' from *Barbarians* (1979), 'Ratatouille' from *St Kilda's Parliament* (1981), both from Faber & Faber. **Paul Durcan**: *A Snail in My Prime: New & Selected Poems* (The Harvill Press, 1993), by permission of the author and Blackstaff Press.

Lauris Edmond: *New & Selected Poems* (Bloodaxe Books/Oxford University Press, NZ, 1992), by permission of the Lauris Edmond Estate. **T.S. Eliot**: extracts from *East Coker* (1940) and *Little Gidding* (1942), from *Four Quartets*, from *The Complete Poems and Plays* (Faber & Faber, 1969). **Hans Magnus Enzensberger**: 'The End of the Owls', tr. Jerome Rothenberg, by permission of the author; 'Explaining the Declaration' from *Lighter Than Air*, tr. David Constantine (Bloodaxe Books, 2002).

Faiz Ahmed Faiz: *The Rebel's Silhouette: Selected Poems*, tr. Agha Shahid Ali (University of Massachusetts Press, 1991/1995). **U.A. Fanthorpe**: *Collected Poems* (Peterloo Poets, 2004). **Helen Farish**: *Intimates* (Jonathan Cape, 2005), by permission of the author. **Paul Farley**: *The Boy from the Chemist is Here to See You* (Picador, 1998), by permission of Macmillan Publishers Ltd. **Fiona Farrell**: *The Inhabited Initial* (Auckland University Press, NZ, 1999). **Vicki Feaver**: 'The Way We Live Now' from *Close Relatives* (Secker & Warburg, 1981), by permission of the author; 'Crab Apple Jelly' from *The Handless Maiden* (Jonathan Cape, 1994), by permission of the Random House Group Ltd. **James Fenton**: 'Wind' from *The Memory of War and Children in Exile: Poems 1968-1983* (Penguin Books, 1983); 'Jerusalem', 'The Ideal', 'The Mistake' from *Out of Danger* (Penguin Books, 1993); 'Let's Go Over It All Again', first published in *The New Yorker*, 14 May 2001, all by permission of Peters, Fraser & Dunlop Group Ltd. **Roy Fisher**: *The Dow Low Drop: New & Selected Poems* (Bloodaxe Books, 1996). **Nick Flynn**: *Some Ether* (Graywolf Press, USA, 2000). **Cheryl Follon**: *All Your Talk* (Bloodaxe Books, 2004). **Duncan Forbes**: *Taking Liberties* (Enitharmon Press, 1993). **Linda France**: *Red* (Bloodaxe Books, 1992). **Tom French**: *Touching the Bones* (Gallery Press, 2001). **Erich Fried**: 'What Happens' from *100 Poems without a Country*, tr. Stuart Hood (Calder, 1978); 'Conversation with a Survivor' from *Love Poems*, tr. Stuart Hood (Calder, 1991). **Cynthia Fuller**: 'Guests' by permission of the author.

Deborah Garrison: *A Working Girl Can't Win* (Random House, NY, 1998). **Jack Gilbert**: 'Measuring the Tyger', 'Searching for Pittsburgh' and 'The Great Fires' from *The Great Fires: Poems 1982-1992* (Alfred A. Knopf, NY, 1995); 'Hunger' by permission of the author. **Susan Glickman**: *Hide & Seek* (Signal Editions/Véhicule Press, Montreal, 1995). **Denis Glover**: *Enter Without Knocking* (Pegasus Press, NZ, 1971). **Luis Enrique Mejía Godoy**: 'Revenge', tr. Dinah Livingstone, by permission of the translator. **Linda Gregg**: *Things and Flesh* (Graywolf Press, USA, 1999). **Andrew Greig**: *Into You* (Bloodaxe Books, 2001). **Chris Greenhalgh**: *Of Love, Death and the Sea-Squirt* (Bloodaxe Books, 2000). **Lavinia Greenlaw**: 'Tryst' from *A World Where News Travelled Slowly* (Faber & Faber, 1993); 'Zombies' from *Minsk* (Faber & Faber, 2003). **Jane Griffiths**: *A Grip on Thin Air* (Bloodaxe Books, 2000). **Philip Gross**: *Mappa Mundi* (Bloodaxe Books, 2003). **Vona Groarke**:

Flight (Gallery Press, 2002). **Thom Gunn**: *Collected Poems* (Faber & Faber, 1993). **Jen Hadfield**: *Almanacs* (Bloodaxe Books, 2005), by permission of the author. **Donald Hall**: *Old and New Poems* (Houghton Mifflin, USA, 1990). **Choman Hardi**: *Life for Us* (Bloodaxe Books, 2004). **Kerry Hardie**: 'The Hunter Home from the Hill' and 'Autumn Cancer' from *A Furious Place* (1996); 'She Replies to Carmel's Letter' and 'What's Left' from *Cry for the Hot Belly* (2000); 'Sheep Fair Day' from *The Sky Didn't Fall* (2003), all from Gallery Press. **Michael Harlow**: *Giotto's Elephant* (McIndoe Publishers, NZ, 1991). **Michael Hartnett**: *Collected Poems* (Gallery Press, 2001). **Tony Harrison**: *Selected Poems* (Penguin Books, 1987), by permission of Gordon Dickerson and the author. **Gwen Harwood**: *Collected Poems* (Oxford University Press, 1991), by permission of John Harwood. **Robert Hass**: *Human Wishes* (HarperCollins, USA, 1999). **Kaylin Haught**: 'God Says Yes to Me', first published in *The Palm of Your Hand*, ed. Steve Kowat (Tilbury House Publishers, USA, 1995), by permission of the editor and author. **Seamus Heaney**: *Opened Ground: Poems 1966-1996* (Faber & Faber, 1998). **W.N. Herbert**: *The Big Bumper Book of Troy* (Bloodaxe Books, 2002). **Zbigniew Herbert**: *Selected Poems*, tr. Czeslaw Milosz & Peter Dale Scott (Penguin Books, 1968). **Tracey Herd**: 'The Survivors' from *No Hiding Place* (1996), 'Ophelia's Confession' from *Dead Redhead* (2001), both from Bloodaxe Books. **Bob Hicok**: *Plus Shipping* (BOA Editions, USA, 1998). **Rita Ann Higgins**: *Sunny Side Plucked: New & Selected Poems* (Bloodaxe Books, 1996). **Selima Hill**: 'Being a Wife' from *Trembling Hearts in the Bodies of Dogs: New & Selected Poems* (1994), 'Please Can I Have a Man' from *Violet* (1997), 'Hairbrush' and 'House' from *Bunny* (2001), all from Bloodaxe Books. **Edward Hirsch**: *Wild Gratitude* (Knopf, NY, 1986), by permission of Alfred A. Knopf, division of Random House, Inc. **Jane Hirshfield**: 'Knowing Nothing', 'Not-Yet', 'A Room' from *Lives of the Heart* (HarperCollins, USA, 1997); 'Red Onion, Cherries, Boiling Potatoes, Milk – ' from *Given Sugar, Given Salt* (HarperCollins, USA, 2001). **Tony Hoagland**: *Donkey Gospel* (1998) and *What Narcissism Means to Me* (2003), both from Graywolf Press, USA, all poems reprinted in *What Narcissism Means to Me: Selected Poems* (Bloodaxe Books, 2005). **Matthew Hollis**: *Ground Water* (Bloodaxe Books, 2004). **Miroslav Holub**: *Poems Before & After: Collected English Translations* (Bloodaxe Books, 1990). **Marie Howe**: 'How Many Times' from *The Good Thief* (Persea Books, NY, 1988); 'What the Living Do' from *What the Living Do* (W.W. Norton & Company, 1998). **Ted Hughes**: *Collected Poems* (Faber & Faber, 2003). **Pearse Hutchinson**: *Collected Poems* (Gallery Press, 2002).

    Helen Ivory: *The Double Life of Clocks* (Bloodaxe Books, 2002).

    Anna Jackson: *The Pastoral Kitchen* (Auckland University Press, NZ, 2001); **Kathleen Jamie**: *Mrs and Mrs Scotland Are Dead: Poems 1980-1994* (Bloodaxe Books, 2002). **Esther Jansma**: 'Descent', translated by James Brockway & Esther Jansma of 'De val', from *Hier is de tijd* (De Arbeiderspers, Amsterdam, 1998), by permission of the author. **Randall Jarrell**: *The Complete Poems* (Faber & Faber, 1971). **Elizabeth Jennings**: *Recoveries* (André Deutsch, 1964), by permission of David Higham Associates. **Rodney Jones**: *Things That Happen Once* (Houghton Mifflin, USA, 1996); **M.K. Joseph**: *Inscription on a Paper Dart: Selected Poems 1945-72* (Auckland University Press/Oxford University Press, NZ, 1974).

    Kapka Kassabova: *Someone else's life* (Bloodaxe Books/Auckland University Press, NZ, 2003). **Patrick Kavanagh**: *Selected Poems*, ed. Antoinette Quinn (Penguin, 1996), reprinted here by permission of the Trustees of the Estate of the late Katherine B. Kavanagh and the Jonathan Williams Literary Agency. **Jackie Kay**: 'Twelve Bar Bessie' from *Other Lovers* (1993); 'Somebody Else' from *Off Colour* (1998), both from Bloodaxe Books. **Brendan Kennelly**: *Familiar Strangers: New*

490

& Selected Poems 1960-2004 (Bloodaxe Books, 2004). **Jane Kenyon:** *Otherwise: New and Selected Poems* (Graywolf Press, USA, 1996). **Galway Kinnell:** *Selected Poems* (Houghton Mifflin, USA, 2000; Bloodaxe Books, UK, 2001). **August Kleinzahler:** *Green Sees Things in Waves* (Farrar, Straus & Giroux, Inc., USA; Faber & Faber, 1998); **Rutger Kopland:** *A World Beyond Myself: Selected Poems*, tr. James Brockway (Enitharmon Press, 1991). **Robert Kroetsch:** *Advice to My Friends* (Stoddart, Toronto, 1995), by permission of Stoddart/House of Anansi. **Stanley Kunitz:** *Collected Poems* (W.W. Norton & Company, 2000).

Philip Larkin: 'Poetry of Departures' and 'Toads' from *The Less Deceived* (1955), reprinted in *Collected Poems*, by permission of The Marvell Press; 'An Arundel Tomb', 'The Whitsun Weddings' and 'The Trees' from *Collected Poems*, ed. Anthony Thwaite (Faber & Faber, 1990). **Michael Laskey:** 'A Tray of Eggs' from *Thinking of Happiness* (Peterloo Poets, 1991); 'The Tightrope Wedding' from *The Tightrope Wedding* (Smith/Doorstop, 1999). **Radmila Lazic:** A Wake for the Living, tr. Charles Simic (Graywolf Press, USA, 2003; Bloodaxe Books, UK, 2004). **Li-Young Lee:** 'From Blossoms' from *Rose* (1986); 'Little Father' from *Book of My Nights* (2001), both from BOA Editions, USA. **Tom Leonard:** 'Four of the Belt', from *Intimate Voices: Poems 1965-1983* (Galloping Dog Press, republished Etruscan Books, 2003), by permission of the author. **Denise Levertov:** *New Selected Poems* (Bloodaxe Books, 2003), by permission of Laurence Pollinger Ltd. **Primo Levi:** *Collected Poems*, tr. Ruth Feldman & Brian Swann (Faber & Faber, 1988/1992). **Gwyneth Lewis:** *Keeping Mum* (Bloodaxe Books, 2003). **Philip Levine:** 'The Simple Truth' from *The Simple Truth* (1996); 'Every Blessed Day', 'What Work Is' from *What Work Is* (1999); 'Starlight' from *Ashes* (1979), reprinted in *New Selected Poems* (2002); all from Alfred A. Knopf, Inc., NY. **Sarah Lindsay:** *Mount Clutter* (Grove Press, NY, 2000). **Joanne Limburg:** *Femenismo* (Bloodaxe Books, 2000). **Liz Lochhead:** 'Rapunzstiltskin' and 'I Wouldn't Thank You for a Valentine' from *True Confessions and New Clichés* (Polygon, 1985); 'My Way' from *The Colour of Black & White: Poems 1984-2003* (Polygon, 2003); by permission of Birlinn Ltd. **Gerald Locklin:** *The Iceberg Theory* (Lummox Press, 2000), by permission of the author. **Michael Longley:** 'Detour' from *Selected Poems* (Jonathan Cape, 1998), 'The Waterfall' from *The Weather in Japan* (Jonathan Cape, 2000); 'The Pattern' and 'Echoes' from *Snow Water* (Jonathan Cape, 2004); by permission of the Random House Group Ltd. **Thomas Lynch:** *Grimalkin and other poems* (Jonathan Cape, 1994), by permission of the Random House Group Ltd. **Roddy Lumsden:** *Mischief Night: New & Selected Poems* (Bloodaxe Books, 2004). **Thomas Lux:** *The Street of Clocks* (Houghton Mifflin, USA, 2001; Arc Publications, UK, 2003).

Norman MacCaig: *Collected Poems* (Chatto & Windus, 1990), by permission of Random House Group Ltd. **Gwendolyn MacEwen:** *Magic Animals* (Stoddart, Toronto, 1984), by permission of Stoddart/House of Anansi and the Estate of Gwendolyn McEwan. **Gerry McGrath:** 'Noticing a man unable...', previously unpublished poem by permission of the author. **Don McKay:** *Birding, or desire* (McClelland & Stewart, 1983). **Kenneth Mackenzie:** *The Poems of Kenneth Mackenzie* (Angus & Robertson, Sydney, 1972), by permission of ETT Imprint, Sydney. **Archibald MacLeish:** *Collected Poems 1917-1982* (Houghton Mifflin, USA, 1985). **Louis MacNeice:** *Collected Poems*, ed. E.R. Dodds (Faber, 1979), by permission of David Higham Associates Ltd. **Kona Macphee:** *Tails* (Bloodaxe Books, 2004). **Antonio Machado:** *Border of a Dream: Selected Poems*, tr. Willis Barnstone (Copper Canyon Press, USA, 2004). **Derek Mahon:** *Collected Poems* (Gallery Press, 1999). **William Matthews:** 'Grief' from *Time and Money* (1995); 'Misgivings' from *After All: Last Poems* (1998), both from Houghton Mifflin,

491

USA. **Glyn Maxwell:** *The Nerve* (Picador, 2002), by permission of Macmillan Publishers Ltd. **James Merrill:** *Collected Poems*, ed. J.D. McClatchy & Stephen Yenser, by permission of the Literary Estate of James Merrill at Washington University and Alfred A. Knopf, division of Random House, Inc. **W.S. Merwin:** 'For the Anniversary of My Death' from *The Lice* (1967), reprinted in *Selected Poems* (Atheneum, 1988); 'Losing a Language' from *The Rain in the Trees* (Alfred A. Knopf, Inc., NY, 1988); by permission of The Wylie Agency. **Anne Michaels:** *Poems* (Bloomsbury, 2000). **Czeslaw Milosz:** *New & Collected Poems 1931-2001* (Ecco Press, USA; Penguin Books, UK, 2001); **Gabriela Mistral:** *Selected Poems*, tr. Ursula LeGuin (University of New Mexico Press, Albuquerque, USA, 2003). **Adrian Mitchell:** *Heart on the Left: Poems 1953-1984* (Bloodaxe Books, 1997), by permission of Peters, Fraser & Dunlop, with an educational health warning: Adrian Mitchell asks that none of his poems be used in connection with any examination whatsoever. **Elma Mitchell:** *People Etcetera: Poems New & Selected* (Peterloo Poets, 1987), copyright © Harry Chambers. **Dorothy Molloy:** *Hare Soup* (Faber & Faber, 2004). **Esther Morgan:** *Beyond Calling Distance* (Bloodaxe Books, 2001). **Mihangel Morgan:** 'Conversation', tr. Martin Davis, from *The Bloodaxe Book of Modern Welsh Poetry: 20th-century Welsh language poetry in translation*, ed. Menna Elfyn & John Rowlands (Bloodaxe Books, 2003), by permission of author, translator and Cyhoeddiadau Barddas, Llandybie. **Sinéad Morrissey:** 'Genetics' (first published in *Metre*) and 'The Wound Man' (first published in *Poetry London*) by permission of the author. **Howard Moss:** *Finding Them Lost* (Scribner, 1965), by permission of the Howard Moss Estate. **Erin Mouré:** *Wanted Alive* (Stoddart, Toronto, 1983), by permission of Stoddart/House of Anansi. **Edwin Muir:** *Collected Poems* (Faber & Faber, 1963). **Paul Muldoon:** 'The Sonogram' from *The Annals of Chile* (1994); 'Symposium' from *Hay* (1998); 'The Loaf' from *Moy Sand and Gravel* (2002); all from Faber & Faber Ltd. **Richard Murphy:** *Collected Poems* (Gallery Press, 2000). **Carol Muske-Dukes:** *Sparrow* (Random House, NY, 2003). **Howard Nemerov:** *Collected Poems* (University of Chicago Press, 1981), by permission of Margaret Nemerov. **Pablo Neruda:** 'Sweetness, Always' from *Extravagaria*, tr. Alastair Reid (Farrar, Straus & Giroux, 1974); 'Love Sonnets' from *100 Love Sonnets/Cien sonetos de amor*, tr. Stephen Tapscott (University of Texas Press, 1986; 'Births', 'Horses', 'Ode to the Onion' from *Full Woman, Fleshly Apple, Hot Moon*, tr. Stephen Mitchell (HarperCollins, NY, 1997). **Eiléan Ní Chuilleanáin:** *The Girl Who Married the Reindeer* (Gallery Press, 2001). **Nuala Ní Dhomhnaill:** *Pharoah's Daughter* (Gallery Press, 1990). **Grace Nichols:** *The Fat Black Woman's Poems* (Virago, 1984). **Norman Nicholson:** *Collected Poems* (Faber & Faber, 1994). **Dorothy Nimmo:** *The Wigbox: New & Selected Poems* (Smith/Doorstop Books, 2000). **Alden Nowlan:** *Between Tears and Laughter: Selected Poems* (Bloodaxe Books, 2004). **Naomi Shihab Nye:** 'Kindness' from *Words under the Words: Selected Poems* (Far Corner Books, USA, 1995), 'So Much Happiness' © 2001 by permission of the author

Julie O'Callaghan: *What's What* (Bloodaxe Books, 1991). **Bernard O'Donoghue:** 'Going Without Saying' from *Gunpowder* (Chatto & Windus, 1995); 'Concordiam in Populo' from *Outliving* (Chatto & Windus, 2003); by permission of the Random House Group Ltd. **Dennis O'Driscoll:** 'Home' from *Quality Time* (1997), 'Missing God' from *Exemplary Damages* (2002), both from Anvil Press Poetry; 'Life', first published in *The Irish Times*, by permission of the author. **Sharon Olds:** 'Beyond Harm' and 'Waste Sonata' from *The Father* (Secker & Warburg, 1993); 'Forty-one, Alone, No Gerbil', 'My First Weeks' and 'This Hour' from *The Wellspring* (Jonathan Cape, 1996); by permission of the Random House Group Ltd and Alfred A. Knopf, division of Random House, Inc. **Mary Oliver:** 'Some Questions You Might Ask' and 'The Summer Day' from *House of Light* (1990), reprinted in *New and Selected Poems* (Beacon Press, USA, 1992), and 'How Everything Adores Being Alive' and 'Look and See' from *Why I Wake Early* (Beacon Press, USA, 2004), all four poems also reprinted in *Wild Geese: Selected Poems* (Bloodaxe Books, 2004), by permission of Beacon Press and the author. **Michael Ondaatje:** *The Cinnamon Peeler: Selected Poems* (Picador, 1989), by permission of the Ellen Levine Literary Agency, Inc. **Kathleen Ossip:** *The Search Engine* (American Poetry Review, 2002). **Alice Oswald:** *The Thing in the Gap-Stone Stile* (Oxford University Press, 1996), by permission of PFD and the author.

Heberto Padilla: *Legacies*, tr. Alastair Reid & Andrew Hurley (Farrar, Straus & Giroux, Inc, 1982). **P.K. Page:** *The Hidden Room: Collected Poems*, volume two (The Porcupine's Quill, Canada, 1997). **Grace Paley:** *Begin Again: Collected Poems* (Farrar, Straus & Giroux, Inc, USA, 2000). **Tom Paulin:** *Liberty Tree* (Faber & Faber, 1983). **M.R. Peacocke:** *Speaking of the Dead* (Peterloo Poets, 2003). **Pascale Petit:** *The Zoo Father* (Seren Books, 2001). **Robert Phillips:** *Spinach Days* (Johns Hopkins University Press, 2000). **Marge Piercy:** 'In the men's room(s)' from *Circles on the Water: Selected Poems* (Alfred A. Knopf, NY, 1982); 'The low road' from *The Moon Is Always Female* (Alfred A. Knopf, NY, 1994); these poems and 'The watch' by permission of the Wallace Literary Agency Inc and the author. **Robert Pinsky:** *Jersey Rain* (Farrar, Straus & Giroux, 2000). **Ruth Pitter:** *Collected Poems* (Enitharmon Press, 1990). **Sylvia Plath:** *Collected Poems*, ed. Ted Hughes (Faber & Faber, 1981). **Clare Pollard:** *Bedtime* (Bloodaxe Books, 2002). **Jacob Polley:** *The Brink* (Picador, 2003). **Katrina Porteous:** *The Lost Music* (Bloodaxe Books, 1996). **Minnie Bruce Pratt:** *We Say We Love Each Other* (Firebrand Books, USA, 1992). **Jacques Prévert:** *Selections from Paroles*, tr. Lawrence Ferlinghetti (City Lights Books, 1958; Penguin Books, UK, 1965), by permission of City Lights Books. **Alison Pryde:** *Have We Had Easter Yet?* (Peterloo Poets, 1998). **Sheenagh Pugh:** 'Sometimes' from *Selected Poems* (1990), 'What If This Road' from *Id's Hospit* (1997), both from Seren Books. **Al Purdy:** *Being Alive: Poems 1958-78* (McClelland & Stewart, Toronto, 1978).

Deborah Randall: *The Sin Eater* (Bloodaxe Books, 1989). **Peter Reading:** *Collected Poems 2: Poems 1985-1996* (Bloodaxe Books, 1996). **Victoria Redel:** *Already the World* (Kent State University Press, Ohio, 1995). **Deryn Rees-Jones:** *Signs Around a Dead Body* (Seren Books, 1998). **Adrienne Rich:** extract from 'An Atlas of the Difficult World' and 'Final Notations' from *An Atlas of the Difficult World* (W.W. Norton & Company, 1991); 'To the Days' from *Dark Fields of the Republic: Poems 1991-1995* (W.W. Norton & Company, 1995); by permission of the author and W.W. Norton & Company. **Maurice Riordan:** *A Word from the Loki* (Faber & Faber, 1995). **Aleksandar Ristovic:** *Devil's Lunch: Selected Poems*, tr. Charles Simic (Faber & Faber, 1999). **Theodore Roethke:** *Collected Poems* (Faber & Faber, 1968). **Aidan Rooney-Céspedes:** *Day Release* (Gallery Press, 2000). **Anne Rouse:** 'Her Retirement' from *Sunset Grill* (1993), 'Spunk Talking' from *Timing* (1997), both from Bloodaxe Books. **Tadeusz Różewicz:** *They Came to See a Poet: Selected Poems*, tr. Adam Czerniawski (Anvil Press Poetry, 2004). **Carol Rumens:** *Poems 1968-2004* (Bloodaxe Books, 2004).

Eva Salzman: *Double Crossing: New & Selected Poems* (Bloodaxe Books, 2004). **Carl Sandburg:** 'Prayers of Steel' and 'Limited' copyright © Holt, Rinehart and Winston, © both renewed 1944 by Carl Sandburg, reprinted by permission of Harcourt, Inc., USA. **Carole Satyamurti:** *Selected Poems* (Bloodaxe Books, 2000). **Gjertrud Schnackenberg:** *Supernatural Love: Poems 1976-2000* (Bloodaxe Books,

493

2001). **Ruth L. Schwartz:** *Edgewater* (HarperCollins, NY, 2002). **David Scott:** *Selected Poems* (Bloodaxe Books, 1998); **Frederick Seidel:** 'Men and Women' from *Sunrise* (Viking Press/Penguin Books, NY, 1980); 'Dune Road, Southampton' from *Going Fast* (Farrar, Straus & Giroux, Inc, USA, 1998). **Vijay Seshadri:** *The Long Meadow* (Graywolf Press, USA, 2004). **Jo Shapcott:** *Her Book: Poems 1988-1998* (Faber & Faber, 2000). **Henry Shukman:** *In Doctor No's Garden* (Jonathan Cape, 2002), by permission of the Random House Group Ltd. **Catherine Smith:** *The Butcher's Hands* (Smith/Doorstop Books, 2003). **Ken Smith:** *Shed: Poems 1980-2001* (Bloodaxe Books, 2002). **Elizabeth Smither:** 'Mission Impossible', 'A cortège of daughters' and 'The sea question' from *The Tudor Style: Poems New & Selected* (1993); 'On the euthanasia of a pet dog' from *The Lark Quartet* (1999); both from Auckland University Press, New Zealand. **Gary Snyder:** *Turtle Island* (New Directions, Inc., USA, 1974). **Cathy Song:** *Picture Bride* (Yale University Press, 1983). **Marin Sorescu:** *The Biggest Egg in the World*, ed. Edna Longley (Bloodaxe Books, 1987). **William Stafford:** *The Way It Is: New & Selected Poems* (Graywolf Press, 1998). **Pauline Stainer:** *The Lady & the Hare: New & Selected Poems* (Bloodaxe Books, 2003). **John Steffler:** *Wreckage of Play* (McClelland & Stewart, Toronto, 1988). **Gerald Stern:** *This Time: New & Selected Poems* (W.W. Norton & Company, Inc, 1997). **Wallace Stevens:** *Collected Poems* (Faber & Faber, 1955). **Anne Stevenson:** 'The Victory', 'The Mother', 'Musician's Widow' from *Collected Poems 1955-1995* (2000), 'Who's Joking with the Photographer?' from *A Report from the Border* (2003), both from Bloodaxe Books. **Greta Stoddart:** *At Home in the Dark* (Anvil Press Poetry, 2001). **Ruth Stone:** 'Curtains' from *Second-Hand Coat: New & Selected Poems* (David R. Godine, 1987; Yellow Moon Press, Cambridge, Mass, USA, 1991); 'Poems' and 'In the Next Galaxy' from *In the Next Galaxy* (Copper Canyon Press, 2002). **Mark Strand:** *Blizzard of One* (Alfred A. Knopf, NY, 1998). **Matthew Sweeney:** 'The Box' from *The Bridal Suite* (1997), 'The Appointment' from *A Smell of Fish* (2000), both from Jonathan Cape by permission of the Random House Group Ltd. **George Szirtes:** *Reel* (Bloodaxe Books, 2004). **Wislawa Szymborska:** 'Love at First Sight' and 'Reality Demands' from *View with a Grain of Sand: Selected Poems* by Wislawa Szymborska, tr. Stanislaw Baranczak & Clare Cavanagh (Harcourt Brace & Company, 1993); 'The Ball' from *The New Yorker*, 13 January 2003.

   Genevieve Taggard: *Collected Poems 1918-1938* (Harper & Row, 1938), © renewed 1966, Harper & Row, Publishers, Inc. **Sharon Thesen:** *News and Smoke: Selected Poems* (Talonbooks, Burnaby, BC, Canada, 1999). **R.S. Thomas:** 'Lore' from *Selected Poems 1946-1968* (Bloodaxe Books, 1986); extract from *Counterpoint* and 'A Marriage' from *Collected Later Poems 1988-2000* (Bloodaxe Books, 2004). **Rosemary Tonks:** *Iliad of Broken Sentences* (The Bodley Head, 1967), copyright © Rosemary Tonks 1967. **Gael Turnbull:** *Might a Shape of Words and other transmutations* (Mariscat Press, 2000). **Chase Twichell:** *The Snow Watcher* (Ontario Review Press, USA, 1998; Bloodaxe Books, 1999).

   César Vallejo: *Selected Poems*, tr. Ed Dorn & Gordon Brotherston (Penguin Books, 1976), by permission of Gordon Brotherston. **Fred Voss:** *Carnegie Hall with Tin Walls* (Bloodaxe Books, 1998).

   Derek Walcott: *Collected Poems 1948-1984* (Faber & Faber, 1986). **Sarah Wardle:** *Fields Away* (Bloodaxe Books, 2003). **Andrew Waterhouse:** 'Now the City Has Fallen' and 'Climbing My Grandfather' from *In* (The Rialto, 2000); 'Speaking About My Cracked Sump' from *2nd* (The Rialto, 2002). **Susan Wicks:** *Night Toad: New & Selected Poems* (Bloodaxe Books, 2003). **C.K. Williams:** 'The Shade' from *New & Selected Poems* (1995), 'The Dress' from *Repair* (1999), 'The

Hearth' from *The Singing* (2003), from Farrar, Straus & Giroux, Inc. (USA) and Bloodaxe Books (UK). **Miller Williams:** *Imperfect Love* (Louisiana State U. Press, Baton Rouge, 1986). **Anne Winters:** *The Key to the City* (University of Chicago Press, 1985), by permission of the author. **Vincent Woods:** *The Colour of Language* (Dedalus Press, Dublin, 1994), by permission of the author. **Gerard Woodward:** *After the Deafening* (Chatto & Windus, 1994), by permission of the Random House Group Ltd; **W.B. Yeats:** *The Poems*, ed. Richard J. Finneran (Macmillan, 1991), by permission of A.P. Watt Ltd on behalf of Michael B. Yeats. **Saadi Youssef:** 'The Mouse' from *Without an Alphabet, Without a Face: Selected Poems*, tr. Khaled Mattawa (Graywolf Press, USA, 2002); 'Night in Al-Hamra', uncollected translation by Khaled Mattawa, by permission of the translator and author.

Adam Zagajewski: *Without End: New and Selected Poems* (Farrar, Straus & Giroux, 2002), by permission of Farrar, Straus & Giroux, Inc.

Every effort has been made to trace copyright holders of the poems published in this book. The editor and publisher apologise if any material has been included without permission or without the appropriate acknowledgement, and would be glad to be told of anyone who has not been consulted.

My editorial commentaries include quotations from various sources. I am greatly indebted to Dennis O'Driscoll for those included in his 'Pickings and Choosings' selections in *Poetry Ireland*. Emily Dickinson's comment on poetry was noted by Thomas Wentworth Higginson after their first meeting on 16 August 1870 and published in his account of their correspondence in 1891.

Other sources: (18a) William Stafford's remark is recorded by Kim Stafford in his memoir *Early Morning: Remembering My Father* (Graywolf Press, USA, 2002), p.135. (18b) James Tate: *American Poetry Review*, September/October 1997. (18c) Paul Muldoon: *Princeton University Library Chronicle*, Spring 1998. (21a) Eamon Grennan: *Irish Times*, 11 September 1999. (21b) Seamus Heaney: BBC 1, March 1998. (49a) Julia Casterton: *Poetry News* (Poetry Society), Winter 2002/03. (49b) Lucille Clifton: *Baltimore Sun*, 29 September 2002. (49c) Tony Harrison: *Permanently Bard: Selected Poetry*, ed. Carol Rutter (Bloodaxe Books, 1995), p.167. (49d) John Keats: Letter to C.W. Dilke, 22 September 1819, *The Letters of John Keats*, vol. 2, ed. Hyder Edward Rollins (Harvard University Press, 1958), p.179. (107a) Paul Muldoon: BBC Radio 4, 2001. (107b) Charles Causley: *Poetry News* (Poetry Society), Winter 1998. (107c) Seamus Heaney: *The New Mexican*, 26 September 2003. (179a) John Burnside: *La Traductière*, No.17, 1999. (179b): U.A. Fanthorpe: *The Guardian*, 13 February 1999. (211) Kathleen Jamie: 'Holding Fast – Truth and Change in Poetry', in *Strong Words: Modern Poets on Modern Poetry*, ed. W.N. Herbert & Matthew Hollis (Bloodaxe Books, 2000), p.280. (257a) Mark Doty: *Charlotte Observer*, 14 March 2003. (257b) Wallace Stevens: *Letters* (Alfred A. Knopf, New York, 1960), pp.341 & 500. (305) Edward Hirsch: *Washington Post*, 13 January 2002. (353) Adrian Mitchell: *Poetry Review*, Autumn 1997. (397) Charles Simic: *The Age*, 9 March 2003. (443a) Fleur Adcock: BBC Radio 4, August 1999. (443b) Wallace Stevens: 'Adagia', *Opus Posthumous* (Faber & Faber, 1990).

INDEX OF WRITERS

497

INDEX OF TITLES & FIRST LINES

503

509

511